# THE PAINTED TABLE

## SUZANNE FIELD

### THOMAS NELSON
*Since 1798*

NASHVILLE   DALLAS   MEXICO CITY   RIO DE JANEIRO

Published in Nashville, Tennessee, by Thomas Nelson. Thomas Nelson is a registered trademark of Thomas Nelson, Inc.

Published in association with the literary agency of The Benchmark Group, Nashville, TN: benchmarkgroup1@aol.com.

Thomas Nelson, Inc., titles may be purchased in bulk for educational, business, fund-raising, or sales promotional use. For information, please e-mail SpecialMarkets@ ThomasNelson.com.

Scripture quotations marked NIV are taken from the Holy Bible, New International Version®, NIV®. Copyright © 1973, 1978, 1984, 2011 by Biblica, Inc.™ Used by permission of Zondervan. All rights reserved worldwide. www.zondervan.com

Other Scripture quotations are from the King James Version of the Bible.

**Library of Congress Control Number: 2013949986**

ISBN 978-1-4016-8970-4

*Printed in the United States of America*

13 14 15 16 17 18 RRD 6 5 4 3 2 1

*For my Father*

*You prepare a table before me*
*in the presence of my enemies.*
*You anoint my head with oil;*
*my cup overflows.*

PSALM 23:5 NIV

# CONTENTS

# THE BEGINNING

1858

etal teeth rip through the rough, mottled bark and bite into white cambium. Steady strokes saw forward and back, grating, rasping. Two hands push, grate; two hands pull, rasp, lacerating the ring of yellow sapwood. The blade advances, traverses golden heartwood, more sapwood, more cambium, then needs merely to touch the last of the bark.

The sacrificial birch tips, then plummets; its startled branches cry out, rudely raking upright brothers. Severed from stump and root, the tree crashes onto the rich Valdres Valley soil—a brutal amputation, but necessary to be rendered a gift of love.

A gift that will one day be abased, and another day redeemed.

# PROLOGUE

1921

A damp, colorless dress, pinned to the clothesline, tosses about in the blustery prairie wind. Arms outstretched, Joann lets the fabric flap against her thin, seven-year-old frame. She aches for her mother's hands that will never again extend from the empty sleeves that twist and turn about her head, caressing her face.

"Momma . . . Momma." The wind snatches away her whispers.

The dress belongs to Joann's oldest sister now. Evelyn began wearing it last month when her own tore beyond repair. It is an ill fit for her; Evelyn at fifteen is more plump than Clara had ever been. Seeing the dress stretching across her sister's frame is a daily offense for Joann. Joann's dress, and four others of various sizes, each faded and threadbare, flutter nearby.

Not far from the line, Evelyn, Maxine, and Dorothy bend to pick stunted vegetables. Their pa warned that the well might go dry if they watered the patch more than every few days. The heat of August is fast approaching and it hasn't rained on the North Dakota prairie since June.

Life on the prairie farm is at once strong and proud, fragile and impoverished. "Not much here today," Evelyn says. "We'll make soup again, plenty of broth." Their buckets hold a few turnips, onions, carrots, and shriveled pole beans. The potatoes are not ready to dig.

Pa and Lars and Rolf have a second pair of work clothes to wear on washday, overalls, faded and patched. But the girls, until the laundry dries, each wear only a chemise undergarment, stitched of muslin by their mother, modest enough to wear in the presence of brothers and Pa. Evelyn pins a shawl over her shoulders to conceal her already ample torso. Pa turns a deaf ear to her embarrassed, whispered requests for a brassiere from the mercantile in Steele.

In the house, carefully folded away in the big black steamer trunk, are six white batiste dresses. They were supplied by generous neighbors so the sisters had "something decent to wear" for their mother's funeral four months earlier. Shortly thereafter, Uncle Jergen, a circuit pastor, came and insisted that all his brother Knute's children be baptized at once. So the "good" dresses were worn a second time.

Beneath the tossing clothing, Joann sinks down onto prickly grass, unaware of a long, black rat snake coiled near the clothesline pole, its yellow eyes trained on her. She watches her pa's two work horses fifty yards away searching in vain for green shoots. Beyond them are fields of parched crops and boundless miles of dry grass. She shields her eyes from the sun and watches the white chickens strut daintily in the barnyard. Once, and only once, Joann had playfully imitated their jerky gait on her rickets-bowed legs.

"Look at me!" she demanded of Maxine. "I'm pretty-walking, like the chickens!"

Maxine snickered. "Those legs of yours will never walk pretty, Joann."

Lars chimed in, "*Cluck-cluck-cluck*, Joann."

Pa and the brothers unload lumber from the wagon, stacking it beside the barn. They returned last evening from a fifty-mile trip to the Valley City lumber mill. The horses had done well to pull the heavy wagonload and had earned their extra oats. Knute is proud of these black muscular giants. "A stronger pair I never seed," he often declares, his English marked by the undulant accent of his native Norwegian.

The unloading is strenuous work for Rolf and Lars, only thirteen and twelve, and small for their age. Every day tests their young muscles. But their pa, an immigrant farmer trying to survive, cannot coddle them. God saw fit to give him only two sons among seven daughters.

Knute Kirkeborg does the work of several men, in spite of one short, lame leg, but the stubborn prairie always asks for more. At times he can be a harsh man, appearing to be angry at the world, when mostly he is angry at himself. He shouldn't have taken his friends' dare to jump from the roof when he was twelve. The mishap caused his right leg to stop growing. Yet he knows it also prompted him to become clever and resourceful.

As a Norwegian boy of seventeen, he heard about earning passage to America by working in the bowels of a freighter. He could have a new life in that promised land across the Atlantic where so many Norwegians had fled. There he could till virgin flatland and grow fields of grain like Norway's mountainous terrain never could. There he could prove himself whole. His godly family was more sorrowful about their oldest son's bitterness over his short leg than his leaving. Leaving for America they could understand. They gave him their blessing.

Knute was handsome and could be beguiling. High cheekbones and an aristocratic nose distracted women from his limp. Making his way west, he met young Clara in Minnesota and quickly won her over. Part French and third-generation American, he deemed her a prize. She accepted his dreams as her own, gathered her belongings into a cedar-lined trunk, made arrangements for her treadle sewing machine to follow, and together they headed out to break the rude soil of central North Dakota.

There, in spite of ever-increasing demands of motherhood, Clara tended well to her domestic tasks. Her food preparation was in the French manner, ingredients chopped finely, not left in chunks common to Scandinavian dishes. Whenever possible, her meals had flavor and color, and she considered *lefse* a poor substitute for bread.

Knute has long talked of building an addition to the barn. Now that he has the lumber, he will need to hurry so they can store extra wheat and oats for the animals come fall. Extra, that is, if it rains. He needs more fodder; he's added a third cow.

As the three lug and pile the rough boards, they pay no heed to a mother partridge rapidly scuttling her young through tall brown grass not fifteen feet away. Neither do they notice the chickens periodically interrupt scratching to cock their heads to listen. Then, with distraught fluttering and squawking, they strut here and there in mindless circles.

Suddenly, there is a bawling. The cows, head-to-tail, are plodding determinedly toward the barn. Why? It's only been a short time since morning milking and many hours until the next. Knute notes the cows, then the frantic chickens. On his good leg, he whirls to the west. *Smoke!* An evil ribbon of black along the horizon stretches as far as can be seen to the north and south.

"Fire! Prairie fire!" he shouts. "Lars! Put da cows in da barn! Rolf! Run get da horses! Hurry!"

Rolf takes off running. Knute and Lars prod the cows. "It's still far off, but dere's a stiff wind!" Pa shouts. "We'll get dem horses harnessed, put 'em to da plow!"

Lars, pale and shaking, gathers up leather harnesses from their place in the barn. "Get da blinders," Knute barks. "Can't let 'em see da fire."

The girls in the garden, and Joann under the clothesline, hear the commotion and see the smoke. Color drains from each face. "Prairie fire! God, spare us!" Evelyn entreats. "Maxine, Dorothy, we've picked enough, we better go to the house." She can only pretend to be calm. "Joann! Joann!" she calls. "Come along now." At an early age, these prairie children learned to recoil when adults spoke of flames, hideous flames, approaching from afar, licking up all creation in their path.

Joann rises from the ground and lunges awkwardly toward the others. Her legs tremble, her heart pounds like a hammer in her chest. The rat snake races past her, slithering purposefully from west to east. Joann sees it, screams, and spurts ahead to grab Dorothy's skirt.

The washtubs and scrub boards outside the house remind Evelyn of the laundry. She thrusts her vegetable pail toward Maxine. "I'll go back for the dresses," she says. "Can't let 'em . . ." She almost says *burn*. "Girls, go in the house," she calls back over her shoulder. "Check on Helen and Francis and then stay inside."

She snatches clothing off the line with an eye on the smoke that now ascends into pillars. Not heeding instruction, the younger sisters gather into a tight huddle, mesmerized by the ominous horizon edging the flatland. Their chatter is high-pitched and nervous. Five-year-old Francis scampers out of the house and Maxine scoops her up. Evelyn hurries toward them, her arms full of laundry. She deposits it in the house and returns to stare wide-eyed with the others. Joann moans with fright and buries her face at Evelyn's waist.

Knute and the brothers manage to catch the horses' unwilling heads, strap on the blinders, and hitch the muscular animals to the plow. They whinny and paw the ground with mighty hooves. A quick check confirms that the wide leather bands are secure. Knute climbs up and stands astride. He slaps the reins and pulls right. "Haw! Haw!" he commands.

The beasts jolt forward and Knute guides them to the western edge of his cleared property, one hundred or more feet beyond the barn. He yanks the lever to lower the plow, and the pull begins. The curved metal teeth dig through the dry earth. He urges the reluctant horses to their full speed and the plow begins to cut a wide swath of ground for a generous distance north, and then south. Back and forth, back and forth he drives them, yelling, straining at the reins with all his might each time they reverse direction. The hard soil looks darker when turned, once again fertile.

Periodically Joann dares lift her head for a quick look. Each glimpse prompts an impassioned wail. "Stop! Fire, go away!"

Dorothy grips the sides of her face. "The barn and the shed," she despairs, "they'd . . . they'd burn up so fast." She doesn't dare speak of the house. Knute built the few wooden buildings with his own hands, finishing the clapboard house only four years before, so his family could finally move out of the sod house. Clara had insisted that raising children in a house of mud and grass was not civilized, even after he limed the inside walls white, hoping to placate her. He had often reminded her that sod houses don't burn.

The boys rush to join the clutch of girls and all stand close, paralyzed. The wind has increased, snatching up and whirling particles of earth. The girls feel the itching sting of dry dirt against their faces and through their thin clothing.

"What's Pa doin'?" demands five-year-old Francis, eyes wide with fright as she struggles in Maxine's firm hold.

Although they are huddled close, Lars yells to her over the howl of the wind, "He's plowin' a firebreak!"

"So we don't burn up," Rolf adds. The boys' voices, which mimic their father's "old country" speech patterns, crack with fear. Rolf is the first to note a sinister stripe of bright orange in the distant sky beneath the black smoke.

"Looks 'bout a mile out," he shouts. "Maybe closer. An' the wind's blow'n' mighty, straight outta the west." In spite of their plight, Rolf, the older brother, sounds proud to announce the information.

It isn't long until the dreaded odor of smoke whips its way across the flatland. They cover their noses. What were whimpers from Joann and Francis are now terrified sobs. Evelyn puts her arms around as many sisters as she can to prod them into the house. She doesn't try to corral the boys, who suddenly, with buffoonery and false bravado, whoop and leap, mimicking the horses, dismissing from their minds that unless the firebreak works or the wind shifts, voracious flames may devour them.

Joann tugs desperately at Evelyn's arm. "We need to run away," she shouts. "Come on, Evelyn, we need to run away!"

"No, Joann, hush now, don't pull on me. There's no place to run," she says.

Joann, in the vise of fear, breaks away from the others and darts into the house. She scuttles across the floor and dives beneath a great sturdy wooden table that dominates the room. She hunkers down on the plank flooring, surrounded by a protective barricade of rough wooden benches. Knute had made the benches crude but serviceable, like the other pieces of rudimentary furniture in the house. Not like the table, with its ornate vine motif carved into the entire length of its apron.

In the doorway, Evelyn casts a last fearful look toward their pa as he cracks his whip in the air. In spite of the blinders, the sweating horses toss their heads indignantly as they strain forward.

"Go! Faster! Faster!" she hears Pa yell.

Evelyn quickly shuts the door and turns to tend to her sisters. Although she is only fifteen, they have been her responsibility since early spring when Clara, their precious, almost continuously pregnant mother, finally proved not strong enough for homestead life. When the ninth baby came, Clara's health gave out.

Evelyn sees that sixteen-month-old Helen is still asleep in her box bed. She considers, for a moment, that she and Dorothy should prepare the vegetables for soup, carry on as if great danger were not rushing toward them. But the smell of smoke is seeping into the house, and with it, panic. Chopping vegetables is out of the question.

"God, save us!" Maxine implores.

Beneath the table, seven-year-old Joann hunches, arms tightly hugging her legs. She repeats the words in a whimper, "God, save us."

The boys tumble into the house, slamming the door behind them. Helen awakens, senses tension, and screams. Evelyn picks her up and paces back and forth, jostling the child on her hip.

From her floor-level view, Joann watches Evelyn's worn brown shoes traverse the room. Always, but at this moment more than ever, Joann craves to be held. But Evelyn, try as she may, is still a girl herself and, like her mother before her, can only do so much.

Maxine, Dorothy, and Francis shove aside the long benches in order to invade Joann's space. Perhaps their awkward runt sister has found some inexplicable safety there where she spends so much time. Joann covers her head with her hands and tries to make herself smaller, although there is room for all. The table is extended by three generously sized leaves.

The girls have noted an aura of mystery around this ancestral table that Uncle Jergen brought to them all the way from Norway some years ago. It had come by steamship, then train, then wagon. They heard Pa tell their mother he hadn't wanted to accept it. Perhaps it reminded him of things he wanted to forget. Only because his brother had come such a long way had he felt obliged to keep it.

Joann found refuge under the table long before Clara died. From here she watched her mother nurse baby Francis, then later, baby Helen. Joann didn't know that for a nutritionally depleted mother, the act of nursing is an arduous sacrifice. Although Clara had little time to give lingering hugs to the older ones, she always spoke kindly to them. No one doubted her love. But Joann's lingering ache for her mother's unavailable embrace prompted her to slip between the table benches, seeking a substitute place of comfort. Still, comfort sometimes embraces her here.

In the night, it is not unusual for Maxine, the largest sister, although not the oldest, to crowd Joann from their shared bed as she turns. In response, more than two years ago Joann began to leave the bed sometimes and, being careful not to bump and topple a bench, wrap herself in a quilt beneath the table in the main room. Here she needn't suffer a knee in her back and she can be alone, until returning before dawn. The space beneath the table, surrounded by a fence of benches, has become a haven. Other than to give occasional ridicule, her daytime visits there are generally ignored by her siblings, who are used to her idiosyncracies. Her father has never noticed her there.

Rolf and Lars, still in a bewildered mix of exhilaration and hysteria, race back and forth between the two small west-facing windows as they report on the steadily advancing wall of flame.

"Pa's makin' dem horses fly!" Rolf yells.

"Fire's gettin' closer!" Lars screeches. Evelyn grabs his arm, pushes him under the table, and crouches down herself with the crying baby. Rolf follows.

"Don't look out!" Evelyn commands. "Stay down right here. And pray!"

"God, save us! God, save us!"

The house darkens as outside smoke swirls around it, seeps inside, hot. It feels like thistles in their throats. Fists are clenched, as they were when they came into the world.

"Mama, Mama!" Joann cries. Others join in.

"Pa!" Lars whines. "Why don'tcha come in?"

They hear the racing flames roar angrily close. Will they survive this terrible day?

*Crack!* The west windows, blackened with smoke, break in the heat, intensifying the children's terror. The dark room spins. Joann swoons and slumps into unconsciousness.

The others, terrorized by the sound of the inferno, cough from the smoke and sob, clinging to each other with racing hearts, keeping their eyes tightly shut. *Will the plowed earth stop the fire from reaching the house? Or will the wind carry it over? Are Pa and the horses . . . ? Oh, God!*

When the fire passes, spreading its fury eastward, the roar diminishes. Under the table, what seemed like an eternity has been close to thirty minutes.

*Pa. Where's Pa?*

They clamber from beneath the table and stumble toward the door, leaving Joann's limp figure behind.

"Open it real slow!" Evelyn orders, dreading what they will see. They spill into the smoke-filled yard, choking in the acrid stench. Through the haze, they see their father near the barn. Black with ash, he leans over the plow seat, retching inhaled smoke. The horses, soaked in sweat, snort as they drink lustily from the watering trough. As far as can be seen, what once were wheat fields now smolder in red and black desolation—all the way up to the freshly turned earth— *but no farther.*

"Pa!" they cry.

Knute steadies himself and raises his head.

*They are safe.*

"Boys," he calls hoarsely between dry coughs. "Boys. Unhitch da team. Wipe 'em down. Wipe my horses down good."

In the house, time has no boundaries for Joann in her unconsciousness. She sees herself months earlier, hunkered beneath the big table, listening . . .

*Knute is urgent. Clara whimpers in protest. There is muffled struggle. What's wrong? She should help her mother—what should she do? She is bewildered, frightened, and engulfed in guilt, knowing instinctively she has heard something she was not meant to hear . . .*

The voices drift and return, bringing conversation from a different night. Her father is harsh . . . *"I tell you again, Clara, if this one's a girl, we'll hafta give it away . . ."*

*Her mother pleads, cries bitterly . . . "People have a duty to keep and raise their children, Knute!"*

*"I can't hardly feed all the girls I got now, and not one of 'em can do the work of a man. In town I heerd about a couple who want a baby, any baby."*

*"No, Knute! It will kill me if you give this baby away! It will kill me!" . . .*

Joann's dream-like state meanders to a crack of lantern-glow around her father's bedroom door. The bedroom where her mother no longer sleeps . . .

*The door opens. Knute, with his uneven stride, goes to Clara's trunk, not seeing that one of his daughters, wrapped in a blanket, is hunched beneath the table, watching. He places an envelope into a box in the trunk and returns to the bedroom. The light around the door goes out . . .*

Joann stirs from unconsciousness. For several moments she refreshes her bearings. The fire! She jolts upright. Where are the others? Is she the only one to survive? New panic subsides when she hears her siblings outside. Joyful with relief, she dashes to join them.

Throughout the summer and long after, Joann continues to try to sort out the loss of her mother. Over and over she reviews all she knows: another baby girl was born. Her mother named her Mavis. She remembers the newborn's cry and her mother's hysterical sobs when the next day Pa picked them each up, carried them to the wagon, and drove away. There were stains of birthing blood on her mother's clothing and the bedding she left behind.

He had returned the next day without them, saying they needed to stay in a hospital for a while. He made several trips to Steele during the next weeks, and when he came home he did not answer questions. Finally, one evening Knute told them their mother had died and he had given their baby sister to "someone." He did not say to whom. When they asked Evelyn why their mother had died, Evelyn said simply, "She bled to death."

It was that same night, under the table, that Joann, stunned, had fixed her eyes on a ribbon of light around her parents' bedroom door, refusing to believe that her mother was not there, lying in bed, nursing the new baby. Then she had seen her father come from the bedroom and limp to Clara's trunk and place the envelope in it. Why had he moved so stealthily? At other times, when he rose in the dark to go to the outhouse, he was not particular about being quiet. She knew instinctively that the paper was not for her eyes, yet because it might have something to do with her mother, her curiosity became unbearable. She felt compelled to see it.

She waited several nights for an early morning when the moon was full, casting cold light through the two small west windows. She slipped from beneath the table and padded over to the trunk, cringing, fearing that her brothers in the loft or her sisters behind the blanket covering their door frame might hear. They would scoff, call her crazy, and tell Pa. He might get the razor strap he uses not exclusively on the boys.

She raised the high, curved top of the trunk, releasing the sweet smell of cedar. She saw the carefully folded white batiste dresses. Had her mother looked down from heaven and seen her girls wearing them at her funeral? In a wooden box with a slide-off lid, right on top, Joann found an envelope with handwriting on the front. Her fingers fluttered as she picked it up and tiptoed to a moonlit window. "Certificate of Death, Clara Isabelle Kirkeborg."

Death. Such a hated, incomprehensible thing that had taken her mother away. She pulled a paper from the envelope and tamped down her nervousness in order to absorb the official-looking document. Some of the words she comprehended. Others she made herself memorize, determined to understand them later—"hysteria," "exhaustion from acute mania," and "Hospital for the Insane."

Throughout the next two summers, when infrequent rains come, they often bring hail. Knute's renewed efforts to turn his girls into field workers fail, his sons prove to be barely competent. The proceeds from his farm cannot support his large family. Back in Norway, after his unfortunate accident, herding the family's sheep up rugged mountainsides became too difficult. He'd tried his hand at fishing. Whenever weather permitted, he cast his line into the swift mountain streams with great success. Now, on the parched prairie, he yearns for icy water to rush against his legs. Just a few hundred miles to the east is a place legendary for its lakes and forests. Evelyn can manage without him for a couple of weeks. He heads for northern Minnesota.

On one of the largest and deepest lakes the state has to offer, Knute finds a fishing resort for sale. He buys it on credit and sends a letter to Evelyn, with instructions to bring her five sisters on the train. He includes details of how the boys are to stay behind long enough to oversee transporting the furniture and other belongings. He writes that he is corresponding with another prairie farmer who has an interest in buying the animals. They will have a new home. Knute will be a fishing guide for tourists, his boys can look after equipment and clean the fish, and the girls, he has plenty of girls, will cook in the lodge and clean the cottages.

As preparations are made to leave, Joann stands staring at the big table. For more than two years, the space beneath the ancestral piece has beckoned her, promising solace. In this private, mysterious sanctuary, she communed with impressions and thoughts that would suddenly come to her. Soothing thoughts, she believed, came from her mother. She could not guess the origin of others, those that made her heart race and her hands clammy. Those that magnified her young life bereft of love. It has been under this table that she has seen things she was not meant to see, heard things she was not meant to hear. It is the place where the words she read on her mother's Certificate of Death embedded themselves into her psyche. Words that would hound her forever.

## CHAPTER ONE

# THE DRAFT NOTICE

1943

Joann looks down two stories from behind her gauze-curtained window. She watches absently as a twenty-ton behemoth snorts, grinds gears, and backs onto the sidewalk below. She often stands here, hoping to catch a cool breeze and eager for the first glimpse of her husband returning from the dairy. Even when it's too early, just seeing the street that will carry his ten-year-old Chevrolet comforts her.

Two sooty figures hasten to guide a shiny chute toward an open basement window. The beast revs, squeals, and tips its midsection high into the air. Black lumps of coal rumble, plummet, then crash through the chute. Only when lusty screams come from the nearby bedroom does Joann return to the moment and realize that the scene below is odd. A coal delivery in June? This war! Nothing is normal anymore.

She rushes into the bedroom to shut the window beyond the crib. The frightened face of her almost-two-year-old pushes against the slats. Her mother snatches her up, holds her awkwardly.

"Don't be afraid, Saffee. It's just coal to keep Daddy's little girl warm when winter comes." She speaks without mother-to-baby nuance. The screaming does not abate. Joann places her on the double bed, sits down nearby, and bounces. "Sa-ffee, Sa-ffee, Sa-ffee." The baby is not quieted.

She stops the bouncing and tries reasoning. "Maybe the coal men have to come now. They might be off to war by winter, just like . . . just like . . . your daddy."

The next afternoon when the child awakes, she screams again. Sweat-soaked, she buries her head in her mother's shoulder, hiding her eyes from the window, even though now the shade is pulled and the limp curtains drawn shut.

Why is her baby crying? "Sapphire! Stop!"

Joann hadn't desired a baby. She had never been fond of babies. But she had wanted Nels—and having a baby came along with having him. Neither gave a thought to the fact that he would be a father who had been essentially fatherless, and likewise, she a mother who had been essentially motherless.

The nurse had pestered her to declare a name for the birth certificate. From her recovery bed, Joann thought about it for three days, until the evening she peered out at a deepening blue summer sky, its first stars twinkling.

*Sapphire, that's it. Like the sky. Or even better, Sapphira.*

"What could be more romantic than being named for the wild beauty of a night sky?" she had gushed to Nels. He arched one eyebrow and scratched his head.

"Oh, Nels, you just don't have a flair for the dramatic like I do."

She was right. He was used to down-home names like those of his sisters, Bertha, Ida, and Cora. No highfalutin names, those. Still, he gazed at her with tenderness and pride, his wife-become-mother.

"You name 'er whatever you want, honey," he said. "Just so you like it, that's the important thing."

The nurse wrinkled her nose. "Sapph*ira*? Isn't that someone in the Bible?"

"Oh yes! I think so. Probably a beautiful queen!" Joann chortled.

"No, Mrs. Kvaale, I sort of remember maybe she was a bad person."

The hospital chaplain confirmed that the nurse was correct.

Later, when Joann noticed her baby's eyes were indeed blue, and not knowing they would soon turn to hazel, she settled on Sapphire Eve. "It was meant to be," she said. "When I saw that blue evening sky, I just knew."

The ink was hardly dry when she regretted the choice, but couldn't say exactly why. Perhaps it was the "fire" sound of it. Later, as she leaned over the bathtub, scrubbing stubborn stains from diapers and flinching at hungry cries from the crib, she decided that Sapphire was too fine a name for this baby. The beauty of an evening sky, indeed. She began to call her Saffee.

Every morning Nels leaves their small apartment before dawn to deliver glass bottles of milk door-to-door, returning in the late afternoon. The dairy job alone would be enough to cover their expenses, but the apartment building's aging owner had inquired if Nels might assist with caretaking in exchange for rent. "It'll just mean keepin' the furnace stoked in winter an' the front grass cut in summer, an' a few other things. Nothin' much," Mr. Resslar said. Nels agreed, even before asking about the "few other things," which turned out to be shoveling snow, burning trash, and trimming the front hedges.

Stoking the furnace only sounded easy. Every cold morning, which in Minnesota is almost every morning of fall, winter, and spring, Nels hurries into coveralls at 4:00 a.m. and heads for the basement. He shovels out yesterday's clinkers from the gaping boiler belly and shovels in new coal until it again belches heat. The task takes almost an hour. He barely has time to clean up, slip into his whites, eat breakfast, and get to the dairy by 5:45 a.m.

As each day wears on, Joann keeps an eye on the clock and goes to the front windows a dozen or so times. She misses him when he's gone, worries about him, craves his affection.

It's almost four o'clock. Joann tucks the ironing board into its alcove in the kitchen and lowers the burner under a simmering chicken. Cooking is a skill Joann is teaching herself. When her family moved to northern Minnesota, her older sisters cooked for the resort guests; Joann and the younger girls cleaned cottages. Knute maintained this arrangement until each girl was eighteen. Only then could they begin high school.

Those resort years, like the prairie years before, took a toll on everyone in Joann's family. And they took Knute's life—he drowned in a boating accident a month after Joann left home.

Humming along with a Sousa march, compliments of WCCO, Joann carries Nels's freshly pressed white uniform toward the bedroom.

"It's almost time for Daddy to come home!" she calls to Saffee, who is sprawled on the living room carpet, chewing and drooling on a rubber teething ring.

"Da-ddy!" the toddler says brightly through a flow of saliva.

Joann hangs the uniform in the closet and pauses at the bureau mirror to run a brush through her dark curls. She turns her face this way and that, at once vain and highly self-critical, then returns to her post at the living room window. From it she can watch mothers push babies in buggies, and men with hats and business suits hurry to what must be very important appointments. She's noted that some pass by about the same time each day. If they would look up, they might see her.

Someone is coming in the main entrance. She moves nearer the door, head tilted to one side. It's the two old gossips from the first floor. Who are they chewing up and spitting out today? Their voices fade.

With Nels due any minute, military music is not the mood Joann desires. She sits down at the desk and turns the radio dial.

"*. . . moments in the moonlight, moments of love . . . lost in the thrill . . .*"

Ahh, much better—the velvety voice of that new crooner, Frank somebody.

She draws their wedding photograph toward her across the desktop, leaning forward to give it close inspection. How many times has she wished she could readjust the veil of her white satin hat? Why hadn't the photographer told her it fell crookedly across her forehead? The gardenia corsage against the navy blue suit looks lovely. She still recalls its fragrance.

She studies the groom's solemn face and, as always, sighs. If she would have only known why her usually jovial Nels had been so out of character that day, she could have set matters straight. His mood remained alarmingly dark for two weeks after the wedding. Only a few days earlier he had been ecstatic, flushed with anticipation. But when he showed up at the church, he was irritable, said he was sick. After the ceremony he didn't want their picture taken. But the photographer was waiting.

Looking at the photo, Joann lets her mind range over the disappointing first days of marriage when she wondered why he spoke to her so harshly, wondered what had happened to his ardor . . .

*"Hold me, Nels. Hold me. I thought you loved me."*

Her quandary continued until the day he came home from work and found her napping on the couch. She propped herself up on an elbow, brushed away damp stray locks of hair from her face, and said apologetically, "I'm always more tired during . . . well"—she wasn't sure how to say it—"during . . . my time of the month."

Nels's jaw dropped. He fell to his knees beside her, pulled her to him, embracing her so tightly she thought he might hurt her. "I thought . . . I thought maybe . . . I'm so sorry! I've treated you so bad." A sob escaped him. He reddened and quickly wiped his eyes on his sleeve.

Joann, stunned by the disclosure, freed herself from his arms and sat upright. He took her face in his hands. "Joann, tell me you're mine, all mine, and never . . . never been with another man."

"Nels! Of course I haven't! Why did you even think it?"

He told her that when they had moved up the wedding date from

September to May, the boys at the dairy called him a "rube" and, in so many words, said she was in "a family way." They teased that her father might show up at the wedding with a shotgun. At first Nels was mad, then he began to believe them. He recalled how popular she was at the dances. There was a flirty way about her. He had seen the guys looking at her, whistling when she passed by.

Now, almost three years later, Joann is oddly conflicted. Although the memory is embarrassing, she can't resist a grin. She has to admit she enjoyed all the attention she got at the Friendship Club dances. She'd never had anyone's notice until she left home and came to St. Paul. Her bent "chicken legs" had filled out. They are not shapely, but they love to dance. When she realized her curves brought attention, she naively became a flirt, making sure it was all flash and no fire. She had never wanted to cause Nels any hurt.

Nels couldn't dance well if his life depended on it, and his grammar is atrocious. She can understand the reason for his grammar, he having been raised in a Norwegian-speaking home, but she cannot excuse it. Joann, like all of Clara's daughters, speaks good English, without the accent Knute passed on to his boys.

When Joann was obligated to exchange school for the dirty linens of fishermen, a sympathetic teacher occasionally brought her books of poetry. From then on, Joann steeped herself in rhyme. So it is not unusual that as she looks at the wedding photo she says, "Oh, Nels, 'How do I love you? Let me count the ways.'"

She's loved Nels from the beginning for his unreserved devotion to her, his sunny disposition, and his talk of getting ahead in life in spite of humble beginnings and lack of education. He was a good man, so there seemed no reason to delay marriage. She insisted on moving up the wedding date, unable to bear the thought that he might slip away. If only she had known . . . Thank goodness, since those first regrettable days Nels has continuously showered her with the affection she had hoped for, and twelve months into the marriage, their baby was born.

Saffee whimpers and looks for something else to gum. Spying the cotton teddy bear Joann made for her, she toddles across the room.

At the desk, another romantic melody scatters its stardust while Joann studies a second photograph. It is a portrait of Nels, displaying his engaging smile and prominent teeth. She had insisted he have the picture taken last summer to capture what he really looks like. With a sigh, she puts the wedding photo into a drawer. She's tired of seeing that veil askew.

She hears Nels on the stairway. Smoothing her carefully curled hair, she hurries to the door, eager for him to embrace her tightly, as he always does. She is surprised when his hug is perfunctory. He tosses his white cap and sinks into the secondhand sofa, ignoring his daughter's uplifted arms.

"It came," he says simply, waving an envelope in her direction.

"Oh, Nels." She switches off the radio and rushes to sit beside him.

"It says report for duty at Fort Snelling. Monday."

"Monday! So soon?"

Joann opens the letter addressed to Nelson Kvaale. She reads one word: "Greetings," and looks at him pleadingly.

"I was hoping . . . I was hoping you'd be deferred awhile longer . . . because . . . because of the baby . . . I don't want you to go, Nels."

"You know I hafta go, Joann . . . it's the right thing to do. But I've decided something."

He tells her that the draft board at Fort Snelling is only taking men for the army now. He's decided he wants navy and he will tell that to the board. Too many American boys are dying in foxholes over in Europe, he says. He'll take his chances in the Pacific.

The baby plops onto the floor at his feet and tugs at his shoelaces. He reaches down. "Come up here, Sapphire, up to Daddy." He lifts her onto his lap and she snuggles against him, wiping a wet chin on his shirt. Nels puts his lean, sinewy arms around his little family and holds them close. Joann begins to weep.

"Now, Muzzy." For some reason he'd given her this nickname after Saffee was born.

"Don't cry. It won't do no good." She is numb.

Saffee squirms, wiggles off Nels's lap, and slides down to the floor. Noticing her, and seeking diversion from news she cannot yet absorb, Joann bemoans her recent frustrations with the fussy baby, especially when the coal delivery frightened her.

Nels interrupts. "The coal came?" Not expecting it this early, he had pushed the bin away from the chute when he swept the basement. The floor must be covered with coal. Tomorrow he'll need to rise early and shovel it up before the building owner discovers it. He sighs.

"It's a few minutes to news time," he says. She gets up and switches on the radio again. Ever since the war started he's never missed the five o'clock broadcast.

"That's Glenn Miller," she says, trying to steady her voice. "Makes me think of the night we met." She sits down at his side, puts her head on his shoulder as they listen and remember.

"New Year's Eve, the Friendship Club," he says, stroking her arm. "As soon as I saw you, you were mine. Even if those other fellas were thick as flies 'round you. You sure had a way of attractin' 'em. But I knew you'd end up with me."

Holding his hand, Joann feels a rush of gratitude that he completely forgave her for causing suspicion in those early days. Now she is sorry she brought up the past at all. He continues the reminiscence, telling her she had looked pretty good in "that there" red sweater.

"Pretty good?"

"Well, no. Gorgeous." He turns serious again. "Yeah," he says, "and when I'm gone, promise to keep yourself, well, covered up with somethin' when you're out, okay?"

Flattered, because she knows she attracts male attention, she says, "What should I wear, a tent?"

The brief levity passes. Drafted. He'll be leaving. Joann puts her face into her hands and sobs.

At their feet, Saffee whimpers and raises chubby arms. "Up, Daddy, up!"

About nine they ready for bed, speaking low so as not to wake the little one in her crib. Nels sets the alarm clock for three thirty.

At 12:50 a.m., Joann still tosses in their bed. With whiffling snores, Nels embraces sleep with the same enthusiasm he gives his waking hours. How can he sleep tonight, knowing he's going off to war? She's already lost both mother and father. By her own choice she's essentially lost her siblings. And now Nels? She presses her hands against her face, sensing her irregular breathing. Across the room, the baby sighs in slumber.

From the start, Joann hated the idea of Nels shoveling coal into a hot furnace.

"But, Joann," he countered, "it's not dangerous. In fact, it's a *wunnerful* thing! Who else gets free rent nowadays?"

She relented, but regularly cautions him to be careful around the flames.

As she listens to his breathing, she worries that Mr. Resslar will ask her and the baby to move out when his stoker leaves for war. How will she live without Nels? She's even lonely when he's at work.

Tomorrow he'll get up . . . so early . . . She finally drifts into troubled sleep . . .

*"Joann! Joann!"* . . .

. . . and a new episode of her recurring nightmare . . .

*Nels scoops flames, tosses, shovels, tosses, shovels . . . Joann is propelled toward the hideous conflagration . . . "Nels! Nels! Hide me!" . . . Burned faces sneer, taunt, laugh . . . Tongues of fire uncoil, lick at her . . . Armies of menacing, charred figures march lockstep . . . "Hide me! Please hide me! Where can I hide?" . . .*

Joann slams upright, hands grip sheets, breath heaves to expel imagined, smothering smoke. *Who is crying? Her mother? Her sisters? Who is burning?* She bounds from the bed unsteadily, crazily.

*"I'm coming! I'm coming!"* With heart pounding, she snatches up her startled baby from the crib, holds her tightly in the darkness, and slumps against the wall.

Encroaching fear advances like a cancer.

## CHAPTER TWO

# WAR

At the door early Monday morning, she clings to him. "Now, sweetheart," Nels pleads, "don'tcha go worryin'. Today is only the meetin' with the draft board. I'll call you before they pack me off to boot camp." But Joann doesn't try to be brave. He cups her face in his hands as they kiss; she wills it is not their last.

By the time he calls Wednesday night, she is frantic. "I've been so worried! Why haven't you called sooner?"

He tries to soothe her. Tells her that in the military everything takes a long time and there are always long lines of inductees at the telephones. "But guess what? I'm a navy man!" He sounds proud. "Took three days of arguin' with the Fort Snelling draft board, but in the end, I won." He will go to Idaho for boot camp, he says. To a place called Farragut. He leaves tonight.

"Tonight? How can you sound happy about it?" she demands, one hand gripping the receiver, the other clenching and unclenching.

"Oh, now, Joann. You know I'm not happy 'bout goin' to war or leavin' you; just happy I won the argument so I don't have to go to the fightin' over in Europe. Besides, bein' a sailor suits me more."

"*Suits* you!" She abruptly stands to her feet. "How can anything about going off to war *suit* you?" Just as abruptly, she sits again, rubbing her temple. Doesn't he understand? He is her life.

Nels tells her it must be done. "But it's going to be so *hard*!" she whines. "For me too, you know."

There's a painful silence. She attempts to pull herself together and asks how he convinced the draft board to transfer him to the navy. He says that after three days a sergeant got tired of his face and stamped his papers.

Her fingers race through her hair. "What does that mean?"

Nels hesitates. "Well, they might have it in fer me."

She tightens her grip on the receiver. "*In* for you?"

He tells her that when the navy sees that the army didn't take him, they might think he is a troublemaker. The sergeant told him that as a consequence, he might be assigned to hazardous duty.

She catches her breath. "*Hazardous*? Like what?"

He cautions her not to "go gettin' upset." He tells her, then wishes he hadn't, that he might be assigned to a ship that carries ammunition. One, he supposes, "that's a prime target fer Japs."

"*No!*" The room swims. She feels faint.

"Ah, gee, Joann, now don'tcha go worryin'. Oh, an' everythin's secret, a course, so don't go tellin' nothin' I said. It's time to catch the train. I'll write ya every day, Joann. Promise. I love you."

Joann pleads with Nels's mother. Will she keep Saffee at the farm? It won't be for long, just until she finds a job in San Francisco. She can't possibly care for a child and job hunt at the same time. Why is she going? She must be near the ocean so she can see Nels when he gets shore leave—he's on an ammunition ship and she hasn't seen him for months. She can hardly stand the worry. She'll come back on the train for her, maybe by Christmas. Saffee's well behaved for just turning three years old. She'll love the country, the chickens, the kittens in the barn. There's one thing, though—can she have her own cup to drink from instead of sharing the dipper on the water crock? Oh, and, of course, the outhouse, no place for a child—can she have a chamber pot inside? Good. It's settled then.

Good-bye, little one, be a good girl, do what your grandmother tells you. I'm going to the edge of the war to see your daddy. I'll be back for you.

# CHAPTER THREE

# SAN FRANCISCO

Joann had tried to make Saffee look acceptable, choosing her best dress, a blue-and-white stripe. But now it is travel-rumpled and barely reaches the top of the little girl's stocky legs. She's grown taller during their separation.

On the three-day train ride, Joann had coached her. "Now remember," she said, "you can't make any noise at Pearlmans'. They aren't used to noise. And don't make any mess—I have enough to do. I wonder if anyone's cleaned while I've been gone. I can't imagine anyone washed the floors."

They step through the service entrance into the huge kitchen of the stately house. Saffee surveys the black-and-white tile floor and whispers loudly, "Yer right, Mommy. Dis floor's dur-rty."

Maude, Joann's seventyish, aristocratic employer, is brewing tea. Hearing the comment, she looks up, startled, appraises the child, then chuckles. "Well! Joann! I daresay it's good you're back."

For three months, Joann was Maude's housekeeper and caregiver for her one-hundred-year-old mother, Grandma Pearlman, before she revealed she had a three-year-old back in Minnesota. Hoping to have proved herself an able employee, she finally dared ask to retrieve her daughter by train, promising that Sapphire would present no trouble in the home. She would be seen and not heard. Well, if they wish, her daughter would not be seen either.

*Seen and not heard. Like the child Joann, under a table.*

Maude and her husband, Henry, object to her leaving for even a few days. How could they get on without her? Grandma Pearlman needs constant care. And there's the cleaning and the laundry—especially the laundry—Grandma's bed needs constant attention. Well, perhaps Dora, the night aide, can stay around the clock a few days. Can Joann be back in a week?

True to the agreement, Saffee is usually hidden away in the Pearlman house. By day, she stays alone in the small bedroom where mother and daughter share a narrow bed. She gazes wistfully out the window, seeing little more than the side of the next house. She peeps out the door and listens to distant conversation and the clatter of household routine that echoes, retreats, then returns. She traces the knobby rows on the chenille bedspread with her finger, counting. But five is as far as her knowledge of numbers goes.

In other regions of the house, Joann attends to Grandma Pearlman's every need and every whim. At night, she is too exhausted to play or even talk much with a lonesome daughter.

It isn't long before Dora quits the night shift and Joann is on call around the clock. When the buzzer sounds, as it does numerous times in the night, she leaves the bedroom to attend to duty. Saffee also awakens, since she is often not tired enough to sleep deeply at the end of an inactive day.

Occasionally, as Grandma Pearlman sits staring out at the winter rain, she remembers that somewhere in the house is a child and asks Joann to bring her. When Saffee arrives, the old woman has usually nodded off, her head bent alarmingly to the side. If she is awake, she puts a dry, blue-veined hand on Saffee's arm and speaks to her briefly in a querulous voice. The conversation is always the same. Grandma Pearlman admonishes Saffee to always "be good" and obey her mother. Saffee shyly dips her head and doesn't speak.

"Well, what do you say, girlie-girl?"

Puzzled, Saffee says, "Nothin'."

"Nothing?" Grandma Pearlman furrows her brow. "Hasn't your mother taught you manners? It's best to say, 'Yes, ma'am,' not . . ." The old woman pauses, struggles to find the pocket of her black shawl, and brings forth a handkerchief to wipe away escaping spittle.

"So," she demands again, "are you going to be a good girl?"

Saffee guesses she should offer a "yes, ma'am," but the unfamiliar words won't come.

For a few moments, Grandma Pearlman's eyes seem to penetrate Saffee's face. Then the old woman sighs, again fatigued. Saffee stands quietly at her side, wondering why Grandma Pearlman looks as she does, smells as she does. She waits until the gray head falls forward in slumber and then she walks away.

When Easter approaches, Henry and Maude make plans to invite their two great-grandchildren for Easter dinner. On Saturday morning, Henry spends considerable time in the backyard. About noon, Joann rushes into the bedroom. All she can see of Saffee are her high-top white shoes sticking out from under the bed where the girl is studying a parade of ants.

"Saffee, get out from under there, quick! Mr. Henry says he wants to show you something." She pulls Saffee by the ankles, helps her up, and brushes off her dusty dress. Joann leads her daughter out through the back door, trying to smooth her hair as they hurry.

Stepping into the squinty sunlight, Saffee sees tall, bony Mr. Henry smiling proudly as he surveys a thornbush. The sun sparkles on hundreds of sugared gumdrops that the man has laboriously stuck onto every thorn he could find. Saffee catches her breath at the thrilling sight and steps closer.

"Oh! It's candy!" she says. She reaches out an eager hand and pulls off one luscious piece.

"No! No! It's not for you! It's for my Philip and Katherine. They're coming tomorrow." Mr. Henry, suddenly embarrassed, glances at

Joann. "Oh . . . well. You can keep it, of course . . . yes, you may have one."

Saffee steps back quickly and hesitantly puts the soft, sweet treat into her mouth. Although seen through welling tears, the gumdrop tree is the most tantalizingly beautiful thing she has ever beheld.

But it is for someone else.

"Saffee, hurry up now, eat your oatmeal," Joann says as she stands at the kitchen sink filling Grandma Pearlman's water pitcher. "I see Beanie coming up the walk." Even after a year, Beanie, the sizable, middle-aged Irish woman the Pearlmans call "Cook," is not used to having a child "underfoot" in her kitchen at mealtime.

Beanie doesn't usually move fast, but today she bursts into the kitchen and blurts, "Joann, where'd you say that man a yours is at?"

Alarmed, Joann almost lets the pitcher slip from her hands. "He's on a navy ship."

"I know—but where's the ship exactly now?"

"I don't know, his letters can't tell me where it goes. Everything's secret in war. What's the matter, Beanie? Tell me!"

Saffee pauses her spoon in midair listening to the distressed exchange.

"Oooh," Beanie moans, shaking her hands up and down as if that will help her to think more clearly. "Well, what's the *name* of the ship he's on?"

"Nels told me not to tell anyone. He said no reckless talk." Desperate to know Beanie's news, and knowing that his ship is the USS *Alamosa*, Joann reveals, "His ship starts with the letter *A*."

"Saints be praised." Beanie sinks into a chair at the table across from Saffee as if to catch her breath. She tells Joann that her husband, Johnny, was on his way home from the rail yards near Suisun Bay at ten o'clock the night before and heard "a terrible 'splosion." She says it was "one a them 'munition ships," but she can't remember its name. "It was *Byron* or *Bryan*, or somethin'. Yeah, that's it, the USS *Bryan*. I *knew* it din't start with *A*. Blew up high in the air when they were loadin' it. Johnny sez that's only 'bout twenty-five mile from here. Didju hear it?"

"I must have been asleep," Joann says, her head bent in relief. The pitcher is overflowing. She leans weakly against the sink and turns off the tap.

Not comprehending the conversation, Saffee says, "Mommy, when we gonna have shigger again? I like shigger on my oatmeal."

Lacking no drama, Beanie continues her report, telling Joann she heard that the explosion had lit up the sky like red and orange fireworks. Her husband wouldn't be surprised if everyone in the area had burned. Joann is shaking. She sinks into the chair beside Saffee and through clenched teeth declares, "I hate this war."

"Mommy!" Saffee hits her spoon against the cereal bowl, splashing milk.

"Saffee, stop it!" Joann snaps. "Maybe we'll have sugar when the war's over." Then more softly, "I hope."

Beanie stands and puts her plump arms around Joann. "Sorry to give ya such a scare, Joann."

"Thanks, Beanie. It's okay."

It's been a long time since anyone has offered Joann a comforting embrace. When will her man hold her again? A ship blew up, an ammunition ship. *"Hazardous,"* he had said. What an awful word.

## CHAPTER FOUR

# SHORE LEAVE

1944

In the middle of the night, Saffee often awakens to see Joann reread-
ing letters from Nels. When a packet of mail arrives about every two
or three weeks, Joann eagerly tears them open and cries. Having no
one else with whom to share her lonesomeness, she sometimes reads
to Saffee, even though all the child understands is that her daddy
is gone and her mother is sad. At such times especially, Saffee, like
the young Joann, yearns to be held, but her mother is too tired, too
stressed to realize it.

"'The sun is so hot on deck we don't wear shirts and we look like
lobsters,'" Joann reads to Saffee one evening. "'I wonder if I'll ever
get used to the constant pounding of the ship's ingine and the rope
hamick they spect us to sleep in.'"

Joann is sorry about her husband's discomforts, but in addition,
Nels's substandard English continues to be a source of consternation.
"Oh dear," she laments to Saffee, "your daddy doesn't spell any better
than he talks." She'd naively assumed before they married that she
would teach him a thing or two in that department.

He writes about the "rough charcters" he serves with, and how he seems to find more favor with "the brass" than they do, getting recognition for his eagerness to do well. Although the ship is camouflaged as a merchant vessel, there are opportunities to "fire our big guns" at the enemy. He's not a very good shot yet, he writes.

One letter relates that a Japanese radio station plays American music over the intercom by day and at night broadcasts the sultry voice of a woman named Tokyo Rose, who coos steamy, generalized accusations of GI wives misbehaving back home.

"I know it's propaganda to brake down our morale," Nels writes, "but sometimes the other men on bored get pretty riled up by it. I'm just glad I don't have to worry about you, Joann. I know our love will never be corrupted, no matter what crazy Rose and these guys say."

One day, poring over a newly arrived letter, Joann exclaims, "As if *being* on an ammunition ship isn't bad enough, *now* he tells me it's manned by *criminals* released from prisons!" Looking at Saffee, but not seeing her, Joann's voice falls to a strained whisper. "Japanese subs thick as the fish in the water . . . crazy bombers in the air . . . and now *criminals* right on his ship. Maybe the military doesn't mind losing *them*—but what about my Nels?"

Alarmed by her mother's distress, Saffee asks, "Mommy, what's a crim-nal?"

Joann rips open the next letter. It contains more disappointment. He's getting shore leave in Portland, Oregon, not in San Francisco! She drops the letter and puts her head into her hands.

"Joann." Maude straightens to full height, somewhat taller than her housekeeper. "Of course I understand you want to see your husband, but remember, we already let you go several days to get your girl, and now you want to leave again? I hardly think you'd expect *us* to keep . . ."

Joann interrupts, her words tumbling rapidly as she pleads. "You know that Sapphire doesn't get in the way at all and she's very quiet. The train trip only takes one day, I'll stay the next day, and then I'll come right back."

"That would be three days. My goodness." Maude folds her arms across her narrow chest and takes a few steps away as she ponders the situation. "This war is so disruptive," she says under her breath. "Gasoline rationing. Food shortages. And now the help . . ." She turns around and says more gently, "Please stop wringing your hands, Joann. I'll discuss it with Mr. Henry and let you know."

Maude and her husband give their reluctant permission for Joann to take a three-day trip to Portland, leaving Saffee at the house. Joann meets Nels and they spend fifteen hours together, mostly at an inexpensive waterfront hotel. When she returns, she is pregnant.

"Mommy! I rode an elephant! I rode an elephant with Mr. Henry!"

"I know, Saffee. I know. You've told me five times." Joann is surprised, and pleased, that Maude and Mr. Henry treated her little girl to the zoo. Saffee had had the time of her young life, and the unexpected gesture makes Joann feel less guilty for leaving "Daddy's little girl" behind when she went to Portland.

A few weeks later, when she is certain, Joann excitedly writes to Nels about the baby.

> *Maybe this one will be a boy! Nine months from Portland is sometime in May. Please come home by then, Darling! His name will be Nels Jr., of course. But if it's a girl, I think May would be a good name, don't you?*

He answers.

> *A family of four—wow! I'm trying to imajine us with two kids. I hope*

*I'll be able to get my job back at the dairy after the war. I hear it's against the law for GI's jobs to disppear. Take good care of yourself, sweetheart. I wish you didn't have to work so hard. Remember, I'm gonna live thru this war and be back to take care of everything—and everybody. I hope I get there before the new baby does.*

Joann conceals her pregnancy from Maude and the others as long as she can. But halfway into the fourth month, fatigue and a ballooning belly rule she must tell. Not eager to house a woman in "that condition," especially whose husband is nowhere to be seen, the Pearlmans quickly decide she will have to leave. They offer to help her find an apartment. Joann has saved almost every penny she has made under their employ, as well as Nels's pay that arrives every month. She is prepared to make do, at least financially.

On her last day, Grandma Pearlman is irritable and refuses to say good-bye to Joann. "Who knows what your replacement will be like?" she whines. But with her slender, blue-veined hand, she motions Saffee to draw closer and lifts a tissue-paper-wrapped package from her lap.

"This is one of my milk-glass plates," she warbles. "I'm a hundred and one years old now, and this plate is as old as I am. It's for you, girlie-girl. Don't break it." Glancing at Joann, she adds, "Your mother will take care of it for you."

Not sure how she should express her delight, Saffee grins broadly and says, "Yes, ma'am."

Joann and Saffee move to a sunbaked, stucco apartment building built into a typically steep San Francisco hillside. They settle into a top-floor, two-room unit, accessed by an outdoor stairway. When the

Murphy bed is lowered in the living room, it fills most of the space. There is a window seat where mother and daughter look far into the distance, all the way to a sliver of ocean where a man they know crisscrosses dangerous waters. The kitchen is just large enough for a two-burner stove, an icebox, and a small table. In this private, pleasant place, while they wait for the baby, and in spite of Nels's absence and the demands war has placed upon Joann, Saffee and her mother have the best months they will ever have together.

## CHAPTER FIVE

# THE BABY SISTER

**M**airzy doats and dozy doats and liddle lamzy divvy. A kiddley divey too, wouldn't you?"

"Sing it again, Mommy! Sing it again!" Saffee begs, laughing and bouncing on the Murphy bed. Joann repeats the song, enjoying its silliness as much as Saffee.

"What are you singing, Mommy? Tell me!"

"If the words sound queer and funny to your ear, a little bit jumbled and jivey, sing, 'Mares eat oats and does eat oats and little lambs eat ivy.'"

It still doesn't make much sense to her, but Saffee happily joins in the next round of "A kiddley divey too, wouldn't you?"

Singing each evening as they lounge on the bed, their spirits lift in a magical way. Mixing off-key voices with laughter, Joann sings in something of an alto range and Saffee mimics with her four-year-old lilt. They sing as loudly as they dare, bouncing gently in time on the bed, in deference to Joann's "condition."

"My Bonnie lies over the ocean, my Bonnie lies over the sea . . . Oh, bring back my Bonnie . . ."

When they tire of singing, Joann reads poetry.

*And they wonder, as waiting those long years through*
*In the dust of that little chair,*
*What has become of the Little Boy Blue*
*Since he kissed them and put them there.*

Joann weaves a blue ribbon through the cloverleaf-shaped cut-outs around the edge of Grandma Pearlman's milk-glass plate and places it on a shelf above the sofa. Saffee beams. The beautiful plate is something of her very own.

While Saffee naps, Joann, a study in loneliness, spends more and more time at the window seat. Pairs of chatting women, most likely military wives, stroll with their young children along the pine-needle-strewn path of the wooded hillside next to the building. Joann notices the seeming ease in which they converse. Occasionally, at the bathroom mirror, she enters into barely audible, imagined conversations with these unsuspecting women. She refrains from such dialogue when Saffee is nearby.

Indulging her weaknesses, Joann rarely suggests that she and Saffee leave the apartment. When they do venture out for short walks on the hillside path, Joann stays on the alert for dogs and averts her eyes from passersby. She can't hide her bulging middle, but she tries to mask her insecurities with head-held-high aloofness, all the while holding tightly to her little girl's hand.

When a friendly neighbor invites Saffee to her son's birthday party, Saffee cries and adamantly refuses to go. In front of the boy's mother, for appearances' sake, Joann briefly insists that Saffee should agree to go. But, of course, she cannot. The left-out mother has taught her daughter to be a left-out child. In her four years, she has never been in the company of other children.

It is no coincidence that one of their favorite songs goes:

*Oh, little playmate, come out and play with me,*
*And bring your dollies three,*

*Climb up my apple tree.*
*Look down my rain barrel,*
*Slide down my cellar door,*
*And we'll be jolly friends, forevermore . . .*
*I'm sorry, playmate, I cannot play with you,*
*My dollies have the flu,*
*Boo-hoo-hoo-hoo . . .*

To prepare for the baby, Joann and Saffee, holding hands, brave a cable car ride to a downtown department store. They return with infant clothing and diapers.

In late March, Joann feels cramping. It's too soon. She telephones a San Francisco hospital for advice and a nurse tells her to go to bed and stay there. She is not reassured.

How can she manage? Who will buy groceries? She's been concerned for some time about who will care for Sapphire when it's time to go to the hospital by taxi. She knows instinctively that this is the kind of thing family is designed for. But she, like most all her sisters, had left the family the day after graduating from high school. Run away from home and each other. Blown to the wind. For Joann, and, she suspects, for the others also, by then it was too late to bond, to behave like a family. Joann had taken a bus to a new season, a fresh life in St. Paul that brought her a little fun, a husband, and a child. She had no intention of ever again communicating with family. Especially Maxine. Especially Rolf. But now, alone and afraid, she must think about them again.

Of the sisters, Dorothy, although imperious at times, had been the only sibling who was not exactly kind, but at least tolerant. She wrote Joann a couple of letters that she has kept but did not answer. She shuffles through her stationery box. Yes, the first one has a phone number.

Perhaps Dorothy will be willing to help. She knows how hard it is to have a husband in the Pacific; her George is an officer on the

USS *Ticonderoga*. She is living, she wrote, with her two children, in the home of a cousin in Iowa for the duration of the war.

Hoping for a miracle, Joann calls and pleads with her to come. Dorothy, a more capable woman than Joann, agrees to leave her children for a short time in the care of the cousin and take the train to California. Until she arrives, Joann is beside herself. From her bed, she frets to Saffee, "*You* gave me twenty hours of hard labor, Saffee. I don't know if I can go through that again."

On a sunny spring day, Saffee watches out the window as her mother steps from a cab. The blanketed bundle in her arms is baby sister April. Aunt Dorothy carries the sleeping infant up the outer stairway as Joann relates that it was an easy birth, "compared to the first one."

"Look, Saffee!" Joann gushes. "Look at the baby. See how tiny she is. Isn't she beautiful?"

In the hospital, Joann wrote Nels the news. She tells Dorothy how she anticipates his surprise to learn he's the father of two, a whole month earlier than expected. "He probably wanted a boy this time," she says, "but I'm sure he'll be happy with a girl."

Joann places the sleeping infant on the bed and begins to unpack her small overnight bag. She thinks about her own father, recklessly sacrificing his wife's health hoping to produce male farmworkers. She knows; she had been a secluded witness. Sometime later, of course, she had understood what was happening. Perhaps that was the night her mother began to grow a seed. A girl seed. The last one. Sometimes sounds of their struggle still replay in Joann's mind, as do Clara's pleas from that other night. *"No, Knute! It will kill me if you give this baby away! It will kill me!"*

At the remembrance, a tear threatens to slide from Joann's eye. She quickly blinks it away so Dorothy doesn't see. Their mother's words had come true and explained what Joann read to be the cause of death on the certificate in the wooden box. Memorized words that have not diminished their foreboding.

Dorothy stays two more days. Joann is grateful for her help but cringes at the once-familiar caustic voice, characteristic of all her sisters. They share war information, scanty as it is, gleaned from their husbands' letters. Joann learns that two kamikaze planes hit and seriously damaged George's aircraft carrier three months earlier. Hundreds of men had been killed, burned in fires on deck, Dorothy tells her. "I'm so thankful that George was spared."

Joann trembles. A fiery attack in the same waters traversed by her Nels. The *Alamosa* could just as easily be hit and burned. Is the whole world ablaze?

Impulsively, she tells Dorothy scenes from her troubled nightmares. "It's that prairie fire. It still haunts me," she says, steadying her hands.

"Oh, Joann, it was such a long time ago," Dorothy scoffs. "We all have to move on, you know."

Joann bristles. How can her sister dismiss the horrific event? She will not mention to Dorothy that sometimes, even in *day*dreams, the fire still burns within her, visions of flames rushing over their mother's grave. What good would it do? Dorothy too is a daughter of hardship, a motherless sibling. Joann came to the conclusion some time ago that none of her siblings emerged from their needy upbringing unscathed. All of them, but less so Dorothy, were difficult people. It was with relief that Joann had left home after high school, with no desire to see any of them again.

Their conversation moves on. Dorothy speaks with sadness of their mother's death. "Can you imagine birthing nine babies at home with no medical assistance?" She recalls how weak Clara had been as she lay in bed and how they had all seen the blood. How their father, beside himself, made a pallet for her in the wagon and carried her, and then the baby, out of the house. "And then Pa wasn't able to tell us that she had bled to death, had Evelyn tell us."

*Hysteria. Acute mania. Hospital for the Insane.* It seems clear that Dorothy does not associate these words with their mother. Does not know the cause of her death. Just as well. They would have little impact on self-assured Dorothy. She would not relate.

"Back then," Dorothy says, "the mysteries surrounding the whole matter of giving birth prevented us from asking very many questions." Joann tries to change the subject, but her sister muses on, speculating how their lives might be different had Clara survived.

"Don't get me wrong," Dorothy says, "tragic as it was, in some ways I think her early death made me a stronger person. I became independent, and that was good."

Joann says nothing. Clearly Dorothy is contrasting herself with Joann's inadequacies. To Dorothy, she must still be the frightened girl whimpering under the table, aching for her mother's attention. Childhood emptiness rushes back and stabs her. Joann knows that she still is that little girl.

When Dorothy leaves, Joann makes a few changes. She arranges for weekly grocery delivery, and each evening she makes a bed for Saffee on the sofa. Baby April shares the Murphy bed with her mother.

As Joann strokes the downy head of her nursing baby, pleasant maternal feelings rise within her. She anticipates that this child will bring her comfort, make life good again. These are not the feelings she experienced with her firstborn, the one standing before her now, watching with her usual soberness. The newness of marriage and first motherhood, the war that made them move across the country, the months spent washing Grandma Pearlman's soiled sheets—all these had hindered closeness with the first child. But now, this new one brings hope for happier days. The war will end. Nels will come home. They will return to Minnesota.

Saffee watches her mother cuddle baby April and sing soft lullabies. She watches Joann kneel at the bathtub every day to scrub diapers, then hang them on a rack to dry. She watches her bathe April in a metal tub on the kitchen table. They no longer bounce on the bed and sing "Mairzy Doats." As April grows, Joann frequently comments that she is the "spittin' image" of Nels.

Joann is worried, then frantic, when no letter comes from Nels for four weeks, then five. Has his ship gone down and no one has told her? Finally, an envelope arrives containing an astonishing message.

Dear Joann,

I got yer letter. So the baby was born April 11th! Swell! Wasn't it sposed to be near the end of May?

Please don't tell me Tokyo Rose is right. When I hear that woman, I can't help having doubts—even about you. Some men out here have gotten walking papers from girlfriends back home—and there's even been a few divorce papers. How low. Its hard enuf just being out here and not knowing if I'll live thru it.

Your all I have to live for, Joann. Thinking about some other man holding you is driving me crazy. I'm sorry to write this. I hope I'm just brainwashed and it aint true. It's hard to think straight out here.

I still love you,

Nels

P.S. Some nerve to name her after the month!!!

Joann is devastated, hurt, and angry. She expected him to be happy. Disregarding that he has the highest morals of any man she's ever met, and disregarding that he's written that he never takes island shore leave with the other sailors because he wants no part of their "carouzing," she retaliates.

Dear Nels,

You're accusing me again? I thought you were over that. I thought you trusted me—as you should. And you're a fine one to talk. I read in a magazine about GIs on shore leave—taking "liberties" with those gorgeous, curvy island girls—the ones who don't wear anything but beads around their neck.

Love to you too,

Joann

She mails the letter and quickly regrets it. She writes a profuse apology. His letters from then on are few and convey no passion of a lonesome husband at sea.

CHAPTER SIX

# THE HOMECOMING

1945–1946

August 15. The war is over at last. Nels will be coming home. Daddy will be coming home.

"Saffee, take this little flag, go outside, and run all the way down the hill to the end of the street," Joann instructs. "While you're running, wave the flag and shout as loud as you can, 'The war's over!' Go on, now. Run!"

"Mommy! Come with me!"

"No, I can't. I need to stay with April."

"I can't go alone!" She stamps her right foot in protest. "I won't go!" Never has she been expected to do such a public thing. Never has she been outdoors alone.

But Joann insists. After minutes of argument, Saffee grabs the flag, dashes outside, and with tears streaming, fearfully runs down the long San Francisco hill. She does not shout the wonderful news but sobs, incredulous that she must do something so intimidating.

They wait.

Nels's ship does not release him for almost ten more months. His letters during this time are lukewarm. On one hand, Joann is grieved that he doubts her faithfulness, as he had before they married. And now again, skewed by her emotional immaturity, she is not *completely* sorry for inadvertently causing jealousy, even when it is needless.

Finally, he calls to say that he's on his way from Portland to San Francisco. Joann and Saffee are beside themselves—Saffee with happy anticipation, Joann with nerves. When they hear him coming up the stairway, they expectantly open the door to a man with a heavy sea bag over his shoulder and a taut, unsmiling face that Saffee barely recognizes.

"Daddy? Daddy! You're home!" Saffee reaches for him to pick her up, but he thrusts past both wife and daughter and shows no interest in the sleeping, almost-one-year-old child on the bed. To Saffee's great dismay, her parents begin to yell angry words.

Within a few days, Joann is able to convince Nels that April is indeed his flesh and blood. "See, Nels, look at that grin. Just like yours! A baby never lived who looked more like her father."

Convinced, yes, but traumatic months of doubt at sea did permanent damage. April is a child of his flesh, but will never be a child of his heart.

# CHAPTER SEVEN

# ST. PAUL

1946

Saffee slouches in a living room chair, one leg slung over the armrest. As is often the case, her young mind, uncluttered by experience or preoccupation, scrutinizes the present moment. Singsong floats down the stairway as April, playing in her crib, forestalls a nap. Why is her little sister always so happy and busy?

On the floor is a rag doll that Joann made for Saffee that she has never cared for. What does one do with a doll? Why does April cuddle and coo over Saffee's neglected toy? She's dragged it around so much its yarn hair is all but gone.

Saffee listens to her parents as together they attach shelves to a kitchen wall. They aim to make their newly purchased, modest home more livable. Joann gives minute instructions and Nels tries to comply patiently and precisely, "to keep the peace." No matter what Joann and Nels are doing, decisions rarely involve discussion, since Joann usually makes up her mind quickly about things, then closes it.

After three weeks back in St. Paul, the Kvaales, other than Saffee, are fairly comfortable. It's their first house and their first backyard. April finds delight toddling barefoot in the grass, picking dandelions and chasing squirrels.

"Watch your sister," Joann often says. Saffee doesn't mind being in the backyard, but she's uneasy in the front. She's seen older children in the vicinity, to say nothing about a few dogs. She is comfortable with neither.

As she slumps in the chair, idly bouncing a leg, laughter from outdoors interrupts her boredom. Curious, she steps out onto the screened front porch, just far enough to investigate unobserved, as her mother might have done. In the adjacent yard, five girls in summer dresses, perhaps slightly older than Saffee, giggle and shout, jump and run, as they bat about a blue rubber ball, the largest ball Saffee has ever seen. She does not yearn to join them, but is curious enough to watch.

"Here. Send it over here. It's *my birthday*, you know!" a bubbly blond girl cries. The frivolity continues until an aproned woman steps out of the house and calls, "Midgie! Everyone! Come in for cake and ice cream." The laughing girls skip and tumble into the house.

Saffee remembers that her own birthday is coming. The one, she's been told, that means she must soon attend something called kindergarten. She goes inside to the kitchen. Nels is nailing shelf supports onto a wall according to Joann's carefully considered pencil markings.

"Daddy, when it's my birthday, will you buy me a big ball?" Saffee asks.

Nels pounds the last nail and laughs. "A ball? What would you do with a ball?" he teases. He lifts a shelf to its place. "Balls are fer boys, ain't they?" Teasing is Nels's usual mode of communication with Saffee. It amuses him and aggravates her.

She turns to her mother. "Mommy, I saw some girls next door having a party. They were playing with a big, big ball. The girl who lives there is Midgie."

"Nels!" Joann exclaims. "That top shelf tips to the right. Anything I'd put on *that* would roll right off."

Saffee ambles out the back door to sit on the steps. She idly watches a robin hopping here and there in the grass. He cocks his head to listen, then pecks the ground. Hop, cock, peck. She admires his orange breast and beady, bright eyes and most of all his perkiness. If she could have this incredible creature for a pet, she would not be lonely.

At supper, Saffee asks Nels how she might go about catching a robin. He tells her the only sure way is to put salt on its tail. So easy! She is thrilled with the anticipation of capturing a friend.

The next morning Saffee finds Joann stirring bright yellow dye in a steaming galvanized tub that covers two burners of the gas stove. Eagerly, Saffee asks if she might have some salt. "Don't bother me, Saffee. I'm dyeing sheets to make curtains and this dye's very hot—stay away now."

"But, Mommy, Daddy says if I put salt on a bird's tail I can catch him! Pleeease give me some salt?"

Joann reaches into a cupboard. "Here," she says, sprinkling a few stingy grains from a shaker into Saffee's ready hand. "That's enough."

Saffee skips outside and sits on the step, waiting for her robin. Presently, a wren swoops down onto the grass and begins to search for tasty morsels. Well, any bird will do. Saffee darts at the wren, tossing salt in its direction. The bird takes flight, carrying with it Saffee's hope for a friend. She tears back into the house.

"Mommy! It didn't work, my bird flew away!"

Joann, stirring intently, doesn't seem to hear.

*"Happy Bir-ir-thday, Sa-pphire! Happy birthday to you!"*

The family sits in the kitchen alcove brightened by windows newly curtained in yellow. Saffee blows out five candles. While Joann cuts the cake, Nels brings in a large pink balloon from the next room. Granted, it's the biggest balloon Saffee has ever seen, but there is no escaping the fact that it is not a ball.

When their cake is finished, Joann washes April's sticky fingers and Nels lifts her from her high chair. Brownie box camera in hand, Joann says, "Saffee, let's go outside now and take a birthday picture of you and the new ball."

Saffee picks up the balloon with both hands and follows. Under her breath she says, "It's not a ball."

"Me ball, Saffee?" April begs. "Pleeease?"

Nels notices a girl in the next yard and calls to her, "Are you Midgie? Come on over here. Have your picture taken with Saffee."

Saffee pulls her shoulders up toward her ears. "Daddy! No!" she hisses. As far as Saffee is aware, no one in the family, least of all her, has yet spoken to anyone in the neighborhood.

Midgie slowly crosses to the Kvaales' yard with a wary smile.

"Oh!" Joann has an idea. "Midgie, I've heard you have a great big ball too. Go get it for the picture."

Midgie glances at Saffee's balloon. "Well, okay," she says hesitantly. The young neighbor goes back to her house and returns with her blue ball. Joann poses the two older girls and April, and then prominently places the ball and balloon in front of them on the grass.

"Smi-ile! Saffee, I said smile. Come on, *big* smile." She snaps the picture. "There. Now, girls, you play nice," Joann directs over her shoulder as she and Nels turn back to the house.

April jumps up and down, squealing, "Me ball! Me ball!"

Saffee picks up her balloon and steps a few feet away from Midgie. "Want me to throw it at you?" she asks.

"Sure," says Midgie.

Saffee lifts her birthday present over her head and gives it a toss. "There."

Immediately, a gentle breeze catches the balloon. The girls watch it float to the top of a tree and alight on a branch. *Pop!*

April stretches her short arms to the sky, calling, "Come back, ball! Come back, ball!"

"Be quiet, April." Saffee seizes her sister's hand and retreats across the yard and into the house.

Midgie watches them go.

The kindergarteners, their faces full of dreams and wonder, sit on the floor and sing with high voices, hardly in unison, *"Si-ilent night, ho-oly night . . .'round yon vir-ir-gin mother and Child."*

Singing along, and contentedly rocking with the rhythm, Saffee admires the lopsided green paper wreaths adorning each of the classroom's tall windows. *It's Christmas!* She's not quite sure what it's all about, neither the tinsel part nor the spiritual part, but this year she's been touched by the magic of it. On sudden impulse, she purses her lips and begins to blow with enthusiasm.

Astonished, Miss Jessup says, "Sapphire Kvaale! We don't whistle Christmas carols! Go stand in the cloakroom!"

Hot tears of mortification and contempt flow freely as Saffee buries herself behind her wool winter coat that hangs alongside a forest of others. Hadn't her mother said that kindergarten would be fun? On the first day, Saffee knew she had been duped when she and her classmates had to tearfully bare their arms for polio vaccinations. Every morning boisterous, chattering children hurry by her as she dawdles four blocks to the intimidating redbrick building. She is usually late. The heavy outside door never yields to her pull. She leans against it, nose running from the cold, until someone passes by in the hall and opens it for her. In the classroom, she is tongue-tied when others speak to her. If forced to reply, she mumbles, hiding her face in her hands.

But this morning she had not been late because speculations about Christmas prompted her to be happy. Her father had placed a tree right in their living room and her mother had strung it with colored lights and added silver tinsel. There had been talk of a baby named Jesus and Christmas presents. How wonderful it all was. Why wouldn't whistling be an appropriate expression of joy? Now she hears her classmates sing, *"Oh, what fun it is to ride in a one-horse open sleigh."* She stares at the wood floor, made muddy with melted snow from eighteen pairs of rubber boots.

That evening Saffee sits at the supper table stirring patterns of gravy into her mashed potatoes, round and round, round and round, until she has a plateful of uniformly brown mush. Her right foot kicks a steady tempo against the table leg as she broods over the morning's humiliation.

She had been so proud of learning to whistle, and she didn't have that many things to feel proud about. Certainly not the playground races she always lost or the paintings she always smeared. But she had learned to whistle! . . . and foolishly dared reveal her new talent. During naptime, snot-nosed Alan had pointed a pudgy finger at her and sing-songed, *"Saffee's sappy, Saffee's sappy,"* and then, *"Sappy, sappy, sappy."*

She formulates a desperate emergency plan: she will stop going to kindergarten. Of course, she'll need parental cooperation.

"Mommy?" She waits for a reply, but Joann stares into some middle distance between here and there and doesn't respond.

"Mommy, listen." Still no answer.

*"Mommy!"*

"Eat yer potatoes, Saffee," Nels says.

"Mommy! *Please*, listen to me!"

April bangs a spoon on her high chair. "More?" she begs, pushing her bowl around the tray.

Saffee watches her mother absentmindedly spoon another helping of applesauce from a serving dish and plop it onto April's "no-touch" plate, divided so that foods don't mix.

"Mommy! I need to talk to you!"

Her father frowns. "Don't bother your mother, Saffee," he says sternly.

In spite of Nels's jovial, back-slapping ways in public, his unmistakable message to Saffee is that she must suffocate all spontaneity. Spontaneity is a problem. Bland is good. So be as bland as cold mashed potatoes. Therein is safety; safety is a virtue; risk is not to be tried. Saffee instinctively knows that his instructions are meant to avoid igniting her mother's "nerves," and she is sure he would also want her to exhibit this restraint at school. Whistling had violated her father's limiting philosophy.

Saffee shovels potatoes as fast as she can, swallowing with difficulty around the growing lump in her throat. She must get away from the table, but will be prevented if her plate is not clean.

"I'm done!" she blurts and tramps from the kitchen.

Her tears are angrier now than they were in the cloakroom. She's always hated her mother's silent staring. And she hates kindergarten. She will *never* go back.

Saffee stands biting her lip in the middle of the darkened living room, lit only by the strings of lights glowing on the Christmas tree. She stares at their reflected colors on the light gray carpeting that her mother is so proud of. Joann never misses a chance to comment, "It's a Gulistan, you know!" Whatever that means, it must be something wonderful.

Saffee quietly opens a drawer of the corner desk and pulls out her cigar box of crayons. She holds up a fat one to catch a glimmer of light. Purple. Her chin trembles and her heart beats wildly as she presses the crayon in a diagonal line from corner to corner across her mother's gray carpeting.

In the dim light, unaware that the waxy crayon has failed to leave any mark on the carpet, she dashes up the stairs to her bedroom. Under the covers, she waits for the desperate deed to be discovered.

She sleeps.

## CHAPTER EIGHT

# THE HIGHWAY MAN

1948

A gurgling radiator in the girls' bedroom struggles to keep January drafts at bay. Joann tucks blankets securely around April as Saffee stands at her sister's crib, watching. "Mommy, can I stay up later tonight? A second grader shouldn't hafta go to bed same time as a three-year-old."

"I suppose, for a while, but put your nightgown on now."

Joann goes downstairs. Saffee sheds her wool sweater and corduroy overalls and dives into a flannel nightgown, a quilted robe, and a pair of matted slippers.

She scampers out of the bedroom and creeps down the stairway. She loves to lie on the carpet and listen to her mother read, but it isn't a time of closeness, like those first happy weeks in the San Francisco apartment. Nowadays, when she reads verse, Joann communes only with her own melancholia. Tonight perhaps she will read "The Raven," Saffee's favorite, although very scary, poem.

*"The moon was a ghostly galleon tossed upon cloudy seas . . ."*

Saffee recognizes "The Highway Man," a poem that, in Saffee's opinion, is almost as good as "The Raven."

Joann sits in the armchair on many lonely winter evenings, wrapped in a blanket, lost in melodramatic rhyme. To her consternation, Nels is only home on weekends now. The dairy is rapidly expanding across the state, much of its success due to Nels, the milkman-become-sales-manager. In this new position, he acquires country dairies, hires distributors, and keeps grocers happy with the dairy's service.

Nels believes that his work is of more benefit to his family than his presence. The division of labor—he brings home the bacon, Joann raises the girls and runs the house—is taken for granted and never discussed. Nels is quite capable of doing his part, he assumes Joann is likewise. To him, his diligence through winter's cold and summer's heat means they will have all they need to live on, plus savings in the bank. To Joann and his girls, it means he is little more than a stranger. Once again, Joann feels empty.

> The road was a ribbon of moonlight over the purple moor,
> And the highwayman came riding—
> Riding—riding—
> The highwayman came riding, up to the old inn door.

Lying on the floor, her chin cupped in her hands, Saffee listens to the familiar story of tragic Bess, the innkeeper's black-eyed daughter who pulls the trigger bound to her bosom, sacrificing her own life to signal a warning of danger to her lover.

"The man is a thieving scoundrel," Joann has explained to Saffee, "but he's so-o-o handsome that he steals her heart away."

Saffee doesn't understand the nuances of the story, but no matter, poetry is, for Saffee, at least, distant communion with her mother. With increasing passion, Joann continues . . .

*Then look for me by moonlight,*
*Watch for me by moonlight,*
*I'll come to thee by moonlight . . .*

The poem grows long. Saffee's head sinks onto the carpet. She can't stay awake to hear the familiar, gripping climax, when the highwayman rides at a gallop brandishing his rapier high, only to be *"shot . . . down like a dog on the highway . . . with the bunch of lace at his throat."*

Several poems later, Joann hears Saffee's gentle snore and looks her way. "Saffee . . . Saffee," Joann orders from her chair, "go to bed now; you've been up way too long. There's school tomorrow." Saffee yawns and climbs the stairs. Joann goes back to her poem and reads so late she's too sleepy the next morning to ready her daughter for school.

"Get your own cereal, Saffee," she calls from her bed. "Button your coat and zip your boots. I'm going to sleep 'til April wakes up . . . don't be late now."

Saffee doesn't need the last reminder. She no longer dawdles along the four blocks to school nor plops down in the snow halfway to consider whether to go on at all. Now that she's learned to read, a skill that makes her feel alive, bordering on important, she finds security sitting in her own desk, part of an orderly row of other desks. At home she has a small collection of children's books, pages tattered from turning.

At the same time that books become doors promising light for Saffee, her mother begins to spiral downward into darkness.

## Chapter Nine

# Discontent

Throughout the winter, Joann grows more resentful of Nels's absences. She broods. She frets. She gives minimal attention to her daughters, choosing instead radio episodes of *The Guiding Light*, *The Right to Happiness*, and *The Romance of Helen Trent*. The romantic poets continue to be her nighttime companions. She asks Nels to buy her a spiral-bound notebook. In it she tries her hand at her own poetry. At times throughout the day she whispers a word or phrase that fancies her, rolls it around in her head, tries it out on the mirror, and when satisfied, scribbles in the notebook, murmuring. At first her poetry dissects loneliness. The loneliness she learned as a child. Then she begins to fantasize what her life would be like with a man more handsome, more entertaining than Nels. She wonders if perhaps he also desires . . .

As is Saffee's habit, she watches her mother. She notes that Joann's hands, when quiet, are fists. Not fists that pummel, but neither do they stroke, or pat, or beckon. Their clench seems to restrain something within. At other times the same hands are fastidious, precisely stacking towels for the shelf as if on display, then moving on to pound flour with the edge of a saucer into sinewy round steak until it is pink and flaccid.

It's not unusual that when Nels returns home from work, Saffee hears her parents argue.

"Don't you forget, Nels," her mother will say, "I was *alone* all those years you were at sea, working my fingers to the bone and so worried about you. When the war was over, I thought you'd stay *home*."

"I work hard for *you*, Joann," Nels will counter, "so we can have things. Don'tcha understand?"

On weekends, Nels pays bills, buys groceries, and tends to neglected household chores.

With little to occupy her time and mind, baseless suspicions spread across Joann's void. She quizzes Nels about what he does at work each day and what he does each night.

Exasperated, Nels sputters, "If you'd just git out, Joann, *meet* folks, make some women friends—"

She cuts him off. "Gregarious is for *you*, Nels"—she tosses her head—"*not me*."

In February, Joann declares, "If I don't see more of you, Nels, I'm going to die! So I've made a decision—I'm going to travel with you."

"Joann, don't talk nonsense. What about the girls?"

"I don't know about them, Nels, but I'm just *not* going to be alone in this house anymore."

Nels knows that his wife's feelings, although not understood, cannot be treated casually. Wearied by her discontent, he offers a compromise. "How 'bout if we move, then? If we get a place more the middle of my territory, I can be home more."

Joann agrees and shakes off some of her recent melancholy. The next three Saturdays, with Saffee and April in tow, they travel miles of highways, bordered by drifting snow, to evaluate small towns that dot the interior of the state. On the third week, they consider Miller's Ford, a community of four thousand residents, where fathers work, mothers keep house, and children grow up to follow suit.

"I can see it's a decent place," Joann says as they explore. "Churches outnumber beer joints more than two to one." She's made a careful count. "And there's a minimum of garish neon signs," she adds. Nels notes there seems no need for traffic lights. "Uptown," Main Street has a variety of stores, a movie theater, and a bank. They drive past a two-story redbrick school, a small hospital, and a Carnegie library.

The following Saturday they find a six-bedroom, fifty-year-old house for sale on the west end of town. With great enthusiasm, Joann recognizes its potential and leaves behind her season of inertia, replacing it with one of creativity.

"Look, Nels. This huge kitchen could be made into an efficiency apartment to rent out." In her exuberance, she fairly flies to the next room. "The big dining room can be divided, making a small dining room for us, with a new kitchen at that end."

With ideas bubbling like a percolator, Joann quickly notes that the four upstairs bedrooms are large enough to make two more apartments. "And, oh!" she gushes. "The living room French doors downstairs can be closed to give the upstairs renters private access. We won't even have to see them at all," she says, "except to collect the rent, of course." Eventually, however, she will make sure that through those French doors she is able to see and hear *them*.

Nels, more cautious than his wife, tries to temper her, commenting that such a huge remodeling project is beyond him and would need to be hired out. While April scampers with delight from room to room, Joann solicits Saffee's support. "Saffee, wouldn't you just *love* to sit and read on the wraparound screened porch? And here, look out this window, there's a river down that hill, right across the street. You can learn to swim in the summer and skate in the winter." Saffee looks dubious.

The cost of the house, plus the remodeling, would hardly be offset by the monthly rent it might generate, but Nels's new job has increased their income. Encouraged by Joann's sudden buoyancy, he agrees that the purchase is feasible. Does she understand that she will have to oversee the carpenters, electricians, and plumbers? She paces here and there in the empty dining room, takes a deep breath, and assures him she will.

Back in St. Paul, even before the purchase is complete, Joann begins meticulous drawings, detailing her ideas for change. Saffee surveys her work and asks, "Will I have my own bedroom?"

"No. All the extra rooms will be apartments."

Eager to move and begin the work, Joann decides that Saffee can miss the last two months of second grade.

The packing of their belongings is well under way when Joann receives word that Evelyn, her oldest sister, had a heart attack and has died. The news prompts Saffee to ask questions that mostly go unanswered. Other than Dorothy, who came to San Francisco when April was born, her mother never mentions siblings.

After Nels and Joann attend Evelyn's funeral, Joann's ebullient mood plunges. The next day, and the day after that, she sits in the armchair, immobilized, staring into the mists of memory. Partly filled boxes lay neglected in every room.

"Oh, Evelyn . . ." It is a quiet moan, barely audible. "Only fifteen and had to raise us . . . like a mother hen . . . took care of everyone when that fire came . . . except the baby."

Saffee leans against her mother's shoulder and thrusts her face close to Joann's, demanding attention. "*What* baby, Mommy? *What* fire? Who are you talking about?"

Joann, far away, responds in a monotone, "Mother's last little girl . . . and Pa gave her away."

Saffee struggles to grasp the idea of a motherless family—and giving away a baby.

"Mommy, how little were you when"—she flutters her hands—"you know, when your mother . . ."

Joann continues her whispered thoughts. "Hospital for the . . ." Suddenly she exclaims, "No!" causing her focus to momentarily sharpen. "Seven," she says to Saffee. "I was seven when she died. Same as you."

"Not like me," Saffee says quickly, "because I'm almost *eight*!"

Joann reenters her distant place; her hands tighten their grip.

"Mother was delicate . . . surely not cut out to live in a sod house," she whispers. "Not meant to have nine . . . Pa insisted . . . I heard him. He only wanted boys . . ."

Saffee sinks to the floor and sits very still. Joann's emotions surge as she continues, "Then she was gone! Left Evelyn . . . left her to do the work and put up with the boys . . ."

Nels, who has taken a week off from work for the move, comes into the room and interrupts. He reminds Joann that it is Wednesday and the moving van comes Friday morning. She seems not to hear. By Thursday, with little assistance, Nels manages to fill the boxes and make all the necessary preparations.

That afternoon a battered pickup truck stops in front of the house. Saffee doesn't recognize the barrel-chested man in overalls and faded shirt who comes to the door. He removes his dusty cap and fingers it in a self-conscious manner. Nels shakes his hand. "Samuel! What brings you here?"

The man greets Nels, then looks beyond him to where Joann stands. "Hello, Joann. My Ev'lyn"—the big man's face goes red—"she wanted you ta have our ol' table, so I brung it to you." His speech is the dialect of Minnesota Norwegians. "When I heerd"—he puts his cap back on and just as quickly removes it—"at the fooneral that you bought yerselves a place out in Miller's Ford, I din't want you leavin' without it."

Joann sucks in her breath. "Oh my," she says. "The table?" She lowers herself onto a closed packing box.

"Me an' the boys, we're thinkin' a movin' to the cottage on the west side a the farm. It's right on the lake, don'tcha know. Boys, dey like ta fish a lot. Without Ev'lyn, we don't need no big place, don't need no big table. Won't have room. Anyways, it needs ta stay in Ev'lyn's side of the family, don'tcha know."

He apologizes for not bringing the chairs. His boys had been rough on them, and anyway, he adds, they were not the originals. Evelyn told him that when the table was in her childhood home, her father had made benches for it.

Joann looks pale and makes no comment.

## CHAPTER TEN

# THE TABLE

affee and April follow Samuel and their dad to the truck where they watch the unloading of the heavy, disassembled relic. In addition to two large squares for the table's top and four sturdy legs, there are three good-sized leaves and several lengths of apron with a wide pattern of carved vines on each length. Although the finish has been rubbed away, the color of the old scarred wood is still warm, neither light nor dark. Samuel, puffing from the lifting, says he reckons the wood is birch.

"'At's not a tabo," says April, regarding the various pieces of wood piled on the ground.

"When it's all put together it is," Saffee informs her. April squats to get a closer look.

Nels admires one of the legs. "I think maybe this here is called dovetail joinery?"

Samuel agrees, saying that the design allowed the table's disassembly, which made it possible to transport it to America from Norway. He adds that, according to Evelyn, one of her father's brothers brought it from the family homestead to North Dakota for Knute and his family.

"That was quite a trip in those days," Nels says.

Joann has followed them outside and stands expressionless several yards away. "It was Uncle Jergen," she says in a flat voice. The men turn to look at her. "He brought it to our pa, the oldest son. But he didn't want it. And I don't want it either. Our brother Rolf should have it," she says.

Samuel runs sizable fingers through his thinning hair and repeats Evelyn's wishes on the matter. "She had her reasons. Somethin' 'bout it bein' special to you, Joann. You playin' under it or somthin'. All I know, she said it should be yers. The brothers, they ain't married, ya know. It's a piece fer a family."

Joann returns to the house without responding.

Saffee joins April's inspection. She runs her fingers over the tooled vines, tracing the intricate pattern, then turns over an apron piece and studies some lettering on the back. She strains to lift up a length of wood for Nels to examine, asking him to explain what the numbers and words mean.

"Thought you learned how to read, Saffee," he teases. Nels gives the wood a close look and reads a date, "1865. Guess that's when somebody made it. Here, Samuel, can you read it? The words are in Norwegian." Samuel props his glasses atop a large bald place on his head and squints at the lettering.

"Always heard it was Ev'lyn's grandpa who done made it, don't know for sure," says Samuel. "Yup. Here it says, 'Anders Kirkeborg'— that's Knute's father all right—'and Maria Kirkeborg.'" Samuel tilts the wood to catch more light. A twitch of head and shoulders shows discomfort. "Den I think it says somthin' like, 'God . . . is . . . glor-ious,' or some such." It isn't usual for a Minnesota man to speak of God or His attributes, no matter what his personal convictions might be.

The big man suddenly slaps his thigh. "Uff-da! Almost forgot the box." From the truck bed he pulls a wooden box somewhat less than eighteen inches long, tied with sturdy twine. Its top fits snugly between grooves. He extends it toward Nels. "Here's some of her ol' family stuff we had makin' clutter. Found it in Ev'lyn's"—he swallows with difficulty—"closet. Not much in it, just ol' records, baptizim and marriage 'tificates, that kinda thing. Maybe you 'n' Joann won't mind takin' it off my hands?"

"You betcha," Nels says. "I'll just put it with all the other boxes we've got there on the porch 'n' let the movers take care of it tomorrow."

After Samuel instructs Nels how to fit the table parts together for reassembly, the two men make trips into the house, placing the wood on the living room carpeting.

Joann is upstairs.

"My Ev'lyn . . ." Samuel chokes and looks embarrassed for it. "She told me there was somthin' special 'bout this table. Guess lot a life went on 'round it when she was a girl. Then our three put *their* feet under it fer a good while. Well . . . it's yerz now. Thanks for takin' it off my hands."

"We'll take good care of it," Nels promises. With solemnity, they thump each other on the back.

That evening Joann stands in the living room among the packing boxes. A strange, magnetic pull that she had all but forgotten draws her to the piled pieces of birch wood. Her eyes are fixed on the past . . .

*Under the table, young Joann silently presses fists against streaming eyes, taking in great gulps of air, until she can breathe normally again. She wonders why the older siblings no longer cry. Don't they care their mother is gone forever? Where did they put their pain? "Come on out, and don't act like a baby, Joann," Maxine scoffs. "You're too old for that." From the floor-level view, she watches Evelyn's worn brown shoes traverse the room, ministering to the needs of the younger ones . . .*

Part of Joann still longs for a place of safety. As a child, under the table she found an inconsistent safety that alternated with fearful discovery. She claps her fists together. How can a piece of furniture be so bewitching?

Saffee skirts around the cartons, lightly touches Joann's arm, and looks inquiringly into the drawn face and red eyes. Joann has two modes; Saffee dislikes them both. The first is hurry and scurry—washing, straightening, folding, peeling, stitching as if prodded and timed. Now Joann occupies her other mode, marked by an unwavering stare into some middle distance. When there, is she in a silent, vacant universe, or a cacophony more frenzied and peopled than the first? No one knows; she goes there unaccompanied.

"Mommy . . . Mommy, why are you so sad?"

Joann sinks into a chair. Her whispered words drift without direction. "We were under that table . . . hoping to stay alive."

Saffee doesn't ask what she means.

Suddenly, Joann tips her head back and gives a loud, hooting laugh. Her young daughter senses its inappropriateness and draws back, startled.

"They say . . ." Joann's eyes are again fixed, her voice low, but the words tumble fast. ". . . there were curses spoken around this table. They say Pa stood *cursing*"—she spits out the word—"*cursing over each girl* as Mother, lying in their bed, gave birth to one girl after another. He said he needed *farmworkers*, not seven *girls*!"

Saffee doesn't move.

Suddenly, Joann rises and shakes her upper body as if to cast off something distasteful, something that clings.

"I don't think I packed all the towels from the upstairs bathroom cupboard," she says. "I'll go see."

She disappears up the stairway and calls over her shoulder, "Saffee, look around for another empty box and bring it up."

Later, emotionally exhausted by the events of the day, Joann goes to bed early. In her midnight dream . . .

*She rushes to her place of refuge, her head and shoulder bump and* scrape against a table leg. She cries out in pain. Her mother is there, with her, under the table, soothing her, cooing. Above, Maxine yells, "You clumsy girl! What are you trying to do? Knock over the kerosene lamp? Burn down the house? It's all your fault, Joann! It's your fault!" Flames encroach. She is in her mother's arms . . .

## CHAPTER ELEVEN

# REMODELED

Joann's spirits lift once the family completes their move to Miller's Ford and Nels is out of town only two nights a week. For the first time in her life she becomes slightly acquainted with a few neighbors, and she and the carriers, Saffee and April, walk uptown once a week to buy groceries. Each trip is an occasion that requires special attire and grooming for all three. The family joins the First Methodist Church, demanding more attention to appearance, never forgetting white gloves.

Most important, in Nels's opinion, is that Joann has something to do that she thoroughly enjoys—remodel the old house. Her mood sobers noticeably, however, the day Nels assembles the Norway table, as they have come to call it.

"Your grandfather was a real craftsman," Nels remarks as he fits the puzzle-like pieces together without nails or glue.

Joann's appraisal is different. "It's ugly," she says. "I'll need to cover it."

Ignoring the remark, Nels places four of six chairs around it. They are old chairs of traditional style he bought at a yard sale. Joann looks at them with disinterest. In contrast to the table, anyone who knows furniture would say that the chairs have no "presence." Nels planned to put two of them in the basement, but when it is obvious, even to him, that four look lost around such a large table, he adds the others. Now that Joann seems to have come alive again, perhaps they might even have guests.

"Mom? What are you making?" Joann holds up white sheeting that she has sewn together into sections.

"It's a playhouse," she tells Saffee, pointing to the doorway and two green-shuttered windows. Each window has a cross of framing in the center to create four "panes." A row of tulips has begun to "grow" along the bottom edge.

"Oh! Mom!" Saffee dashes back to the bedroom. "April! Wake up! You won't believe what Mommy made us!"

Yesterday April had cajoled Joann into a short game of hide-and-seek. April hid under the Norway table. "You can't find me, Mommy! You can't see me!"

Of course Joann did see April, and remembered another girl. A girl with her own face, looking out from behind a barricade of heavy benches. She, too, was hiding and, like April, others knew she was there, but she wasn't playing.

"*Whatcha doin' under there, Joann? Think I can't see you? You're crazy, Joann, crazy.*"

She thinks about nights in her childhood, under the same table, when she had sensed a light touch on her arm, or her hair, sometimes her legs. She would jerk to wakefulness, hear a scuttling away in the dark, and the creak of the ladder to the brothers' loft. Or did she dream it?

When she discovered that the offender was Rolf, she tattled to her pa. With vehemence Rolf denied it. "She's crazy, Pa, you know that! I done nothin', she's crazy!" Later he yelled louder under the razor strap. Rolf didn't bother her in the night again but took to tormenting her in other ways. It was contagious. Soon Joann, an oddly withdrawn child, became the object of the other siblings' ridicule.

*"You're crazy, Joann. Just plain crazy."*

In the wake of these and other unwanted memories, Joann relived her hurt and loneliness for the rest of the day. Under the table she had been a child without love. To be a child without love is a transgression. She must find a way to cover the table—this symbol of transgression against a child.

Last night the thought came to her that if April wants to play under the table, it must be made into a pleasant place. She would make a playhouse cover.

She rose early and sewed the sheets together, making them fit perfectly. Now, with crayons, she finishes the tulip border.

Throughout the weeks ahead, until the carpenters arrive to turn the house upside down, the playhouse cover is usually in place. Underneath, April tends her dolls and Saffee colors in her Jane Powell coloring book.

"A little camouflage goes a long way," Joann is heard to say.

The table would be hidden every day if Nels didn't insist that the cover come off for their Sunday after-church pot roast.

"It's not right to eat in the kitchen on Sunday," he says. Joann glumly obliges, tossing a green percale tablecloth over the relic from her childhood.

No matter what or where the Kvaales eat, chewing takes precedence over conversation—especially on Sundays when the stringy, inexpensive roast presents a challenge for all. Joann reminds her daughters that God gave them their father's big strong teeth and they should use them without whining. Neither parent is qualified to teach the girls the art of table talk. Joann's studied vocabulary and love of poetic phrases is for impressing herself and doesn't usually fit into mealtime conversation.

Joann's creative accomplishments are inconsistent with someone born in a poor prairie sod house and who has only a high school education. But she has a natural talent for design and renders precise drawings for the main-floor efficiency apartment. There will be compact built-ins, including an eating table, hinged to raise and fold up into a wall. She makes a movable, paper model. "Look at this, Saffee. It'll disappear just like the Murphy bed we had in California."

"I liked that bed," Saffee says, glancing at April.

It appears that all the necessities of a one-room apartment will fit into the allotted space—except a refrigerator. Joann is stumped. Reluctantly, she makes an unsatisfactory decision. Since there will be a door between the apartment and the Kvaales' new kitchen, the tenant will have to come into their place to share the refrigerator.

When the downstairs plans are complete, Joann turns to the upstairs. Nels gives her full rein. The only matter they take care of together is hiring the workmen.

"A person can't be too careful nowadays," says Joann. "Can't trust just *any*one coming into the house, you know."

The sawing and pounding begin and Joann keeps a critical eye on the crew, following them from room to room, peering over their sweat-soaked shoulders.

"They better not steal any materials when my back is turned!" she declares to Nels. If it seems that wallboard or trim is wasted, or too many good nails are left on the floor at night, she gathers them up and doesn't hesitate to mention it. If framing doesn't look square to Joann's eye, it's done over. As the project proceeds, the workers try to sidestep the lady of the house, but sometimes tempers flare.

"Don't those men realize that I have it hard too?" she frets. "I carry the responsibilities of management, to say nothing of noise from power tools, and how about *all this dust*!" Her frustrations alternate with exhilaration, however, as she watches her well-thought-out plans take shape.

Joann's preoccupation with the renovations allows Saffee and April, now eight and four, more freedom than they had in St. Paul.

April makes friends with neighborhood children and Saffee explores the shallows of the Blue River down the bank across the street. She steps timidly into the dark, cavernous spaces under the bridge that spans the river and, from a distance, peers warily as water crashes over the dam. When a truck rumbles overhead, her heart pounds and she scrambles up the side of the bank. More to her liking are the safe treasures found in the public library.

The cloth playhouse cover has done nothing to change Joann's subconscious perception of her unwillingly inherited table. It continues to feature prominently in her disturbing dreams. Perhaps if she would alter . . . In a moment of clarity, she knows what she must do.

## CHAPTER TWELVE

# THE FIRST COAT

Joann throws aside a worn-smooth piece of sandpaper and swipes her damp forehead with the back of her hand. Her fingers are stiff and her back aches, but she hardly notices. She selects new sandpaper with rougher grain and rubs the tabletop with intensity. Rubs away scratches. Rubs away scars and stains. Nearby, a can of primer and a gallon of fresh paint wait unopened.

Nels had objected to her plan. "You've got enough goin' on with all this remodelin'," he said, when really it was her inordinate intensity over the idea that concerned him. It had taken some persuading on Joann's part to get him to drive to the hardware store to buy supplies. He almost always complies with her wishes eventually.

Nels. She applies more pressure to her strokes. Why can't he understand that she must do what must be done? And why hasn't she thought of doing it before? She welcomes the thought of permanently obliterating the anxieties of childhood that for years have taunted her, haunted her with hellish visions in the night. They will be gone.

Or will they?

Is she doing the right thing?

This table . . . why, oh why is it such a puzzle? She gives her head a jerking twitch as if to shake herself free of confusion, and once again she reviews the past. As an insecure child, the table beckoned her. Sometimes it offered her a place of privacy, where she had hopes and good thoughts. Those times made it sacred to her. At other times, under the table, she was betrayed by darkness and foreboding. A paradox. But perhaps sanding and painting—honest toil—will bring about some understanding, maybe even some peace.

She rearranges the drop cloth she's placed on the floor to catch sanding dust and paint, then rubs a stubborn mar with intensity. Her loose, uncombed hair falls forward, a labyrinth through which she must look. When scratches diminish, she is heartened. The water stains, however, formed years ago when water splashed from laundry tubs and washboards, resist obliteration. No matter, the paint will do its work.

Yes. This labor will be worth it. She rubs feverishly, prompting quizzical glances from the two workmen who paint window trim in the adjacent living room. They make excuses to walk through the dining room to get a better look at this peculiar woman. She pays them no heed.

When the tabletop is sanded, Joann decides the vine-covered apron needs no attention. Its original varnish is mostly gone, but it has escaped the ravages of time and misuse. She alternately kneels and sits on the floor, sanding away blemishes on each leg. Fatigue takes hold. She'd intended to prepare a more perfectly smooth surface for the primer coat. Perfect, because everything Joann does must meet her standards. But in her eagerness she concludes that the paint—the paint!—will cover all remaining blemishes. She eats a few crackers to renew her energy, then opens the can of primer.

By late afternoon, the primer is dry. The day's surging emotions and the physical labor have sapped her strength. She will apply the topcoat early in the morning. But she can't resist prying open the lid, just to look at the paint she has such high hopes for. Its smell assaults her. Why did Nels buy oil-based paint? Doesn't he know it has a noxious odor? The color, however, is perfect, soft, reassuring. It seems to have a certain quality—a presence. She will dip her brush into it tomorrow.

But first comes night, and another dream . . .

*A little girl on a plank floor . . . crude benches . . . whispered conversation . . .*

*"Lars, Pa's got the farm insured for lots a money. Hunderds, I'd guess."*

*"Hunderds? This here place? You know what boys like us could do with money like that? We'd be rich!"*

*"It's not for us, you dummy. It's fer if somthin' happens to it, you know, like a cyclone."*

*"Cyclone? How 'bout a fire, like another prairie fire?"*

*"Yeh, Lars, like a fire . . . But it don't have to be no prairie fire, ya know."*

*"Whatcha sayin', Rolf?" . . . Red-orange flames leap . . . "Whatcha sayin', Rolf?"*

*Billows of black smoke mushroom, rise, drift . . . The girl chokes, screams . . .*

At 2:00 a.m., Joann, sweat-soaked, rises from her bed and writes shaky lines in her notebook.

*What is it, who is it that lifts the torch and bids fire rage from the horizon? Who strikes the match to destroy a farm?*

The next morning Joann strokes with wide, sweeping motions. She imagines herself an orchestra conductor, directing, not music, but a flow of color. A flow of healing color. An ointment. Oil-based? Perhaps that was meant to be after all. In spite of its odor, she will believe it to be anointing oil.

Saffee sits on a stool and watches, fascinated, as paint flows from her mother's brush onto the Norway table. "Can I help?" she asks.

Her mother's all-consuming expression does not change.

"Let me help, Mommy."

Joann is curt. "No."

Her mother's unpredictable moods and preoccupations make no sense, but Saffee knows when to be quiet. She retreats to her bedroom with a book under her arm.

As she works, Joann is at first pleased with the effect. The glossy shine of wet paint holds promise. The conductor strokes carefully, rhythmically, for almost twenty minutes. Then the smell begins to bother her. "Noxious." She speaks the word, rolls it around in her head.

Last night's dream troubles her. The North Dakota farmhouse and barn had in fact burned to the ground. There had been suspicion that her pa had arranged the fire and collected the insurance money. How else had he been able to purchase the fishing resort? She doesn't want to think that her brothers had had something to do with it. She doesn't want to think that it was arson at all. Arson was criminal. Rolf and Lars were just pathetic boys. Uneducated, overworked, buffoonish boys.

She plunges the brush into the paint too deeply. Paint rises up to the handle, irritating her. She lets it drip a moment over the can, but is too impatient to wait long enough, choosing instead to slop the excess onto the table, smearing it around into a thick mess. She tries to smooth it over with wider strokes. Like a flash of black lightning, the fire and smoke of last night's dream return. Brushing becomes erratic. Perhaps, after today, there will be no more nightmares. When the tabletop is completely covered with its coat of gray, she kneels to slap the brush back and forth onto the legs. Ample and thick. Smelly. But with promise.

## CHAPTER THIRTEEN

# PSYCHOLOGY

t takes three days for the paint to dry, and for three days Joann studies its effect. It had been a bold thing for her to do, paint the Norway table, but she had felt a distinct compulsion to do so. And for two nights her sleep has been dream free.

It's past time to find a place for the supplies. Again she pushes down on the cover of the remaining paint and carries it with the cleaned brush and canvas drop cloth to the basement. She will put them with Nels's collection of assorted necessities on the shelving near his workbench.

She notices his rows of tools, neatly categorized, and is grateful that he is handy, can fix almost anything. It pleases her to know that her in-house repairman loves her, adores her. Or does he? Lately, ever since she told him she wants another baby . . .

Her train of thought is interrupted as she searches for a space to store the paint can. On the highest shelf there are a number of medium-sized boxes. She recognizes that two of them store Nels's war mementos, but a third one startles her. An old wooden box, about the size of a bread box, tied with twine. How could that box turn up in her basement? Surely it isn't . . .

Her heart thumps as she lifts it down. She unties stubborn knots and removes the slide-off lid. Newspaper clippings, receipts, bills of sale, tintypes of people she doesn't recognize. She cautiously thumbs through until she finds a yellowed envelope. Scrawled across the front is "Certificate of Death, Clara Isabelle Kirkeborg." In spite of painting the table, or perhaps because she painted the table, suddenly Joann fears more than ever that the certificate inside foretells her own fate. She pulls her hand away from the damning piece, as if it were on fire. She does not need to read it. She hastens to return the box to the highest shelf and covers it with the drop cloth.

Wouldn't having another baby, a final baby, prove her stability, change her fate? Unlike what happened to her mother, this baby would not be taken away. And then the words *hysteria* and *acute mania* or words like them would never condemn Joann, would never blaze across her death certificate.

Lodging for newcomers is scarce in Miller's Ford, so the Kvaales' upstairs apartments bring in a steady income. The main floor share-the-refrigerator apartment is harder to rent until, just before the first snowfall, a shy, dithering gentleman named Henry Clement comes and stays for six months.

Mr. Clement is rarely seen, except at suppertime, when the family is seated at their new kitchen's "breakfast" bar. Most evenings, after the "God is good, God is great, we thank Him for our food. Amen," their tenant enters the kitchen with apologetic noises. His slight frame squats before the open refrigerator. He contemplates the items on his designated lower shelf while annoyingly clucking his tongue. It's not clear whether he speaks to himself or to the Kvaales when he inevitably says, "I just can't decide what to have for supper."

From where Saffee sits, she can see there is usually little for Mr. Clement to choose from—perhaps a package of bologna, a carton of eggs, butter, and maybe a head of aging lettuce. As a rule, on his first exploratory visit, Mr. Clement chooses nothing and returns to his apartment, only to reappear once or twice before making a selection.

Saffee and April find Mr. Clement's mid-meal visits amusing, but Joann is put out. One evening, as the Kvaales enjoy pork chops, scalloped potatoes, green beans, and homemade applesauce, the hapless tenant lethargically stares at his near-empty shelf. Saffee wonders if he has fallen asleep in his hunkered-down position. Suddenly Joann blurts, as if to a naughty child, "Henry! You're letting all the cold out! Our electric bill will be sky-high if you keep that door open much longer!"

Mr. Clement's shoulders slump. He stands slowly and turns toward her, his face beet-red. "Oh, I-I'm sorry," he stammers, "I'm so sorry," and makes an empty-handed retreat. "I . . . I just couldn't decide . . ." The door closes softly behind him.

From then on, it seems Mr. Clement makes an effort to shorten his refrigerator gazes, but the number of his mealtime appearances remains about the same.

"Mom, what's this pile of books?" Saffee asks one day as she passes through the dining room. She puts down her opened copy of *Heidi* and riffles through pages of an imposing textbook. "Did you go to the library without me?"

Joann looks up from her study and tells her that the books are Mr. Clement's college books about psychology. She has borrowed them. She glances toward the door that leads to Mr. Clement's apartment and whispers, "I want to find out if our tenant suffers from *neurosis* or *psychosis*." She speaks in an airy way that signals delight in a new word or two.

Joann's married years have been filled with self-education. She no longer resents her father for preventing her from going to high school until she was considerably older than her classmates. By the time she enrolled, she had matured to the point that learning fascinated her.

"What's *'chology* mean, and that other word?"

"*Psy*-chology, Saffee. And you're too young to understand."

But Joann is very intent on understanding. Perhaps it will help her avert her own mother's fate. She pores over Mr. Clement's books for days. But to Joann's disappointment, her study comes to a halt when Henry Clement and his books move away.

"Maybe he moved because he wanted his books back and was too *neurotic* to ask," says Joann.

"Maybe he wanted his own refrigerator," says Saffee.

They were both wrong, of course. What Mr. Clement wanted was something the Kvaales were not skilled in giving—friendship.

## CHAPTER FOURTEEN

# UP AND DOWN

1950

All spring and into the summer, Joann sews draperies, tries her hand at upholstery, and adds touches that give the main floor of the old house a certain distinction, albeit homemade. As she bends over each task, she often repeats scraps of high-minded poetry and melancholy song.

> *Sweet sounds, oh, music, do not cease!*
> *Reject me not into the world again . . .*

After this brief hiatus, Joann's nightmares resume, and something within her urges that she employ her brush again. Although disappointed, she almost dutifully removes her portable sewing machine from the table and spreads the canvas drop cloth beneath. After all, the experiment had brought relief for a while. As does the next application. For a while. And the next.

Baffled by what now seems to have become his wife's obsession, Nels tries to dissuade her, but makes no headway. The sober intensity with which she works restrains the girls from asking questions. Her colors of choice are first yellow, and then red. Now, in late summer, Joann dips her brush into chartreuse.

Nels watches his wife's fervent splattering.

"How do you like it?" she asks with a smirk. "It's vomit green."

"Joann! What's got into you?"

She glares at him. Paint drips from the brush. "This is *my* business, Nels. You stick to *yours*."

He retreats, shaking his head.

Curious about the exchange, Saffee appears in the doorway between the kitchen and dining room. She leans against the wall and watches her mother's deliberate stroking. She recalls how that morning Joann had poured the last of the milk from its waxed carton onto April's cornflakes. When the carton was empty, Joann continued to hold it tipped in midair over the bowl. One more drop finally appeared, then none. Still her mother held the carton, motionless. Was that her frugality or, like it seems now, had she been rendered immobile, abducted into some invisible lair?

Saffee is tired of her mother's complexities. She has always hated the trance-like staring. And now, after months of her mother's painting obsession, which Saffee can't possibly understand, she has grown to hate the Norway table. She heads out the front door and crosses the screened porch. April and her neighborhood friend, Marilyn, are busily drawing stick figures with chalk on the cement walkway.

Saffee says, with disgust in her voice, "Did you see Mom, April? She's painting the Norway table again."

"Yeah, I saw her. It's gonna be green."

"No, not *green*, April." Saffee mimics Joann's I-know-a-new-word voice. "It's *vomit* green."

"The king is having a ball!" April chortles as she dashes through the kitchen one afternoon. "The king is having a ball!"

She turns around and demands of Saffee, "Wash the floor, Cinderella! The king is having a ball!" and scampers away. April has recently seen a Disney matinee and ever since, her play-acting has been insufferable, at least to her big sister. Saffee looks up from her Etch-a-Sketch and appeals to Joann.

"Mother, can't you make her stop? She's bothering me." But Joann's expression says, "Isn't she cute?" Saffee can't help but notice that her mother's cares curiously fade somewhat in the presence of her younger daughter's merriment.

Later, when Nels comes home, April is still at it. "Dance with me, Prince!" she calls, stretching her arms toward him. Nels looks quizzical and scratches his head.

Joann comes from the kitchen, laughing. "April, haven't I told you before your father has two left feet? Here"—she grabs April's waving arms—"I'll dance with you." Giggling and singing, the two twirl together across the living room and out onto the screen porch.

The Miller's Ford residents who venture to make Joann's acquaintance are, for a while, fascinated by her posturing ways and unexpected pronouncements. But it doesn't take long for her singular manner to create a space between them. A young grocery store employee one day asks Joann, with Saffee by her side, if she would like him to carry her two bags of groceries to her car. Joann doesn't drive. With an upward twitch of her head she delivers an outlandish retort.

"Alas, my chariot awaiteth not at the door, young man, and my strength comes from sources you are obviously unfamiliar with." She sweeps a bag from the counter and, with a self-satisfied snicker, floats with majesty to the door. She is oblivious of his puzzled look, as well as gasps from two middle-aged women in the checkout line.

Saffee's face burns. She snatches the other bag from the checkout counter and hurries out. What fantasy world does her mother live in? Why didn't she just say, "No, thank you"?

People of the town, unsure how to cross the divide between stable and unstable, learn to avoid this strange woman. Neither they, nor her family, nor Joann herself, can fathom the nuances of a darkening mind.

# CHAPTER FIFTEEN

# THE SEWING CLUB

1950

Saffee tightens toe clamps around her saddle shoes and buckles brown leather straps. The cement bridge spanning Blue River is ideal for roller skating. Swinging her arms back and forth, Saffee scrapes and slides along the sidewalk, bumping over every crack. The skate key sways on its string and lightly thumps against her chest.

On the sidewalk ahead, Saffee recognizes Mrs. O'Reilly, the mother of a fourth-grade classmate. Saffee drags a front wheel. The narrow concrete walkway, and Mrs. O'Reilly's deluxe size, oblige them both to stop to avoid collision. Saffee would have preferred to zip quickly by. Mrs. O'Reilly greets her pleasantly and admires her polka-dotted shirt and matching shorts.

"So cute. Does your mother sew your clothes?"

Saffee nods.

"What's your mother's name? I wonder if she'd like to join the sewing club. I'll call her."

At supper, Saffee mentions that Mrs. O'Reilly might call.

"A sewing club? Hmm," Joann says. "More likely a *gossip* club, I suppose."

"Why don't you go?" Nels urges. "It'd be good fer ya ta get out, meet some other women."

To Saffee's surprise, Joann does attend the sewing club. Once.

The following morning at breakfast the girls are eager to know about her uncharacteristic foray into small-town society.

Joann, holding her coffee cup with a raised pinky, tells them that it was at a Mrs. Birdwell's house where everything was "hoity-toity." Mrs. Birdwell, she says, collects ceramic parrots of various sizes and colors. Joann laughs with amusement and butters her toast. "Really bad taste."

When asked about the food, she grins and reports that there was pink punch, way too sweet, and little square cakes called *petits fours*. It seemed no one knew the French pronunciation that Joann later found in the dictionary.

The women worked on "silly stuff," like crocheted doilies and pot holders with ruffles. Joann doubts that they know how to make *useful* things, like clothes and curtains. She had let down a hem on one of Saffee's skirts.

Saffee glances at April's red-checked pinafore, proud that her mother sews so ably.

"I bet ya met some nice ladies, Joann," Nels says, obviously hoping she had.

"Nice? Well, maybe, but short on looks, shorter on brains," she scoffs. Joann scoops the last of the scrambled eggs onto her plate and declares, "I won't be going back."

Nels knows it is useless to argue.

That afternoon, flushed from the July heat, Saffee hurries into the house with an armload of books and heads to the kitchen for a glass of water. Which should she read first? *Kon-Tiki* or *Pygmalion*? Her mother, at the breakfast bar, does not acknowledge her. She is scribbling in a spiral notebook, imagination meeting memory, a wry smile on her face. More and more she dashes off lines of doggerel, revising for a number of days until a piece gives her pleasure.

"The library was so nice and cool," Saffee says. "Wish our house was air-conditioned. Most of all, I really wish I could have a bike, Mom. I'm tired of walking all the time. I could have a basket on the front for books and stuff."

Whenever Saffee asks for a bicycle, her parents remind her they live on a "very steep hill," and she'd probably "break her neck."

Gulping water, she watches her mother. "Whatcha writing, Mom?"

Engrossed in her own drama, Joann does not respond. Saffee asks again.

"Talk, talk, talk," says Joann, still not looking up.

Saffee stamps her right foot on the floor and sets the glass on the counter a little too firmly. "I have *not* been talking!" she blurts. "I haven't even been in the house! And all I did was ask for a bike."

"Clean up the water you spilled, Saffee. No, I'm *writing* about talking. All that *yak-yak-yak* last night at the sewing club got me started on a poem." She surveys the page, nodding slightly, clicking her tongue. "Actually, it's turning out kind of good. Maybe I'll read it to you when I'm finished." She bends to resume. "Now, let me be so I can follow where my mind is going."

Over the next two days, Joann labors on what she calls an "essay poem." When relatively satisfied, she summons Saffee and April to a dramatic reading in the living room. Joann sits with one leg elevated on a hassock; her varicose veins are "killing her." The girls sit at her feet.

"The title is 'Ensnared,'" Joann says. "There are three parts. Here's the first one." She reads,

*Advance. Retreat.*
*Offend. Defend.*
*Bumper cars converse, reverse.*
*Teasing push here, sudden jab there.*
*Touché! Good hit!*

For a while, April is swept into Joann's theatricality, which is much like her own. She bobs and sways to the rhythm of the words. Her sister sits very still.

> *Smiling masks belie sweaty palms, stiff necks.*
> *Stupid! I knew I should not have come.*
> *Stomachs knot.*
> *Voices blabber.*
> *Batteries rush toward their own extinction.*
> *Blam! Quiplash! Cornered!*
> *. . . At last, they slither away.*
> *Smoke and mirrors.*
> *Forgettable . . .*
> *But not forgotten.*

The confrontational words startle Saffee. She eyes her mother doubtfully. "What's that got to do with sewing club, Mom?"

"That part just sets the stage for the next two parts, so listen." Joann resumes reading.

> *We bring to the table the raw material of unspoken thoughts . . .*
> *The fabric of our words becomes weightier. Riskier . . .*

The essay poem drags on and on. By the time Joann reads the last part, she is giggling, thoroughly enjoying her own melodramatic absurdity.

> *Beware! Beware the delicate dance! The delicate verbal*
> *dance! . . .*

April has become disinterested and has left the room. Saffee listens, hoping to understand even a little about her mother's stinging reflections on the "verbal dance" and the "raucous undercurrent and pieties" at the sewing club.

> *. . . Naïveté trampled, again . . .*
> *Rude cacophony retains its rule . . .*
> *The Lord is in His holy temple.*
> *Let all the earth keep silent before Him.*

When the work finally concludes, Joann continues to edit, energetically inserting a new word here, hazarding a new line there.

Saffee sits silently. She's too young to fully comprehend that what her mother has read from the notebook reflects a growing paranoia that writes on the tablet of her mind. Yet, on a simple level, Saffee relates.

"Like you said, that was about talking, right, Mom?"

"Right," Joann answers, intent on her editing.

"I don't like to talk to people much either, Mom," Saffee says quietly.

Joann stops writing, looks down at her, and says, "Well, of course, the other night wasn't really *quite* that bad. I *made up* some of it."

"Oh." Saffee pauses. "But still, I don't think I'll ever go to a sewing club."

## CHAPTER SIXTEEN

# TREE OF LIFE,
# TREE OF EVIL

1951

Miss Eilert, a cherubic-faced pillar of the First Methodist Church, sits facing the row of three girls and two boys in the basement Sunday school room. The chilly stone walls suggest a cave unsuccessfully disguised with yellow paint. A labyrinth of ancient, patched pipes and heating ducts crisscross overhead. The children, all eight or nine years old, wear coats dusted by snow during their short walk from school.

To Saffee's relief, a navy blue cape with silver buttons at each shoulder disguises Miss Eilert's prodigiousness. Barrel-bosomed women always embarrass her. But worse, Joann's insistence that Saffee attend this class meant she had to give up her usual after-school ice-skating on the Blue River. Saffee had put up a fuss to no avail, and now she sits hunched in a straight wooden chair, scowling.

"I'm sorry it's chilly," Miss Eilert says. "They don't turn on the furnace during the week."

Hearing her pleasant voice, Saffee's impression of Miss Eilert softens. The woman seems intent, yet kind. The children fidget but show respect.

Miss Eilert begins by holding up a paper cutout from a pile on her lap. "When God created the world," she says, "He placed the first man and the first woman in a beautiful garden called Eden." She presses the cutout of Adam and Eve, discreetly standing behind a bush, onto a flannel-covered easel. Saffee's face flushes pink. She's glad no one in the room knows that her full name is Sapphire Eve, not after this obviously naked Eve, but after an evening sky.

"This is the Tree of Life," Miss Eilert continues. "God planted it in the middle of the garden." Up goes the tree onto the easel.

"And God put another tree in the garden. The Tree of the Knowledge of Good and Evil." Up goes the second tree.

Saffee wonders if there might be a stick of Doublemint in her coat pocket. She fishes. All she feels are wet mittens.

"God instructed Adam and Eve not to eat fruit from the Tree of the Knowledge of Good and Evil. But they disobeyed." Miss Eilert covers the cutout figures with a large black circle.

"This black spot represents sin. When we do something God has instructed us not to do, that is sin. Ever since Adam and Eve, every person born, except One, has sinned. We are not allowed to carry that sin to heaven. We can't live with God unless that sin is washed away while we still live on earth."

The five children wiggle but are still attentive.

Miss Eilert smiles at them. It is a pretty smile. "God has a loving plan to take away sin and make us clean." She removes the black circle and says, "God sent His Son, Jesus, to live as a perfect man on earth."

Saffee listens to the familiar story of the birth of Baby Jesus. She was part of a speaking chorus in the church Christmas program last month. Although she diligently practiced her short solo line, she almost fainted with fright when the moment came to speak it.

As Miss Eilert displays more flannel-backed images, Saffee is able to disregard the unpleasant smell of her wet wool coat. She is startled by the picture of Jesus nailed to a wooden cross and wearing a crown of thorns, His body blood-streaked.

"Jesus allowed Himself to be nailed to a cross to die because He loves us." Miss Eilert's voice is slow, as if to let her words sink in. "The sins of the whole world, even yours and mine, were put on Jesus when He hung on the cross . . ."

Saffee perspires inside her heavy coat.

"Jesus was willing to be punished for *our* sins, even though *He* never sinned. Then . . . three days later . . ." Miss Eilert's smile widens as she presses a picture of an empty tomb onto the board. "He rose to life again . . . and He lives today."

After a brief pause, Miss Eilert and her cape stand up. "Children," she says, "we're going upstairs now. Please follow me." *What is this?*

The sanctuary feels even colder than the basement. Late afternoon light hardly penetrates the stained glass windows. Miss Eilert indicates that the children are to kneel along the curved altar rail.

Before them, lining the back of the altar, vertical brass pipes of the organ stand as if sentinels in the Sabbath-like stillness. Saffee considers the organ to be magnificent. She loves its complex sounds and routinely counts pipes during long Sunday sermons. Now, in the dusk, rising high above her, they create a mysterious holiness.

Miss Eilert whispers, "I've told you about Jesus. I've told you that He died on the cross because He loves us. When we trust our lives to Him, He forgives our sins and His Spirit comes to live inside us. Then God sees us as completely clean. Pure like Jesus. Pure enough to someday live with Him in heaven."

Softly, Miss Eilert begins to sing, *"Into my heart, into my heart, come into my heart, Lord Jesus. Come in today, come in to stay, come into my heart, Lord Jesus."*

The children squirm and don't dare look at each other.

"Jesus loves you," Miss Eilert says. "He wants to wash away your sins, and live in your heart, and be with you always. With Jesus, you will never be alone. When you are happy, He will be there. When you are sad, He will be there." She pauses. Saffee senses that the moment holds inexplicable significance and that her entire life has purposefully led her to it. "If you want Jesus to be your wonderful Savior," Miss Eilert says, "please sing with me."

Miss Eilert begins the song again. With hands clasped, and audible only to herself, Saffee sings, *"Come into my heart, Lord Jesus."*

And He does.

Although it is somehow more understood by her heart than her head, she knows He does. She feels an exquisite happiness.

Minutes later she steps outside and stands still in the gathering darkness. Even though she has often sought to be alone, she experiences a curious relief that she will never be alone again.

She hears the slow-moving, heavy church door close behind her. She looks up and sees menacing snow clouds. Her chest tightens. Within her is a new, wonderful, and undeniable presence of love. But in the air there is another presence that scorns the words she has sung.

## CHAPTER SEVENTEEN

# NANCY DREW

urn off the light. I wanna sleep!" April mumbles.

"Gotta finish this page."

"No! I'm gonna tell!"

Saffee snaps the book shut, just as Nancy Drew's blue roadster is about to zip past the suspicious man with the scar on his left cheek. With a sigh, she turns off the flashlight and flings the sheet from her head.

Every window of the house is open but not a particle of stuffy air moves. Saffee squints across the hallway to her parents' bedroom. Rats! The door is open. But it's late; they're probably asleep. She slides out of bed, careful not to let the springs squeak. Tiptoeing past their door, she hears her father's whiffling snore. With pillow and flashlight, Saffee imagines she looks like her favorite sleuth and suppresses a giggle.

Faint rays of moonlight fall on the playhouse cover over the Norway table. Perfect. She crawls under, clicks on the flashlight, and plumps up the pillow for her head. An area rug that she and April have dragged in makes this a comfortable place to lie. As flashlight shadows play on the white fabric walls, Saffee and Nancy Drew resume a thrilling ride around hairpin mountain curves. Suspense mounts as headlights from behind grow closer in the rearview mirror. Saffee perspires.

*Z-z-z-z.* The high whine of a mosquito blood-hunt. Without taking her eyes from the page, Saffee swats at the pest with the flashlight. The annoying sound gathers volume. She trains the light at the underside of the table, searching for the little demon. Two of them. She slaps and misses. Watching for another chance, she wonders why her mother never paints the underside of the table. The latest topside color is buttery cream and she had carefully painted around the vine, leaving it, well, green.

*Z-z-z-z.* Saffee swats again. Another miss. Following the speedy buzzers, her eyes settle on lettering burned into the back of the apron above her and to the left. She has often read the engraved names of her great-grandparents on the apron's right side, but has puzzled over these words that end with numbers: 128 and 3.

Maybe a cryptic message from Viking days?

She feels a bite on her thigh and slaps. *Z-z-z-z.* Missed again. Irritated, she gives the playhouse fabric a smart tug in order to lift the opposite side, hoping the hungry pests will fly out and away.

*Crash!* A pile of books and Joann's metal box that stores hundreds of buttons land on the hardwood floor not far from Saffee's head.

In the bedroom, a malignant voice whispers, *"Joann! Joann!"*

Saffee's adrenaline spikes and she gives a startled yelp. She rolls to the right, out from under the table, only to become hopelessly entangled in sheeting and slide around on the skittering buttons. She struggles to free herself. Her right hand still holds the flashlight, its rays ricochet off the dining room walls.

Roused from the stupor of sleep, Joann stumbles into the dining room, her face a gash of fright. "Fire! Fire! Come, children!"

On her knees, Saffee still struggles to extricate herself from the shroud of sheeting. Joann impatiently gives her a downward shove. "Get under!" she orders. "It's coming! It's close!"

"Mother!" Saffee yells, dismayed at Joann's delusion. "What are you shouting about? It's nothing! Some stuff just fell off the table!"

Joann, desperate to escape whatever pursues her, slips on the scattered buttons and falls to her hands and knees. Her eyes blaze. "Hurry! Everybody! Get under the table or we'll all burn! It's whipping in the wind, coming for us . . . the *inferno*! Get under the table!"

Nels strides into the room. "Joann! Joann! Whatcha doin'? Whatcha yellin' about?" With effort he pulls his wife to her feet and tries to subdue her flailing arms.

"Saffee, get to bed. Right now!" he orders, as if embarrassed that his daughter is witnessing Joann's unnatural behavior.

Instead, her heart racing, Saffee flips the wall switch. Joann wears a stranger's face as her wild eyes dart around the illuminated room. There is no fire. She ceases her frantic reeling, whimpers, and crumples into Nels's arms.

He guides her back to their bedroom, where disguises of childhood trauma continue to torment Joann's midnight hours. Soon they will lurk by day.

Trembling, Saffee turns out the light, retreats to her own room, and slumps onto her side of the bed. It looks as if April has not moved.

The troubling scene lasted mere moments. Would Nancy Drew be able to unravel the meaning of it? Drama and mystery, so exhilarating on the written page, seem only to plunder real life. Although Saffee is confused, tonight she realizes, with maturity beyond her years, that her mother suffers seriously from some irrevocable trauma from her past.

As she lies in the darkness, listening to the high-pitched whine of a mosquito, it dawns on her that Joann's obsession with painting the table has nothing to do with decorating.

The next morning, after Saffee has picked up all the scattered buttons, according to her father's instruction, she wants to question her mother about last night's peculiar excitement. She stands in the kitchen several minutes, watching Joann intently ironing Nels's work shirts to a shine. It would be of no use to inquire; she is unapproachable. Saffee goes outside.

No one is in the neighboring backyard. She crosses over and climbs into the tire swing that hangs from a limb of a towering elm and idly scuffs her feet in the dirt. The tire spins in lazy circles. Saffee daydreams that her mother smiles, puts down her iron, goes to the back door, and calls her. Invites her to sit down beside her on the step, strokes her hair, and talks to her. Explains things about life and life's mysteries.

She pumps her legs vigorously. Extending her arms and leaning far back, she looks at the pattern of the leafy canopy against the bright blue summer sky. Dapples of warm sun kiss her face and she remembers that she is not alone.

*Into my heart, Lord Jesus . . .*

She smiles and whispers, "Jesus, You're swinging with me."

## Chapter Eighteen

# Palm Sunday

1952

Saffee kicks off her wet boots in the entryway and hears the familiar whir of the Singer sewing machine. She pushes through the French doors and hurries to the dining room where Joann bends over her work. Multiple yards of polished cotton splash pink cabbage roses across the Norway table and spill onto the floor.

"Mom, I need you to make something for the concert."

Joann glances up.

"Hang up your coat. Make what? You know I'm busy trying to finish these draperies for the living room."

Saffee pulls a length of white fabric and a mimeographed paper from a bag and shows them to her mother. The paper has a simple drawing of a square with a hole in the center. Below, it says, "Sirplus, 28 inches."

"What's this?" Joann asks. "What's a sirplus?"

"I don't know, but Mrs. Knudsen says everyone's gotta wear one on Palm Sunday for the *Messiah* concert."

Joann's studied vocabulary is a source of pride. She keeps a note-book of newly learned words she finds in *Time* magazine and practices them on the family. Once, when Saffee questioned this preoccupa-tion, Joann gazed at the ceiling and replied, "Well, Saffee, while I would never promote pretension, a certain erudition has always been considered a virtue." But now, erudition or not, here is a word that puzzles her.

She leans to pick up a well-thumbed dictionary from the shelf of the telephone table, a book the family uses more frequently than the phone directory.

"Of course," she huffs with indignation. "It's sur*plice*. S-u-r-p-l-i-c-e. 'A loose white vestment worn by clergy and choristers at Christian church services.' You'd think that people who aspire to communicate would also aspire to spell. What kind of people are up at that church?"

White lilies, their blossoms like trumpets, edge the entire choir loft. The burgundy-colored robes of First Methodist's chancel choir serve as their dramatic backdrop. Although small in number, the choir sings from Handel's magnificent work with as much passion as larger groups of renown.

*"Comfort ye, comfort ye, My people, saith your God . . ."*

As the adults sing, eighteen fidgety grade-schoolers, each wear-ing a square white surplice, whisper in the vestibule, waiting to make their entrance. Monitored by their director, Mrs. Knudsen, the chil-dren nervously swish green palm branches, shipped specially from Florida. A boy covertly distributes sticks of Black Jack to grinning friends.

Through the glass doors, Saffee stares at the back of the con-gregants' heads. It is a fearful thing for Saffee to "perform" like this before the whole church. If she didn't love the music so much, she could never do it. Her dad and sister are seated out there somewhere. Her mother is not. Everything went wrong this morning. April spilled her grapefruit juice and had to change clothes. Saffee arrived at breakfast wearing her concert attire—a white blouse and dark skirt, topped, of course, by the surplice.

"Saffee!" her mother had exclaimed. "It's all wrinkled! I pressed it so nice last night; what did you do?" Nels said he thought it looked fine, but Joann pulled the garment over Saffee's head and set up the ironing board.

After that, Joann fretted for fifteen minutes at the bathroom vanity mirror, struggling to make her newly home-permed hair behave. Battling frizz with her green-handled hairbrush, she grumbled, "What good is going to church anyway? Bunch of unfriendly, snooty people. The only time anyone from church calls is when they want me to bake a cake. Lot of work and no thanks."

"Joann! We're late!" Nels said. "What's holdin' you up?"

She declared that she would not be going, but Nels insisted.

"Didn't you hear me? I'm not going!" Nels dodged the green-handled hairbrush as it flew in his direction. Joann slammed the bathroom door. Containers were heard toppling, clattering across the vanity counter.

Nels shook his head and yelled, "Joann, I'll never understand you!" He took off his suit coat and threw it across a chair.

April looked pale and started to cry.

"Daddy, we have to leave *right now*," Saffee insisted. "I can't be late for the lineup."

"We can't go to church without your mother."

"Why not?"

"People . . . people would think somethin's wrong."

"But, Daddy, today's the *Messiah* concert. I'm in the junior choir processional. We've *gotta* go."

Nels reached for his coat and as the three strode toward the garage he muttered, "Can't figger out what makes yer mother *so irritable*."

*"Every valley shall be exalted, and every mountain and hill made low, the crooked straight and the rough places plain."*

The words, sung by the chancel choir, pulse through the transom above the door. The fugue-like interplay of voice and organ refreshes Saffee, exhilarates her. She presses her face to the glass for a better view of the director. His robed arms beat the air with contagious confidence. His curly black hair bounces with each bob of his head.

Equally animated, the organist, wearing a bright purple suit (she insists she cannot navigate the organ in a robe), commandeers the tiered keyboards flanked by the tall brass pipes reaching heavenward. On the bench she scoots energetically from side to side because her legs are too short to reach the extreme left and right pedals.

*"And the glory, the glory of the Lord shall be revealed . . ."*

"Everybody! We're next!" Mrs. Knudsen whispers. "Take your places!" She matter-of-factly holds an opened concert program under various chins, into which some of the children spit wet wads of black, chewed gum.

The organ swells. The double doors open and smiling children spill into the sanctuary, branches aloft. Their young voices combine with those more seasoned at the front . . .

*Lift up your heads, O ye gates,*
*and be ye lift up, ye everlasting doors,*
*and the King of Glory shall come in.*
*Who is the King of Glory?*
*The Lord strong and mighty, the Lord mighty in battle.*

As best she can, Saffee puts aside the mishaps of the morning and the disappointment that her mother is not present. She sings with feeling, sensing a thrill of kinship with the words, remembering that she had opened the door of her own heart to Jesus when she knelt at the altar a year ago.

"*Lift up your heads, O ye gates.*"

The joyous words are about Jesus' entry not only into Jerusalem but also into her own life. For an instant, she sees her mother behind closed gates, confined, imprisoned. Saffee sings louder, pushing the picture away.

A number of flailing palms skim ladies' spring hats and gentlemen's heads. April grins and gives Saffee a discreet wave with a white-gloved hand as she passes. Nels smiles too.

After the concert, crescendos of "Hallelujah" continue to resonate within her. She asks Nels for permission to walk the six blocks home rather than ride in the car.

Her shiny black shoes step lightly along the wet pavement, skirting narrow, hurrying rivers of melting snow. The exquisite melodies will soon vanish into the spring air, no matter how fervently she bids them stay. She walks the quiet Sunday streets, palm branch in hand, embracing the aura of the music, embracing the closeness of God.

# CHAPTER NINETEEN

# APRIL

Judy Bellingham's light blue eyes are the oversized, pop-out kind that look like they might when she's afraid.

"Saffee, why is your mother yelling so much?" Judy's voice is muffled from under a pillow. "I want to go home!" She pulls up her head.

"You can't," Saffee says, watching Judy's eyes. "Your parents are gone. Your mom wants you to stay here overnight."

"I don't care, I want to go!"

"Judy, I can't sleep with the light on," says April from the floor where she has made her bed, pretending she is venturing to the center of the earth.

"When I'm scared I gotta have the light on," the guest whines.

The verbal altercation between Joann and Nels continues through the closed bedroom door.

The next day, Mrs. Bellingham retrieves Judy from the inhospitable home. When they are gone, Nels draws Saffee and April aside. "Don't be bringin' people in our house," he says. "It's not a good idea."

"Look at me, I'm Queen Esther!" April sings, waltzing through the living room. A strap of Joann's old pink nightgown clings to her small right shoulder; the other side has slipped to her elbow. A gauzy purple scarf flutters from her blond curls. "I'm Queen Esther, the most *bea-oo-tiful* woman in the *whole* Bible!" Joann and April share a love for theatricality.

"Oh brother, April." Saffee sits on the living room floor braiding a bracelet of plastic gimp. She snaps the green-and-white laces in her sister's direction as April lifts the nightgown high for a pirouette. "Get outta here! You're acting dumb again. Mother!" Saffee yells. "April's annoying me!" She often whines this refrain to no avail.

She knows rudeness toward April is not right, but it's a habit she has little inclination to change, since it usually goes unnoticed by her parents. On that snowy afternoon last winter, Miss Eilert said that God's love can change people's hearts. Learning what this means is taking Saffee some time.

Nels is known in the coffee shops of Miller's Ford for his jovial, jester-like personality. Yet at home, spontaneity in his daughters has never been appreciated. "Don't make noise; don't make a mess; don't get your mother upset," he warns. The last is the reason for the first two. Saffee long ago bought into his rules, even though it is obvious their mother is charmed, not disturbed, by her little sister's antics. Antics that continue to befuddle Nels.

"Esther," ignoring Saffee's exasperation, prances out the door and across the porch to the front yard, in search of neighborhood children to join her fun.

Let chatterbox April be entertaining, enjoying quantities of attention and affection at home and elsewhere. Saffee needs none of it. She can't control her unpredictable family environment, but to a certain extent, she can control April. When parents are elsewhere, Saffee is not beyond giving her sister a lecture and a shove. But each rejection only seems to encourage April to annoy the one who refuses to give her adulation.

On a serene, small-town evening in late summer, dark green maple leaves whisper and swish against the side porch screens as if to celebrate the orange and magenta sunset that stretches along the river beyond them. The sounds of baseball faintly ebb and flow from Nels's radio in the kitchen. Saffee is curled up in a wicker porch chair with her current book, *The Wizard of Oz*. Books are her friends. She lives within their characters, looking for her own life. Such fantasy stays in her head and is not "performed" as April would.

From the corner of her eye Saffee sees shadowy movement. The bent form of Lena Bevins slowly climbs four steps and peers through the screen door. Saffee has never been near this woman who lives alone across the street. Both she and her tall, narrow house of weathered gray boards are easily ignored. In summer, if one would notice, Lena, day in and day out, pulls weeds and gathers produce in her half-acre garden of vegetables and flowers. Few know, or stop to wonder, what Lena does in winter.

"I come to take April for a walk," Lena says through the screen. Her monotone is deep, her shy grin reveals gaps between teeth.

Saffee hesitates, stays curled in her chair, then calls, "April!"

April immediately comes leaping onto the porch. "Hi, Lena! You came!"

Before Saffee can think what to say, the two take hands and head toward the brilliant pink and orange sky over Bridge Street. For a moment, Saffee watches them. Lena shambles, April jigs.

Miller's Ford offers indifference to Lena Bevins and other quiet, reclusive women like her, while Joann, voluble and apt to be bizarre, feeds the town's appetite for gossip. This matter, however, is beyond Saffee's young perspective. She resumes her own travel, down a yellow brick road. When it becomes dusk, she squints at the pages as long as possible, then retreats to lamplight in the house, where she is terrorized along with Dorothy by the Wicked Witch of the East.

*April!* How long has she been gone? Lena is *not* the Wicked Witch, she tells herself, but still, weren't the two headed toward the bridge over Blue River? Saffee has glimpsed the cavernous, spooky spaces between the massive cement supports under the bridge. She had shrunk away, recoiling at the mysterious graffiti emblazoned on the giant slabs of concrete. It is a place where a little sister could be swallowed up in darkness in the company of . . .

In a storm of anxiety, she runs to the kitchen. "Mother! Daddy! April's gone, it's dark!" Nels turns off the radio. "She went with that Lena. That strange woman from across the street. And they've been gone a long time. Maybe Lena's going to kill her under the bridge!"

Joann rushes from the bedroom. "Nels!" she shrieks. "What should we do?"

The three stride through the living room and across the porch— just as Lena and April, still hand in hand, come up the walk.

"Here they are," Nels says so only Joann and Saffee hear. "Now, botha you, don't look so upset. It's nothin'." Lena looks intimidated as Joann, arms outstretched, hurries down the steps toward April. Nels and Saffee remain at the open screen door.

"Mommy! I visited Lena in her garden this morning, so now she came to visit me." As is common with April, she doesn't merely speak, she chortles, adding her signature bouncy dance. "We saw the most bea-oo-tiful sunset."

Saffee fumes within; April hasn't an inkling that she has caused her family to worry.

"Tomorrow Lena's gonna let me find ladybugs on her potatoes!"

"The girl sure can sing," Lena intones, it seems with some fondness. "Well . . . bye." She turns and shuffles away into the twilight.

Now that it has turned out to be "nothin'," her parents don't seem concerned that April went off without informing them. Instead, to Saffee's chagrin, Joann says as they enter the house, "Nels. Did you hear how upset Sapphire was? She *does* love her sister. She just *acts* like she doesn't."

Saffee is surprised to hear that her mother has even noticed her lack of sisterly affection, especially since her rudeness has never been corrected. But it is true, something different (perhaps caring?) *had* bubbled up quite unexpectedly during April's brief disappearance. Saffee is profusely embarrassed and determines not to let it, whatever it was, show again.

A few days later, on a bright steamy morning, one of April's play-mates dashes into the Kvaale house, yelling, "April's been hit by a car!"

Joann bolts outside and dashes around the house to cross the alley parallel to Bridge Street, the main road that leads through town. Saffee follows close behind. It's true. Vernon, an attendant at the intersection's service station, saw the impact. He rushed into the street and now kneels beside April's unconscious form. Her custom-ary morning curlers are flattened over the top of her head, forming a crude metal helmet. A tan and maroon Oldsmobile, motor still running, is stopped nearby and its elderly driver stands wringing his hands.

April moans and, with help, is able to sit up. Watching intently, Saffee trembles but this time does not speak out her relief.

## CHAPTER TWENTY

# MR. MASON

1952

A man. Her sixth-grade teacher is a man! Saffee is dumbstruck by the novelty of it. And Mr. Mason is not just any man, but a beautiful man who looks steadily into faces and speaks with an arrestingly gentle voice. The best part is Mr. Mason refers to and addresses each student as "young man" or "young lady." To Saffee, to be so addressed is stunning, revelatory, and dignifying. For the first time in her life she considers that perhaps she is a person of worth. No one before, certainly not her parents, has made an effort to convey that she is.

Furthermore, Mr. Mason goes beyond the customary rote teaching that the class is used to. Instead, he opens to them a world of historical and current events and encourages them to form opinions on issues. Saffee's undeniable crush causes her too much fluster to permit more than minimal classroom participation, but her homework has never been so carefully prepared.

When Mr. Mason teaches the class how to do a simple research paper, Saffee writes about the Battle of Gettysburg. "Well done!" Mr. Mason writes atop her paper. "Gripping! You made me feel like I was there!" Saffee hugs the handwritten pages and determines to keep them forever.

However, when school resumes after Christmas break, the bubble bursts. Mr. Mason announces he has been asked to join the school's administration. He introduces Miss Reynolds, who will finish the year in his stead. In shock, Saffee scans Miss Reynolds: tall and slender, long red hair, very high heels, and, worst of all, fluttering eyelashes. It is hard to miss that Miss Reynolds also is smitten with Mr. Mason.

Saffee walks home in a frozen daze. The first adult in the world to show her respect as a person—gone. For a few months, Mr. Mason had brushed a tint of color onto the dull canvas of her life. Now, the color is expunged. Betrayed, she sits on the edge of her bed and sobs.

Curious, Joann comes into the bedroom. Saffee can hardly speak. She manages to sputter enough information so that Joann realizes, with surprise, that Saffee is experiencing the bitter taste of lost first love. Mother stands staring at daughter.

Finally, she says, "You'll get over it soon enough." She begins to leave the room, then stops.

"It's time to burn the trash, Saffee. Collect everything that's paper and go out with it. Take some matches from the drawer."

Saffee swipes both her hands across hot wet cheeks. "Daddy does that. I've never started a fire." Neither has Joann.

"He's not home. If you're old enough to have a 'flame' at school, you're old enough to light a match."

Saffee cringes at the pun. Still crying, she dumps wastepaper into the oil drum in the backyard near the alley, then timidly strikes match after match against the rough, rusted inner side. Finally, one ignites. She stands still, holding her coat tightly against the winter air, staring through tears at the spreading fire . . .

*We saw it far off, whipping in the wind, coming . . . coming . . . an inferno . . .*

Newspaper becomes cinnamon brown and curls, crackles and turns black.

Heat dries the tearstained face.

## CHAPTER TWENTY-ONE

# VOICES ON THE STAIRS

1953

W hy don't they stop yelling?" April whimpers.

"Give them time." Saffee masks her own nervousness with big-sister superiority. Her first week without Mr. Mason is finally over, but as she and April sit tensely, halfway down the chilly basement stairway, life heightens its gloom. Their parents' strident, garbled voices ricochet in the kitchen above, fade as deliberate footsteps take them into the living room, rise once again as they return.

Nels is no match for Joann's verbal skills. She skewers him in every argument. Saffee recalls that when she did research for her "gripping" paper for Mr. Mason, she read about President Lincoln's volatile wife and thought of her mother.

Catching a word here and there, Saffee realizes this argument is related to Joann's demands that Nels give her another child. A boy, for him, she says. But it is apparent that the desire is more for herself; April is growing up. Saffee has heard Nels tell her mother that her "nerves" couldn't take having another baby.

For some time, Nels has been sleeping on the foldout couch in his den. Of course, no explanation for that has been made to the daughters, but Saffee has speculated. His move from their bedroom has increased Joann's accusations of infidelity. Saffee has seen the hurt in her father's eyes when she hurls barbed remarks. He is a simple, transparent man who lives by a rigid moral code. Her mother's imaginative claims are ridiculous.

Even though it is January, the stairway heat register is closed. Higher up the wall, black windows of night are frosted over. A slit of light comes from under the kitchen door, giving scant illumination. The girls could turn on the back hall ceiling light, but semidarkness seems more comfortable, protective. Saffee stares hard to distinguish the back of her sister's head. April's blond curls pooch out on both sides where her fingers try to stop her ears.

Ever since "April's car accident," Joann has been more diligent than ever to put metal curlers in her hair. The doctor said that she had had a concussion and that those curlers may have saved her life.

Joann's doting has multiplied. April can do no wrong and her every move is reason for applause. At the same time, it seems as if Joann detects some ominous handwriting on the wall. She says because the accident must have done irreparable internal damage, fragile April will need protection forevermore.

"I didn't mean to drop my ring down the sink," April laments. "My hands were soapy—it just slipped off. Why did that make them so mad? Will Daddy have to take the sink apart?"

Saffee sighs. "April, that's not what they're fighting about."

"Really?"

"Aren't you listening? Mother's accusing Daddy of looking at some woman today when they drove to the grocery store."

"So what's wrong with Daddy looking at someone?" April asks.

"Nothing. Unless she's pretty."

During summertime treks to the grocery store, Saffee notices with discomfort how men of the town ogle her mother's curvaceous torso. It seems Joann knows it too and doesn't mind. Doesn't mind at all. But even the thought of Nels ogling another woman, that's a different matter.

In the kitchen, Nels yells, "Joann! I tol' you, I din't even *see* no woman!"

"Sure, Nels, sure," she retorts. "And you never see me either, do you? To me you are cold, withdrawn. You know all I want is—"

"Be quiet, Joann. Keep yer voice down." Their steps retreat again.

From a greater distance, Joann is heard to shout, "My own mother was deprived of her baby too, Nels. Are you aware of what happened to her because of it, Nels? Are you . . . ?"

"Stop," April whines.

Saffee slips into a practiced state of detached loneliness, locking others out, locking herself in. In this place, she is able to endure the din. Then, without warning, she is thrust from her hazy bubble to a heightened sense of awareness. She hears another voice, prominent, yet at the same time quiet and comforting. It enters not through her ears but is present deep within.

*Watch . . . Listen . . . Learn. Your life will be different. Watch . . . Listen . . . Learn.*

Her eyes widen. The moment and the voice are freeze-framed to be remembered all of her life.

Somewhere, probably in sermons, she's heard that God speaks in a still, small voice. Could this be? She takes a deep, uneven breath.

The kitchen door bursts open, spilling harsh light onto the stairway and rudely jolting Saffee back into the tension of the moment. Nels's footsteps are quick.

"Move over," he orders, thumping past them down the steps into the basement. They see him stride in the direction of his workbench.

*Guns. Beyond the workbench are his hunting rifles.* Saffee springs to her feet and races up the steps to the kitchen. "Mother! Mother! Stop arguing!" she screams.

April spurts past them and disappears down the bedroom hall.

White-faced and trembling, Saffee slumps against a wall. "He's getting a gun! This is your fault; why are you always fighting?"

Joann lurches to the stairway railing. Her rashness melts to a whimper. "No, Nels," she calls. "No. I didn't mean it. Everything's okay; don't be mad. Come up, honey. It's okay."

Nels comes up the steps looking puzzled at her change of tone. This woman he loves so deeply bewilders and frustrates him so. There is not a gun but a wrench in his hand. "Gotta take the P-trap off to get the ring," he says gruffly, striding into the kitchen.

Weak with relief, Saffee realizes how out of character it would be for her father to reach for a gun in anger. Countless ensnaring arguments with Joann must sadden him, madden him, make him yearn for peace. "Your mother is never happy unless she's mad about something," he has more than once lamented to his girls.

Saffee trudges to the bedroom and shuts the door. April is face-down on their bed, crying. In keeping with the crummy evening, it would be fitting to say something ugly to April, such as, "Shut up, crybaby." But she doesn't. Instead, she jerks the curtains over the dark windows, hiding icy patterns traced with frost, and lies down on her back beside her.

She stares at the dark ceiling for a long time, wondering about the quiet, straightforward words that were birthed inside her on the steps. *Watch. Listen. Learn. Your life will be different.* She strains to hear more, eyes and ears searching the darkness, but there is nothing.

From Mr. Mason she learned that people have value. That she has value. This simple but profound revelation is changing her thinking. And now a voice—*God's voice?*—seems to confirm Mr. Mason's view. But how could she be worthy of personal words from God? And what is she to do with them?

Three imperatives. *Watch, Listen, Learn.* Maybe she is to recognize some sort of lessons in the unsatisfactory life around her. What is she to learn from her parents' volatile behavior? That parents can scare the bejeebers out of children? Perhaps if one realizes that all people have value, one doesn't carry on so. What with youth's way of taking life as it comes, and no other life to personally compare it to, up to now it has seemed she's had little recourse but to conform to her parents' model. But the words promise change, not conformity. What was it that Mr. Mason said one day about conformity? She struggles to recall a somewhat disgusting image. Oh yes. "Dead fish flow with the stream," he had said. Perhaps she is not destined to flow in her parents' stream.

*Your life will be different.*

Saffee lives within a colorless present that has evolved from her lackluster past. She has never been creative enough to imagine a future that would be any different. But tonight she dares to think that God has.

Minutes pass. She studies April's fully clothed, sleeping form. She slowly pulls up blankets to cover her.

## CHAPTER TWENTY-TWO

# RAGS TO RICHES

1954

While a second load agitates in the humming Maytag washer, together Saffee and Joann match sheets corner to corner and pin them to the taut rope lines Nels has rigged between basement rafters. This morning's threat of rain prevents them from hanging clothes out of doors.

Joann demonstrates the art of pillowcase hanging. "First, be sure to shake out all the wrinkles," she says, giving her sample a smart snap. She limps to a chair to adjust the unsightly rag bindings that have slipped to her ankles. Only because her varicose veins are "killing" her today did she enlist help. Saffee whips a pillowcase through the air as shown and glances at her mother's ropy, swollen legs, then down at her own. She remembers a short, unexpected visit a year ago from Joann's second-oldest sister.

"Saffee, you've certainly got your mother's legs!" Maxine had chortled as she surveyed the hapless girl. Saffee's eyes had narrowed. Why did Aunt Maxine, a virtual stranger, sound delighted by her observation? Was Saffee doomed to hobble around like her mother, legs tied with rags?

Maxine had been horrified when she saw the Norway table of her childhood sporting splotchy paint. The older sister demanded to know why Evelyn had passed the table on to Joann when she had expected to get it herself. "I *never* would have painted . . . Who would want it now, completely ruined?"

Saffee pins laundry to the line, hoping for a rare mother-daughter conversation as they work together. "Mom, I'm reading your book, *Giants in the Earth*," she ventures.

Joann is busy rehanging crooked pillowcases. "I guess life was pretty hard back then." Joann nods her head in agreement but does not elaborate. Saffee is hesitant to ask a pressing question—did Joann know anyone like the book's character named Beret? Isolated Beret, tragically gripped by elements of a dark spiritual world until she was driven insane. Instead, she asks why her mother's family left North Dakota for Minnesota.

Before answering, Joann circulates items in the rinse water with a stout laundry stick and begins to feed heavy wet towels between the washer's slowly rolling black cylinders. "I guess mostly because of the prairie fire," she says. "After that, the prairie was . . . inhospitable."

Casting for safer ground, Saffee asks about washing clothes "back then." She's willing to talk about any neutral subject with her mother, but right now one seems hard to find.

"Well, let's see," Joann says. "I'm not sure if Pa and the boys took their clothes off at all in winter. Of course the girls . . . we did ours more often." She picks up a basket of wrung towels. "Those awful brothers . . ." Her voice trails off . . .

*"I tell you, I saw it. It was all over some ol' rags she had! I think she was bleedin' ta death or somethin'!" "Lars, you peekin' at the girls in the outhouse agin? Don'tcha know nothin'?" "Sh-sh! Crazy Joann'll hear. She's unner da table down there . . ."*

"What about your brothers?" Saffee asks.

"Well . . ." Joann pauses a moment, as if she'd rather not explain what she is remembering. "We'd hide our red-stained rags on thorn-bushes in the brush until they dried . . . could never get the stains out. The boys would find those rags . . . run after us with them, yelling and teasing. It was . . . so *embarrassing*."

For a moment, Saffee is puzzled. When understanding dawns, she stares at her mother with incredulity. Her sense of modesty, even around her mother, prevents her from speaking.

*Red rags? Oh, Mother. There will be no rags in my life. I will be different. Different.*

As fall approaches, Joann once again becomes irritable. She is increas-ingly oversensitive to even the subtlest adversity, such as tenants "tramping overhead." She fuels her suspicious nature by complaining, "Sometimes I see them lingering behind the French doors, peer-ing through the lace curtains into our living room. I'm absolutely shocked at the things they say about us."

While at her sewing machine, making opaque shades for the doors, she is heard to mutter, "Watching me . . . all the time, watching me . . ." At her insistence, Nels installs additional locks throughout the house.

When Nels receives a pay raise in September, mercurial Joann brightens.

"Your daddy makes ten thousand dollars a year now!" she whis-pers to the girls. "But don't tell anyone. Money is a family secret, you know."

Saffee knows. She remembers the day Joann, resembling last year's rummage sale, took her and April to the doctor to update vac-cinations. When Saffee looked in dismay at Joann's faded housedress and unraveling laundry-day sweater, Joann said the doctor would "soak them good" if he thought they were even a little prosperous.

But now, with more income and savings from the rentals, Joann decides it is time to put appearances of poverty aside and build a new house. Five years has been long enough to put up with snoopy tenants. Secure in his career with the dairy, which is rapidly expanding across the state, Nels, a man of easily summoned good nature, agrees to at least look for land. Two miles north of town they find a spacious lot in a newly subdivided area of Miller's Ford called Cottonwood Point. It sits high, overlooking a wooded valley that currently wears radiant colors of autumn.

"We'll have an absolutely *marvelous* view from picture windows in the back!" Joann exclaims as the family walks the property. She whirls in the opposite direction. "And the front will look onto that wonderful grove of cottonwoods. Look how the yellow leaves glitter in the sun!" Her enthusiasm rivals that of when she had found their current house.

To the south is an old apple orchard. Fallen fruit litters the ground. "Our own orchard!" she gushes.

Nels grins. "Does that mean apple pie?"

Saffee and April, comfortable on Second Street, are adamantly against the move. Saffee doesn't want to give up the convenience of ice skating across the street and roller skating on the bridge. April is disappointed to leave neighborhood friends for a place with few houses in sight. The move also means they will suffer the humiliation of riding a school bus.

"Don't be whiney, girls," Joann admonishes them. "It's still the same town, but just far enough out so it won't seem so hoi polloi." Joann has continued to study her dictionary.

The girls appeal to their dad, but he commends Joann's enthusiasm. It seems to confirm his belief that she is stable, merely "nervous" at times. If building a new house will bring her happiness, he says, so be it.

There might be one consolation. "Will I get to have my own room now?" Saffee asks. "I'm *thirteen*, you know."

"No."

Saffee is so indignant that Joann dismissively agrees to compromise. "All right, we'll put twin beds in your room."

All winter Joann draws house plans. When she shows them to the contractor, he is surprised at their precision and says there will be no need for professionally drawn blueprints. Pleased by his approval, she summons the courage to select brick, fireplace stone, and the right windows to frame the "exquisite" views. She can hardly wait for the excavation to begin come spring.

## CHAPTER TWENTY-THREE

# GONE WITH THE WIND

1955

In January, Hollywood's rerelease of *Gone with the Wind* finally arrives in the small town. The *Gazette* touts the classic film with a half-page review. On a blizzardy evening, Joann suggests that she and Saffee go uptown to see it. Nels says they should wait a day and hope for better weather.

"No, now is a good time to go," Joann insists. "On a night like this there will be good seats available." Saffee knows this means she hopes to avoid an intimidating crowd. Saffee is not sure she wants to be seen at the Roxy with her unpredictable mother, and she knows Joann would not go without her. Because she too is very eager to see the popular film, she agrees to go. Ordinarily, they would have walked the three and a half blocks to the theater, even in winter, but because Nels put tire chains on the car that afternoon, and enjoys overpowering snow-packed streets, he drives them uptown through the white flurry.

Ever since she skipped down the yellow brick road of Oz at her first movie, Saffee has determined that flashes of Hollywood magic would ornament her life as often as possible. Over the years, the Roxy has become a retreat where Saffee escapes a humdrum existence and feels very much alive. An assortment of schoolmates often sits on the right side, near the front. With that in mind, Saffee routinely chooses a seat in the middle section, farther back. In the dark, licking a Holloway, she's danced in the rain with Gene Kelly, perplexed the King of Siam, swum with Esther Williams, dressed as stylishly as Audrey Hepburn, and ridden in James Dean's Corvette—all the while looking like Grace Kelly.

"Call me when it's over," Nels says as they exit the car. He drives off, tire chains clanking through fresh drifts and Saffee's mittens left on the backseat.

Joann agrees to split a fifteen-cent box of popcorn but objects to Saffee's request for a Holloway, which, she says, would loosen her teeth. Saffee's tongue explores to see if the damage has already been done. She follows Joann into the darkened, half-full theater and is relieved when her mother selects a row near the back. When seated, Saffee slouches low in her seat.

The red velvet curtains open, and Saffee is willingly abducted into Scarlett's capricious world of extravagant gowns, plantation garden parties, and covert romance with roguish Rhett Butler. When Melanie suffers premature labor and Scarlett must deliver the baby, Saffee covers her eyes. But this discomfort is nothing like what is to come. When the Union Army burns Atlanta and the angry inferno backdrops Scarlett's perilous wagon ride, Joann gasps. She grips Saffee's arm and drags her out of the row of startled viewers, stepping on toes with no apology.

"Mom!" Saffee hisses. "What are you doing?"

"Shh! Sit down!" someone demands.

With Saffee still in tow, Joann shoves through the swinging doors to the lobby. Her eyes dart, looking for a place of refuge, but she sees none.

"Mother! What's going on?"

Joann's face is flushed and her breathing rapid. She stumbles to a far wall and weakly slumps to the floor. Her unbuttoned coat slips from her shoulders. On the wall above her is a framed poster of bare-chested William Holden. He looks down on lovely, placid Kim Novak seated on the ground, encircled by a flowing pink gown. The scene, from a coming attraction called *Picnic*, mocks the show of real life playing on the lobby carpeting below it.

Joann's nervous hands clench and unclench. Fire, again, has triggered a fearful episode.

Seeing her mother's terror, Saffee feels a mixture of compassion and mortification. She looks around, hoping there is no one else in the lobby. Mr. Jenkins, the theater manager, watches them from behind the concession stand with his cleaning rag paused in midair.

"I have to get out of here." Joann's voice is desperate but quiet. She seems to be making an effort to calm herself. "Saffee, help me get home." She waves an arm. "Pull me up."

Saffee steadies the arm and lifts upward but is unable to bring Joann to standing. She is afraid the movie will be over before they can get out the door. She can't let classmates see her struggle with a disoriented mother.

"Come on, Mother. Get up. Let's go."

Joann maneuvers to her knees and with Saffee's assistance inches up the wall, knocking Holden-Novak askew. Once upright, she smoothes her hair and orders imperiously, "Saffee, go to Mr. Jenkins over there. Tell him to give you money back for two tickets."

"No, Mother, I'm not going to do that. We need to leave." Saffee straightens Joann's coat, buttons it, and hurriedly guides her to the front double doors. With a bare hand, she pushes against the cold glass patterned with swirls of ice. The winter storm, which for more than ninety minutes had been forgotten, assaults with cruelty.

Saffee remembers that her dad expects them to call, but she cannot bear the thought of returning to the lobby, soon to be full of people who would gawk at them. They lunge into the wind. Saffee glances back over her shoulder and sees Mr. Jenkins peering out, his face distorted by the ice on the glass door.

Joann, her bare head lowered, heedlessly strides through the drifting snow. Wind quickly penetrates their clothing. Saffee holds Joann's arm firmly with two hands as if worried she might run off, but also to keep them warm. As they hurry along, she is stricken by the role reversal. How has it happened that she, the daughter, is caring for her bewildered mother?

By the time they reach home, Joann's exertion in the cold has restored her senses. Nels, surprised they hadn't called for a ride, meets them at the door.

"We came home early, Daddy, because Mother . . . she didn't like the movie."

Without a word, Joann heads to the bedroom and begins to undress for bed.

Saffee follows. "Mom, do you want me to help you?"

Joann shakes her head no.

Later Saffee lies awake, replaying the frightful evening. It didn't seem that Joann believed she was in real danger from the fire on the screen, unlike that summer night when she tried to push Saffee to some kind of safety under the Norway table. But again flames had triggered irrational behavior.

She's heard that it's illegal to yell "Fire!" in a crowded theater. Saffee shudders. The nightmare could have been even worse.

Movies! Perhaps she will never go to another one. By extension, tonight's experience has eclipsed her fantasy. Phooey on Southern plantations. Phooey on make-believe that has nothing to do with her. For years she has wasted her time being amused, amazed, and aroused by what is not real. She has foolishly built her own dreams around adventures in books and spectacles of Hollywood that will never come true for her.

Real life is the icy sting of cold glass on a bare hand, the lonely darkness of a theater's middle section, a ridiculous movie poster swinging by its frame, and, most of all, a peculiar, tormented mother, crumpled on the floor.

No wonder Joann scolded her last summer. After an engaging matinee of *Daddy Long Legs*, Saffee had parroted Leslie Caron all the way home and neglected to drop the impersonation when she walked in the door.

"And why are you acting so uppity?" Joann demanded. "Don't you come home from a movie and be a smarty. What kinds of things are you seeing there, anyway? That's not how we act in this family, and don't you forget it." Evidently an imaginary life was only for Joann, not for others over whom she might lose control.

Tonight, Saffee sees that her mother was right, and maybe it doesn't matter. When they move to Cottonwood Point, they will live too far from the theater to walk. She sees herself as too old to be driven.

However, when it comes to Saffee's love for movies, tomorrow is another day.

## CHAPTER TWENTY-FOUR

# COTTONWOOD POINT

As the snow melts and the ground thaws, Joann frets about how she will get to the construction site to keep an eye on daily progress of the new house, as she had the remodeling on Second Street. She decides she must learn to drive, something she has previously refused to do.

"Well, Muzzy." When Nels is pleased, he calls Joann by the pet name he gave her years ago. "I been expectin' that ever since I seen you drawed plans for a two-car garage!"

It's no secret that Nels hopes the new house project will help Joann shed some of her other idiosyncrasies as well and "become more like other women."

"Mom? Learn to drive? Good," Saffee says. "Then maybe she'll take me to chorus practice. There's no other way I can get there by seven thirty when we move out to the *sticks* and I have to ride the *bus*!"

April rattles off her list of activities that will also require transportation, including after-school tumbling. Joann reminds her there will be no such dangerous endeavor for her. "You might fall and absolutely *ruin* your kidneys," she warns.

On Saturdays and Sundays, with Nels at her side, Joann nervously nudges a new maroon Ford along nearby country roads. When she ventures onto the streets of town, she traces over and over the route from Second Street to the Cottonwood Point subdivision. The day she returns from her first solo outing, it would be hard to say whether she or Nels is more proud.

Building the new house facilitates a recovery of something that had been stolen from Joann. A driving back of evil gives her renewed vigor for life, at least temporarily. In spite of cold weather, excavation is completed by mid-April. For a few hours each day, Joann, wrapped in a long parka, stands like a sentinel, watching the construction crew lay the cement block walls of the basement. Under a cheerless sky, with the wind wrapping her in its arms, she has plenty of time to think about things—past as well as present.

Receiving compliments from the contractor for her precise drawings and learning to drive have done more to boost her well-being and perspective on life than anything for a long time. So when she remembers her childhood days, when life was observed from under a table, she evaluates the memories more circumspectly than in the past. She remembers the nights her brother Rolf trespassed her shelter, had not molested her but touched her, scaring her. Screams had brought her father, and in the morning, Rolf felt his leather strap. The brothers, both of them, were ignorant and overworked. Now she feels sorry for them.

She thinks about Maxine, the large and bony sister. Maxine, who often hurled scathing and hurtful words and jeered at Joann after incidents with Rolf. In the bed they shared, Maxine, likely troubled, thrashed around in her sleep so much that Joann often had no recourse but to leave it. Today, Joann sees Maxine, in fact all her motherless siblings, as bereft as herself.

Most vivid in her mind is her mother, feeding, clothing, and trying to placate her demanding brood. Joann's pain of neglect had been real but, she decides, it had not been unreasonable to ache for her mother's attention. It is a need she has carried into adulthood. Today, she aches for Nels. He gives her hugs before he heads out the door and again when he returns. She *knows* he loves her, but at night, nothing, depriving her of one last baby. Her mother too had been deprived of her last baby . . . Joann stamps her cold feet and swings her arms not only to keep warm but also to make sure her presence is recognized by the workmen, who probably would take off for a smoke if she weren't around.

Never far from her mind since it reappeared, and even now as she stands watch, is the old wooden box that found its way to their basement shelf and holds her mother's death certificate.

Today, maybe not tomorrow, but today, standing at the building site in the chilly air, she declares that her fate will not be like her mother's. She has designed a wonderful house. She can drive. Nels has often told her there is "nothin' wrong" with her so she "shouldn't act like there is." Today, she believes it. Yet, why then won't he give her another baby?

Looking around her post, she has time to wonder what will eventually be built on lots adjacent to the new house. She decides that Nels should plant a stand of evergreens on the north side of their property to create a privacy screen as well as a windbreak. To the south is the apple orchard. Let people build what they want beyond those trees; the Kvaales won't be bothered.

When the bricks she carefully selected arrive, four burly men unload heavy pallets of red bundles. Joann scrutinizes the delivery. She had imagined a more massive stack. She counts the bricks in one bundle, counts bundles, and multiplies.

"The cheats! They shorted me sixty bricks. They're robbing me blind."

The error is soon corrected. As time goes on, the construction project brings an assortment of such concerns, as well as exhaustion, to Joann. And, as always, when she is stressed, everyone suffers. But in October the Kvaales manage to move into their new ranch-style house.

❖

Later that month, on a gray afternoon when the girls step off the school bus, they are disheartened to see their mother in the open garage, furiously slapping tan enamel onto the old wooden Norway table. They are stunned by her disheveled appearance, her unpinned dark hair falling over her face as she leans into every stroke. She mutters to someone they cannot see and does not look up as the girls approach.

"Why are you making demands again?" they hear her say. "*Yes.* I'm painting. Can't you see? But you lied. *It does no good!* . . . Comfort. *Comfort?* Layer upon layer has given me no comfort. *Won't I ever be free? . . .*"

Alarmed at her mother's mental disarray, and recalling previous histrionics, Saffee hugs her books to her chest. April huddles against her and whispers, "What's she saying, Saffee? Who's she talking to?"

Saffee doesn't answer.

"*Smoke!* The shadow of death." Joann's alarm intensifies. "You are marking me for hell!"

Joann abruptly raises her head and emphatically shakes a heavily laden brush in the girls' direction. "*Stop tormenting me!*" she yells at an invisible phantom. Paint drips down her arm and splatters across the table. The girls want to flee, but their feet will not move. April buries her face in Saffee's sweater.

Suddenly weak, Joann drops her brush and crumples forward, forearms flattened against the wet, glossy table as she continues her garrulous talk. "What's that?" she demands. "You say *He* prepared a snare for me? *He* prepared a trap? *No!* It's not true! *Go away!*"

Slowly, slowly, she strokes with her hands and arms as if fashioning finger paint. She sways back and forth. She no longer smears, she caresses. Her voice, a whisper, turns resolute. "It wasn't a snare. I know it wasn't. 'He . . . prepareth . . . a table' . . . A table before me. *To deliver me from the presence of my enemies!*" She looks heavenward. "Oh, God . . . help me!"

The daughters bolt into the house to elude the disarray that countermands their mother's once rational mind. Behind them, Joann droops over the enigmatic table and cries.

They hang their jackets in the hall closet and dumbly sit on the new kitchen chairs that still feel foreign. Saffee wishes they were in their old house on Second Street.

"You know what I was thinking about on the bus?" April sounds wistful.

"What?"

"I was hoping when we got home Mommy would be in the kitchen, making chocolate chip cookies."

"Sure, April." Saffee rolls her eyes. "Might as well hope for the moon."

April wilts. She sinks her head into folded arms on the kitchen table and begins to cry. Saffee watches her dully.

Suddenly, April raises her tear-streaked face and demands, "Why doesn't she just *get rid* of that awful table if it makes her so upset?"

Lately, Saffee has felt more sympathetic toward her sister, but as usual, she can't resist an opportunity to flaunt her wisdom, valid or not. Furthermore, sniping at April relieves her own tension.

"Get rid of a holy thing? Don't be stupid, April. Why would anyone do a blasphemous thing like that?"

By the time Nels comes home, two days later, Joann has returned to her usual preoccupied, but less episodic, self.

"Muzzy," Nels calls out as he comes in the door. "I see you've been busy. I bet it's nice to have a big garage to paint in, and park your car too."

Since her dad is gone much of the time, Saffee concludes that he must be unaware of the extent of her mother's disturbed behavior. She decides to inform him.

On Sunday afternoon Joann is in her bedroom nursing a head-ache. Although Saffee is hesitant to talk behind her mother's back, she marks her page of *David Copperfield* and summons courage. She trudges to the living room and plops onto the sectional beside Nels, who is reading the newspaper.

"Daddy," she says, hushed, "I need to talk to you about something important."

Nels shifts his toothpick to the other side of his mouth and glances at her.

"Mother was really scary the other day when you were gone, all mixed up."

"Whatdya mean, mixed up?" He puts down the paper.

"In the garage, painting the table *again*, she was talking *crazy*, and paint was flying all over. It was awful, Daddy. I didn't like it!"

"Ahh. She's okay. Dere's nuttin' wrong. She even learnt how to drive."

"*Daddy, listen!* It wasn't normal. April was scared too. Mother acts *so strange* sometimes."

"Nah. She jus' gets nervous and excited about things. Her biggest problem? She thinks too much." He reopens his paper. "You jus' be sure to be a good girl. Don't go gettin' edgewise with 'er. Everything'll be fine."

"*Daddy.*" Saffee is indignant at his assessment and warning. "It's not *my* fault she's so mixed up." Although conversations with her father are usually less than satisfying, she is not going to give up. "I think she needs to go to some kind of doctor or something."

Nels, who doesn't know anyone who medicates mood changes, and wouldn't think much of anyone who does, scowls. "*Nah.* Listen, I tol' you." He takes the toothpick from his mouth and jabs the air for emphasis. "Dere's nothin' wrong with her."

Saffee reminds him that he isn't here all the time to witness his wife's behavior. She complains that she and April are at a loss to know what to do when she gets "all funny." She suggests that perhaps there are hospitals for . . .

"Now don' talk nonsense. She's never goin' to one a *dem* places."

Nels returns to his paper and toothpick. Saffee knows when to say no more but her mind churns. David Copperfield meets a world full of curious people. Had Dickens known her parents, perhaps he would have numbered them with the lot.

In November, the girls take their first ride in the car with their mother at the wheel. She drives at a careful speed, pumping the accelerator. Saffee, up front, hears April whisper in the backseat, "Wow, herky-jerky." They both notice that Joann looks in the rearview mirror almost as much as out the front window. Is she afraid someone behind is following too closely? Or criticizing the way she drives? Twice Joann activates the windshield wipers instead of the turn signals and, worse, doesn't seem to notice them scraping back and forth.

"Mom!" Saffee yells, embarrassed that someone might see them. "It's not raining."

Later Joann asks, "Saffee, what about that morning chorus practice at school? I suppose I could take you."

"No. I don't think I'll go this year, Mom. Maybe next year."

A few days later Joann's right ankle is in a plaster cast. While looking in the rearview mirror as she approached an intersection, she hit a stopped car.

She never drives again.

## Chapter Twenty-Five

# Respectfully Yours

. . . and then the tree caught fire and the whole school burned down to the ground . . ."

In the next room, Saffee surrenders her concentration. Even the great Captain Ahab, harpoon in hand, must defer to Joann when she mentions fire.

It seems that Joann is suggesting to April that out of respect for all who have perished in fires ignited by candles on Christmas trees, the Kvaales should no longer plug in strings of electric bulbs on their tree.

"Never?" April asks.

"Well, I think not," her mother says.

"Let's go tell Saffee," April says, and hurries into the living room, followed more slowly by Joann, on crutches.

"Saffee, Mom thinks . . ."

"I heard, but we don't use candles," Saffee scoffs. "That was the olden days."

"But houses and schools and nursing homes and everything burned to the ground!" April says.

Saffee doesn't understand what good it would do to dispense with

pretty lights in order to remember tragic fires, but she also knows
it will make no difference what she thinks. Joann's ideas quickly
fossilize.

April says, "Mommy, I've always liked Christmas lights."

"A little sacrifice might be a good thing for people nowadays,"
Joann says. "In fact, this might catch on like wild . . . I think I'll dash
off a letter to the *Gazette*."

The day before Christmas, Saffee swishes a dusting cloth over the
living room's built-in bookcase. One shelf holds a few knickknacks,
always arranged just so. A sunshine-yellow dancing girl lunges diagonally from the right corner as if with rapid dash she will thrust
herself to center stage. The ceramic figurine has been on display since
Saffee can remember and, for some reason, seems to convey more
significance in the room than its five inches would indicate. Always
running, never arriving, her gown revealingly presses against her
upper body. She carries her yellow skirt high with outstretched arms,
creating wings of perpetual flight.

Saffee has never liked the piece. The form-fitting gown is immod-
est. Early in their marriage Nels had purchased the unabashedly
seductive piece as a gift for his wife, the dancer. Nels's "two left feet,"
and Joann's encumbrances, emotional and varicose, had eclipsed their
dancing together long ago.

Saffee has memories of her nightgown-clad mother during the
St. Paul years, swaying, swirling, twirling alone across the living room,
dream-like, as Nelson Eddy and Jeannette McDonald belted, *"O
sweet mystery of love at last I've found you . . ."*

"Dancing embraces the light fantastic," Joann would gush. "It's
so romantic." To Saffee, it seemed like carrying on. To young April,
it was an invitation to mimic her mother until she collapsed with
laughter onto the carpet. The gray Gulistan carpet.

During their first weeks in the new house, veins and emotions permitting, and with the phonograph on high volume, a seductive dance from the second act of *Carmen* could still lure Joann into its spell. The staccato rhythms and frenzied climax rewarded her with delight. Saffee chose not to observe these "performances." In her bedroom, trying to ignore the music, she wondered if there had ever been another mother like hers and thinks that if anyone found out about Joann, she would die. But Joann's car accident, coupled with her increasingly pesky veins, knocked the dance right out of her.

Saffee returns the figurine to its place. There has always been a kind of paradoxical exhibitionism in Joann that makes Saffee uncomfortable. Although her mother is increasingly fearful of people, when given the opportunity, her posture continues to tease, "Look at me. Please look at me. See how well I'm built." There is much about Joann, and her own discomfort, that Saffee does not understand. All she can do is accept things as they are.

Joann slides a red curly ribbon from a small package and drops it into the reuse bag. She lets the wrapping paper slip to the floor, then scrutinizes a three-piece manicure set in a cellophane package: scissors, cuticle nipper, and file.

Saffee watches her. As a rule, she and April don't buy Christmas presents for their parents or each other. It has never been expected. But now that Saffee is fourteen, it seems right that she should try her hand at gift giving. She nagged her dad for an increase to her twenty-five-cent weekly allowance, keeping it secret that she planned to buy gifts.

"What?" he teased. "You're overpaid already!" In the end, he gave her three dollars. She added the bills to her savings without a thank-you, frustrated and angered by his teasing.

After purchasing a pair of socks for Nels and a book for April, with four dollars remaining in her billfold, she went to Walgreens and spent over forty minutes trying to select the perfect gift for her mother.

Now she can tell by her mother's upraised brows and downturned mouth that she had chosen unwisely. "I already have a manicure set," Joann declares. "And it's a far cry better than this one. These scissors couldn't cut a thing." She turns over the package. "I could have guessed," she says. "Made in Japan." She sets the gift aside and rolls her eyes. "Where'd you get it, Saffee? I hope you saved the receipt."

"Aw, Joann. It's Christmas. The first one in our new house. Now don't go ruinin' it."

Saffee bends over a good-size box on her lap and fumbles with its ribbon. She is glad her dad has spoken up. Still, she wants to throw him an accusing look because he had not supplied enough money to buy a better gift for her critical mother. Looking up would reveal her tears.

April provides distraction as she squeals with pleasure over a wine-colored outfit for her Ginny doll. There are a number of gifts under the tree that bear Saffee's name, but by its size and shape, she knows that the one she holds contains her every-Christmas ice skates. Since moving to Cottonwood Point, she's been unable to skate on the Blue River, but she hopes her dad will drive her there during Christmas vacation. She rips off the paper and lifts the lid, welcoming the smell of new leather. She holds up a white skate by its shiny runner.

"Mom. This looks so *big*." She peers at the number stamped onto the lining. "Size *nine*? I wear size seven. I'll *never* grow into *these*."

"Yes, you will," Joann assures her. "I'm tired of buying new skates every year; we've already spent a fortune on them."

## Chapter Twenty-Six

# Speaking Truth

1959

"Joann! Joann!"

Another pitiless dream. The same voices.

Sweat-soaked, Joann shoves blankets and sheets aside. Lying immobile on her back, staring at the invisible ceiling, she tries to regain control of her breathing. Fear subsides and discouragement takes its place. Why does the specter refuse to loosen its grip? She must not sleep. She lowers her feet into slippers. The night air is cool but her skin fever-hot. Clad in her nightgown, she makes her way down the hall, tiptoeing past the closed den door, where Nels sleeps. In the dining room she stands immobile, staring at the barely visible, brooding table. Minutes pass. Still she stands; she could not say how long. Finally, she goes into the kitchen, turns on a light, and begins to write in her always-ready notebook.

> The odor of a noxious pyre dogs me.
> A measure of its ash pesters, clings, settles.

*Exchange this curse, O God*
*For the fire of Your Holy Spirit,*
*For the fragrance of Your Christ.*

After dinner, when the dishes are wiped and put away, Joann scours the sink and Saffee retreats to the dining room. At the Norway table, which has been sloppily dressed in charcoal gray for over a month, Saffee intends to hurry through an algebra assignment, then resume chapter six of *Les Misérables*. In the living room, April struggles with the left hand arpeggios of "Für Elise," despairing that her piano teacher expects all pieces first be learned hands separately.

Joann bought the spinet piano shortly after April's concussion and both girls, in spite of their lack of natural talent, began lessons. It was an obvious tactic to keep April, who thrives on active outdoor play, indoors.

For Saffee, playing the piano, even badly, becomes almost as liberating as reading. Joann's recorded music has always captivated her. From what magical places does such music spring? Reproducing even the simplest of melodies stimulates within her a strange desire to someday know the bigger life beyond the insipid Kvaale household.

April's playing, of course, is not for herself, but for performance, and she obliges anyone, not minding at all to play for their few and far between invited guests. When Joann directs Saffee to play for outsiders, sudden queasiness prevents her from playing even one measure.

"Saffee." Joann appears, removing her apron. "Come down to my bedroom."

Annoyed by the interruption, but wondering what the summons is about, Saffee follows Joann down the hall. She notices her mother's slight limp. Joann blames it on childhood rickets and on her ankle, which she says didn't mend properly after her driving accident years before. Joann shuts the door behind them, muting the piano, and sits on the edge of the bed. She indicates a chair for Saffee and gets right to the point.

"I'm going to ask you a question, and I want you to tell me the truth," Joann says. "I want to ask you . . ." She pauses, her hands twist. "I want to ask you if you think there's something wrong with me."

The question stuns. "Wha-what do you mean, wrong?"

"You know, *different* from other people, funny."

Saffee has an urge to be rude. To perhaps say, "Duh."

"I don't know . . ."

"Just tell me, Saffee. Tell me if you think there's something *wrong* with me, not normal."

*Not normal?* What an understatement. Disturbing memories flicker in Saffee's head like a black-and-white news reel. Her mother's trance-like staring. Conversations with an invisible someone. Hallucinations.

Oh, what she could say. Saffee has witnessed her mother's emotional gymnastics most of her life, but a valid evaluation is beyond her. And why is she asking? Joann never seeks her daughter's opinion. Now that Saffee is about to graduate from high school, does Joann consider her finally capable of *having* an opinion?

"Well?" Joann says, impatient. Saffee notes the familiar clenched hands, the pursed lips. She feels cornered.

"I don't know what to say, Mother."

At the piano, April has also become impatient. Discordant notes and premature tempo race through the walls, further scrambling Saffee's thoughts. Doesn't April know that "Für Elise" should float, not gallop?

"I guess I'm not sure what normal is, Mother," she says, knowing she sounds lame. "And anyway, why are you asking?"

Joann takes a deep breath, looks at the ceiling, and says, "I want to know because I want to have another baby, and your father is denying me that . . . pleasure."

"What? A baby?" Saffee doesn't let on she has heard them argue about this. "Don't you think, I mean, do you think you should? I mean, Mother, what are you saying?"

"I want a boy. A cute little boy, fun, energetic. For Nels. It would bring me, us, new life. April is growing up, thirteen already. I know a baby would be a male version of little April."

Nels, Joann tells Saffee, insists that her "nerves" wouldn't take having another child. But that's just an excuse, Joann scoffs. "The truth is that he doesn't find me attractive anymore."

Saffee feels intensely awkward. Shouldn't this conversation be had with a girlfriend, not a daughter? Of course, Joann has no girlfriends.

Joann gets up and goes to the bureau, preens a bit before her mirror, and asks weakly, "Am I, Saffee? Am I still attractive?"

Saffee takes a deep breath and lies. "Mom. Of course you are attractive. And there's nothing wrong with you. You're just *fine*, just *fine*, Mom."

"Are you sure?"

Saffee is unnerved. Her mother is calling for help and she doesn't know how to give it. Worse, she doesn't want to hear any more. She stands, thrusts her hands into her pockets, and takes two or three steps to nowhere.

"Mom, I just told you what I think, but as for having a baby . . ."

Joann sighs, as if resigned that she will get no acceptable answers. She tilts her head back and again looks at the ceiling. "I hope April is almost through practicing," she says, giving closure to the conversation.

"I've got a lot of homework, Mom," Saffee says quietly and turns to leave the room.

"Fine. No, wait, Sapphire." In an instant, Joann's focus has changed. "Come back, one more thing."

"What?"

"Promise me that when I'm old and infirm you'll do something for me."

"Do what?"

"Cut the hairs on my chinny-chin-chin. Promise me now."

No response seems appropriate. Stunned that one minute her mother regarded her as confidante and the next as future caregiver, Saffee quickly retreats to the dining room.

April tries harder, slowly combining arpeggios with melody.

Saffee stares at her algebra book. Her conscience overrides both piano and equations. Guilt about lying crowds out the slight flattery of Joann's asking for her opinion. Of course Saffee believes there is something "wrong" with her mother. Another baby? Absurd. But what could she have said? Both girls have noticed that their dad has been sleeping in the den. Maybe he isn't as oblivious to their mother's mental condition as they had thought.

Saffee copes with her mother by disregarding her, not analyzing her. She consoles herself with the thought that it is mere months until she goes off to college and her own life, one she anticipates will be "different" and, she hopes, better. For now she waits, detached and self-focused.

Bass and treble begin to mingle. April's "Für Elise" flits, almost charmingly, through the air.

## CHAPTER TWENTY-SEVEN

# THE CATAPULT

It is July; college looms. One moment Saffee's heart races with heady anticipation, the next she's filled with suffocating fear.

Clothes are a concern. She needs clothes that give the impression that she belongs at a state university. What do such clothes look like? She has no one to consult and a mother who is unpredictable in stores. Years ago, important shopping was done in Minneapolis, but Saffee is hesitant to take the bus there alone. She will try to piece together what she needs in Miller's Ford's limited dress shops.

At Gilbert's Fine Fashions, she timidly admires neatly folded stacks of sweaters in luscious colors. Any one of them would be a pleasure to own.

A tall, angular clerk, stylishly dressed and coiffed, brows raised, hovers nearby.

"You're the Kimball girl, aren't you?" she says.

"Well, ah . . ." Would it be wrong to correct her? And what does that name, right or wrong, mean to the woman? "No, I'm . . . it's Kvaale and I'm going off to college and—"

The clerk interrupts, "What kind of sweater are you looking

for?" She straightens a perfectly folded stack that Saffee had ever so slightly touched. Saffee feels like a cat at a dog show.

"Kind? Well, I . . . I mean, I don't know. Um, these here are pretty."

"Well"—the clerk sounds impatient—"do you want a cardigan?"

Saffee perspires. Her mother continually spouts obscure vocabulary, but Saffee has never heard her use this word. Everyone else in town probably knows what "cardigan" means.

"Well, uh, I don't know . . . I mean, I don't really care."

The woman gives her a withering look.

"I mean, I guess . . . I'll have to think about it." Red-faced, Saffee rushes for the exit and home to ask her mother what the word means.

"Cardigan? It's a sweater."

"I know it's a sweater, but what kind? A clerk at Gilbert's asked me if I wanted a cardigan and I didn't know what she meant. I was so embarrassed! You're forever using big words, why not that one?"

Joann reaches for her always-handy dictionary.

"You overestimate my erudition, Saffee," Joann says, searching.

Saffee rolls her eyes.

Joann finds that her dictionary defines *cardigan* as a sweater named after a Welsh earl. Not much help.

"I must need a new dictionary," she says, checking the copyright date. "1951." Her face lights up. "I'll get a new one and send this one to college with you."

With the help of a Sears Roebuck catalog, Saffee deduces that sweaters with buttons down the front are called cardigans. Joann orders one for Saffee in tan, "a good neutral color that goes with everything," and then adds another item to the form—the most recent edition of *The American College Dictionary*.

Four more days. Saffee considers each garment as she slides it across the closet bar. On her bedroom floor are two almost-full suitcases, miscellaneous boxes, a portable typewriter, packages of typing paper, carbon paper, and Joann's old dictionary.

April, sprawled across Saffee's bed, watches her sister sort remaining items on the closet shelves. Years of habit prompt Saffee to give her a get-off-my-bed look and April scoots over to her own.

She has packed a new gray tweed suit, a coordinating sweater—pullover—and sensible pumps. Joann surmises that this is what well-dressed coeds wear to class. They had shopped together at Gilbert's to purchase these and other items. To Saffee's relief, her mother was, for once, on her best behavior, and the aloof clerk must have had the day off.

In sportswear, when Joann noticed a mannequin wearing Bermuda shorts and knee socks, she sputtered, "Wool shorts? One might say that's an oxymoron."

"Only you, Mother," Saffee whispered.

"Saffee, that beautiful womanhood would succumb to such outrageous whims of fashion is counterintuitive," Joann huffed.

Saffee doubts she would have the nerve to display her thickish legs in shorts on campus, but if that is the rage, she wishes she could.

Completing her assistance, Joann made Saffee a brown wool straight skirt, and from a sewing magazine, she ordered a lifetime supply of personalized labels: SAPPHIRE E. KVAALE. She stressed how important it is to label every item to be taken. Saffee is grateful for her mother's help.

"I know you don't want me to tell you this, Saffee," April says, "but I'm going to miss you."

Preoccupied with sorting through a bureau drawer, Saffee does not respond.

April continues, "I saw Mother in the basement yesterday, opening up paint cans, checking colors or something. I just hate it when she gets in one of her painting moods. I woke up in the middle of the night because she and Daddy were arguing about it. Did you hear them?"

"No."

April buries her face in her pillow for a few moments and then says, "Saffee, when you're here and they fight it's not so bad, but when you're gone . . . I don't know . . . Maybe we can talk on the phone?"

Saffee is too preoccupied to be sympathetic. "I don't think so. It'd be long distance, you know. They wouldn't allow it." Kvaale long-distance calls are reserved for passing along only the gravest news, such as the death of a relative the girls have never heard of.

"Well, how about letters?"

The coed-to-be ignores the fact that April's voice is cracking. "I'm going to *college*, April. I'll probably be way too *busy* for letters."

"Well, *I* can still write to *you*," April says with resignation and leaves the room.

Saffee pushes April from her mind. She catches a reflection of her furrowed brow in the mirror and leans closer to inspect her face. Will she be the only girl on campus who still must conceal purply-red pimples with pasty-pale medication?

She plops down onto the floor and leans back on her elbows. Idly wagging her feet back and forth, she tries to imagine what lies ahead. She is leaving an insular, unsatisfying home life, but it has been safe, making few demands. Mr. Mason's convicting truism has flashed into her mind lately: "Dead fish flow with the stream." The image sickens her. She does not want to be a dead fish any longer. She wants to get out of the home stream that goes nowhere. But she is afraid.

She might be ready for college academically, but in addition to learning, she supposes that college years are a time to cultivate new relationships and have fun. These things her family has not taught her, while books and movies have only given passive instruction. She hopes to forget her acutely self-conscious years trudging the hallways of Miller's High. She critically views herself as unattractively large, which she is not, and boorish and dull, which, arguably, she can be. Can such a person ever have friends and fun?

Mulling the question, she surveys the familiar bedroom—the white-painted furniture, the homemade flowered curtains, the bedside table with its shelf of books. There she notices the black Bible presented to her at confirmation six years ago.

She was taught that the Bible contains the Word of God, so two or three times she tried to read it. She started at the beginning and soon became bogged down by its unfamiliar style and lists of odd names. The last time she opened it, she found that years before April had glued Green Stamps onto several pages, rather than into a Green Stamp redemption book. Irate, Saffee showed the desecrated pages to Joann, who breezily dismissed the deed. "Well, that just proves the Bible is a redemption book too!" she said, chuckling at her own wit.

Saffee considers that perhaps this is her last chance for some time to look into the old book, since she does not plan to pack it. Maybe there is some encouragement in it for her. Not knowing where to look, she decides to read whatever first meets her eye. She lets the book fall open, beyond the green pages, to near the middle, and reads:

*Thou art my hiding place; thou shalt preserve me from trouble;*
*Thou shalt compass me about with songs of deliverance.*

She reads the sentence again, changing *thou* to *you*. *You are my hiding place* . . . She reads it a third time.

She knows that, much like her mother's life, hers has been spent in hiding places, private and alone, not risking to unveil her innermost being to anyone. Perhaps not even to herself. The verse seems to say that there is some kind of protective place in God. A place away from trouble. This appeals to her reclusive tendencies. But what are songs of deliverance?

She recalls the tense night on the basement stairway, listening to her parents argue. There she heard God's voice: *Watch. Listen. Learn. Your life will be different.* At the time, the promise did not seem to be a song, yet since then, it has lent a certain ever-so-personal lyric to her life. Intrigued, Saffee continues to read.

> *I will instruct thee and teach thee in the way which thou shalt go: I will guide thee with mine eye.*

Saffee stares at the words. She had no idea the Bible would, or even could, communicate to her so directly. Instruct? Teach? Guide? How she desires these things. As strong as her eagerness to leave home is her fear of doing so. She has wondered if she will be able to maintain her comfortably safe distance from people. Will she be expected to speak in classes? Then there is the matter of a roommate. She attached a note to her application requesting a private dormitory room but is afraid it will not be honored.

She reads on.

> *Be ye not as the horse, or as the mule, which have no understanding: whose mouth must be held in with bit and bridle . . . Many sorrows shall be to the wicked: but he that trusteth in the Lord, mercy shall compass him about.*

If God cares enough about her to communicate like this, at the very moment she needs it, maybe she can leave home less afraid. She tucks the Bible between layers of clothes in a suitcase.

# CHAPTER TWENTY-EIGHT

# WHAT'S IN A NAME?

In a sense, Saffee's new life begins because of her name. "Kvaale" places her in the *J* through *L* group for five days of freshman orientation. Somewhere between Monday's health forms and Friday's convocation, she meets Mary, Mary Kvaale, who pronounces her own name as if it is an appellation of honor, even beauty.

"Hello. My name is Mary Kvaale," she says, politely extending her hand, her serene, blue eyes looking confidently into Saffee's. To others, it would have been such a minor thing. But Saffee is stunned. All her life she has painfully resented being stuck with this funny last name, and her first is not at all better. When she cannot avoid admitting to Kvaale, she distorts her mouth and quickly rolls her eyes, showing how distasteful it is to claim. In contrast, Mary speaks the very same name with seeming pride, suggesting that her Kvaale-ness is a sacred trust. Saffee appraises an aura of loveliness that envelops the girl simply because she speaks so softly, so self-assuredly.

Later, when alone, Saffee examines her own reflection in a mirror and says quietly, "Hello. My name is Sapphire Kvaale."

Amazing. Her old life is still written on her face, but something of promise shines in her eyes. She resolves to believe the words she read in the confirmation Bible.

College propels Saffee, a quirky, small-town introvert, into a culture quite foreign. But, from orientation week on, the girl who from childhood has said, *I can't, I won't, I'm afraid*, decides to plant a tiny seed of confidence. However, for some time, as she hurries to and from classes along the crowded mall that flows with a great swell of humanity, she feels empowered, not by confidence, but by her own imagined invisibility. She can't help but wonder what others might notice about her, if anyone bothered to look. Does she bear a physical stamp of her sterile, crazy upbringing? What expressions or gestures reveal her dullness to those who make slight, friendly advances in classes and the cafeteria? She chooses to be polite, but wary.

October 14, 1959
Dear Family,

What should she write? That she is thrilled to be away from the vacuum of her former existence? So thrilled that she has been "beyond words" for almost a month and therefore has been unable to write? It is duty that prompts her to write now; after all, her dad is paying.

I love it here! The campus is full of wonderful people and everyone is so nice to me.

Should she write that after days of observation she does not yet know how to embrace the new, exhilarating life around her? In the past, boredom was so easily obtained. But here, one can hardly be passive; participation is required. In her heart of hearts, how she would love to be swept up in the myriad of activity, the frivolous as well as the seriously academic.

I have a roommate. Her name is Gloria Karson. She's from the suburbs, obviously well-to-do, and has a great personality. I'm sure we'll get

*along fine, even if she is a Lutheran. She reads the Bible every morn-*
*ing before she even gets out of bed!*

For roommates, Saffee has gone from bubbly, extroverted April to
bubbly, extroverted Gloria. April, Mother's little pet, Saffee resented.
Beautiful, self-assured Gloria, with curly red hair and porcelain skin,
she admires and yearns to be like. Gloria's advice on makeup—"That
gloppy cover-up makes you look like death warmed over"—was said
with humor, not ridicule. "Let me show you what real makeup can
do for you, Saffee."

Seeking approval on all fronts, Saffee doesn't want her roommate
to think she's a heathen, so she tells her that years ago she tried to
make sense out of the Old Testament. Gloria suggests Saffee try the
book of Psalms and the accounts of Jesus in the New Testament.

*Gloria thinks my gray tweed suit is quite appropriate.*

"Well, if we ever have to go to a funeral, you'll be all set!" Again,
her statement held humor, not sarcasm, her dimples deepening as she
laughed. "If you'd like, you can borrow some of my pleated skirts and
sweaters until you get more of your own."

She doesn't write that Gloria thinks it's funny that Saffee's every
possession is labeled. "Did you think your roomie was going to steal
your underwear?" she teased, putting her arm around Saffee's shoulders with a friendly squeeze.

*Down the hall is a nice girl named Kathy. We are in some of the same*
*classes, so we sometimes walk across campus together. Across the*
*hall are Charlotte and Jillian from Atlanta, Georgia. I've never known*
*Negroes before. They sure have accents! But that hasn't hindered them*
*from already making a hundred friends! They know some university*
*football players from their hometown. I guess coming from Miller's Ford*
*means I've got a lot of learning to do about different kinds of people.*

Saffee considers that she represents a sort of minority on campus—an outsider by personality and deficient in life experience. One reason she is drawn to Charlotte and Jillian is that they too are from a minority, albeit a different kind. She has been surprised how easily they have assimilated into activities and relationships. Under the influence of Gloria and these other new friends, Saffee begins to discard her insulated, egocentric tendencies.

The best thing: Robert Frost was the convocation speaker yesterday—in person! He's pretty old, with a shock of white hair, just like his pictures. His voice was weak until he started reading "Birches." He actually read "Birches"! (Thank you, Mother, for making it one of my favorites.)

As she listened to the revered poet, Saffee imagined the little old man, once an impish boy, clinging to a bending branch, whooping and hollering, bouncing through the air, then dropping to the ground to watch it spring back. A poem about risk. A poem about fun. A poem that did not at all resemble her own childhood.

About my classes: Psychology 101—The professor is boring, but the subject is fascinating. Mother, years ago did you read about Skinner boxes in Mr. Clement's psychology books? What terrible things. He actually put babies in boxes!

French—Pretty hard, but I like it. Let me tell you about the huge linebacker (second string) who I sometimes sit next to in class. Last week we started talking—in English, of course. Later, I ran into him (not literally, or I'd be dead) in Dinky Town (the quaint shopping village across University Ave.). We went to Bridgeman's and had a cherry Coke. He paid, so I'm calling it my first date!

She doesn't write that when she is called on in class, her face reddens and a shy dumbness comes over her. Twice in French she answered questions with Spanish vocabulary learned in high school.

And her "date" with the linebacker? She was hardly able to say an intelligent word and was so nervous she spilled her Coke on his books, and ever since she makes a point to sit at least three rows behind him in class.

*Well, that's all for now. Gotta work on a four-page paper for history.*

Why mention that her first and only venture to do research for that paper, in the vast, mysterious library, so intimidated her that she did not dare inquire how to locate information?

*Hope you understand I don't have time to write often.*
*Love,*
*Saffee*

She posts the letter, not imagining the kind of ruckus it will cause when it arrives.

## CHAPTER TWENTY-NINE

# SAPPHIRA

Saffee answers the phone in the hallway booth. "Hello?"

"Saffee."

"Oh!"

"This is your mother."

"Yes. I know. Did you get my letter?"

"Yes, it came today, and we want you to come home Friday night on the Greyhound."

"What? *Home?* I just got here!"

"We expect to see you Friday."

"But there's a dorm party Friday night. I've been thinking about going."

"Your dad will pick you up at the station when the bus gets in. Ten o'clock."

"Mother!"

"This is long distance. We'll talk when you get here. Good-bye."

The next day there is a letter from April. In it is no indication that she knows Saffee has been summoned home.

October 21, 1959

Dear Saffee,

I read your letter. College sounds so great! Can't wait to get there myself. What's a Skinner box?

Things around here aren't very good. Mom's been mean to me lately. She calls me bad names and then gives me the silent treatment. It really hurts the way she's changed toward me. And her arguments with Daddy are getting worse. Mom's mostly on her high horse about religious stuff now. Daddy tells her to stop talking foolishness, and that makes her madder. She's bent over her Bible all the time, writing in it. It's like when she wrote a lot in a library book and they made her pay for it. She told them she was translating the words into what they really meant and they should thank her!

With you not here at night I can't sleep very well. I lie in bed thinking about climbing out the window and leaving. I suppose that's ridiculous. When are you coming home?

Love and XXX,
April

Saffee has been away for six weeks. Now she stands in the middle of the living room, hugging her arms to her chest. Why is she uneasy in her own home? Because . . . it is *not* her home anymore. But until she feels less like an interloper on campus, she has no home. She glances around, reabsorbing familiarity: the Audubon Society magazine on the marble-topped coffee table, put there five years ago because its cover coordinates with Joann's décor; the pink fluted candy dish three inches to the left of the crystal lamp, still empty; the yellow ceramic dancing girl, still maniacally lunging on the bookshelf, and no closer to the edge.

Looking out the picture windows to the south, she sees frost-nipped hydrangeas, bent over and dead brown. The apple trees in the orchard have all but shed their leaves. During the summer, a couple named Peterson built a house, then hidden from view, on the lot beyond the orchard. Now, through the bare branches, Saffee can see it clearly. A black Labrador romps in the new neighbors' yard.

Instinctively, she knows that the proximity of the new house and its color are a significant offense to Joann. She can almost hear the protest: "Blue! Have they no sense of propriety?"

Saffee remembers once standing at this window watching April and two young town boys scoop up fallen apples. Their faces glowed with mirth as they shrieked and whooped, lobbing them over the bank into the valley below.

She visually sweeps the living room again, feeling uneasy. It is unusual that the double doors to the dining room are almost closed; it looks dark beyond. She smelled the sickening odor of wet paint when she arrived last night, the smell synonymous with her mother's periodic anguish over the Norway table. She doesn't want to see what new graffiti is there. A familiar, paint-spattered canvas drop cloth extends a few inches out the doorway. She gives it a kick so she can close the doors and sees that the room is dark because newspapers are taped to the windows. She quickly pulls the doors shut. New, worn, track-like marks on the carpet catch her eye.

Her parents are in the bedroom. What's keeping them? Her father said little when he picked her up at the bus last night. This morning they shared a breakfast of cold cereal, and again, he gave no clue as to why she was told to come home. She guesses that it was not his idea. April, he told her, stayed overnight with a friend.

As she waits, she wonders what they will want to know about college life. Her letter mentioned a number of things she is eager to elaborate on, especially her classes. Not that she has ever been in the habit of sharing with them, but now she hopes to be more open, more adult to adult.

She hears a slow shuffle coming down the hall.

"Sit down, Saffee."

Saffee is stunned by Joann's appearance. Her longish dark hair falls free, unkempt. She wears an old, matted chenille robe and supports her body with a crutch.

"Mother. What happened?"

"You mean you don't even remember my car accident? You know very well my broken ankle never healed right."

Saffee wants to mention that the accident was long ago and for years there has seemed to be no need for a crutch. She connects the track on the floor to her mother dragging one foot.

Nels and Joann settle themselves.

"Sit *down*, Saffee," Joann repeats and gives Nels a distinct glare, which tells Saffee she wants him to conduct the proceedings, "as a father should."

Nels is nervous, gruff, and to the point. "Your mother, we, don't want you datin' no colored boys," he blurts.

*"Wh-what?"*

"You heard me."

Saffee stares from one to the other.

"That's why you made me ride more than four hours on the bus? Date, as you say, 'colored' boys? What are you talking about? I haven't even met any."

Nels looks relieved. Joann looks skeptical. Saffee realizes they must have thought the linebacker she had written about was a Negro. He wasn't.

"Those . . . southern girls introduced you. You wrote it in your letter," Joann says. "Get it straight now, we won't allow it!" Saffee knew Joann's intention that Nels lead the conversation would not last.

"Mother, you've got it wrong. I haven't gone out with a Negro, but don't you want me to get along with everybody at school?"

"Getting along is one thing—dating is another," retorts Joann. "We're talking *Negroes* here and you've been fraternizing with them."

Saffee winces; she is committed to telling the truth. She represses last spring's conversation when she insisted there was nothing "wrong" with Joann. "No, I haven't." Saffee looks appealingly at her dad, who sits with head bowed, pinching the bridge of his nose. She wonders if either of her parents has ever even spoken to a person of color.

Joann straightens and tilts her face, posturing regal authority. "*Sapphira!* You are an astonishment!" Her pitch rises. "One's appearance, manner, and behavior should not bring disgrace to one's church, family, school, or God! Sapphira, you have not lied to man but to God."

"What?" Saffee feels sick to her stomach. Moments blur. "Sapphira? Who's Sapphira?"

"I know by your name that you are a liar," Joann insists. She turns to Nels and orders him to get her Bible.

"Aw, Joann, just let 'er be. She says—"

"Get my Bible, Nels!"

He looks at Saffee apologetically and retrieves the book from the bedroom. Joann quickly flips through the pages. Saffee sees they have been heavily annotated.

"Look here, Sapphira . . ."

"Mother, why are you calling me that? You know that's not my name."

"Here you are, right here—read this." She thrusts the worn book toward Saffee, indicating an area marked with red crayon. Joann's unmistakable scrawl almost obliterates many of the words, and sections of the page are shaded with green or yellow.

Saffee reads about a woman named Sapphira, who, after lying, falls down dead. Saffee is speechless. She has been reading the Bible, because of Gloria's encouragement, and has found it instructive and encouraging. How can her mother misuse it? Her mother is not merely eccentric, she is seriously crazy.

Nels clears his throat with a nervous, rough growl.

"See what happens to liars?" Within Joann's irrationality is a note of triumph.

"Mother, you've sent me to a school where there are all kinds of people. They come from all over the country, even the world, and I

think they are all quite wonderful—with probably lots to teach me."
She is fuming. "It never occurred to me to go out with somebody
brown, or pink, or green, but actually, I don't know why not." She is
careful not to say she won't. She needs to think about it.

Joann is not used to being refuted. She looks confused as if
unable to comprehend the show of strength. She struggles to stand,
adjusts the crutch, and rapidly drags herself across the room. Going
down the hall, she shouts, "Sapphira! You are an astonishment! You
have lied to God and man!"

Her mother's irrational theatrics have left Saffee weak, her face
drained of color. She slumps into a chair and looks at her dad. His
shoulders droop, his head is bent. For the first time in her life she is
sympathetic for the burden he carries. She leans forward and says
quietly, "Daddy, Mother needs help. She's *sick*."

Nels raises his head. Struggling for composure, he counters, "She
has good days and bad. Today's a bad one, but she'll be okay."

It baffles Saffee that he continues to deny the obvious.

"I'm so sorry . . . ," he says. "I'm so sorry you had to see her this
way. But there's nuttin' to worry about."

"But, Daddy, what about the crutch? Her ankle is just fine, don't
you think? And you know the crazy way she paints that stupid table
all the time—that's *not normal*, Dad. You know it isn't. Isn't there
someplace you could take her to get some—"

"No! Those places are terrible. She'll be okay," he insists. "I'm
thinkin' of buyin' a trailer in the spring. Maybe we can travel some
on weekends. It'll do her a world of good to get outta the house more.
She'll be okay." He seems to believe it. "Don' worry about it. When
you're home at Thanksgivin', things'll be better."

Saffee studies him as he drums his fingers on the armrests of the
chair.

"You wanna go back to school on the noon bus?" he asks. The
question sounds like an apology. "I'll take you to the station."

## CHAPTER THIRTY

# THANKSGIVING

**N**els sits at the Formica table sharpening knives, a task he has perfected to an art. He deftly circles each blade against the whetstone. "It's all in the angle of the knife against the stone," he says. He holds up a sheet of newspaper to test the butcher knife. When the blade slices razor-perfect, without so much as fluttering the paper, he is satisfied. He will use this knife on the turkey; he has no use for fancy carving sets.

He glances up at Joann, standing at the sink scrubbing the turkey with such vigor it may be in danger of losing skin. "Quill tips," she says, patting the naked bird dry with a clean towel. "Never know when they'll get stuck in a person's throat."

Even though she is stressed over the task of preparing a holiday meal, and has even asked for assistance from her girls, overall she has a little more buoyancy than Nels has seen recently. She did not criticize the produce he bought for the Thanksgiving meal (he has purchased all the groceries for some time), not even the size of the turkey (she had requested sixteen pounds, not seventeen). She limps with determination between stove, sink, and refrigerator, giving instructions to Saffee about making cranberry sauce and April peeling potatoes. Nels notices that her crutch leans against the pantry door, handy but unused. He drums his fingers and clears his throat.

"Joann." At his stern tone, Saffee glances at him over her shoulder. "Joann," Nels repeats, "you've gotta tear them newspapers off them windows before we eat Thanksgivin' dinner."

Joann's demeanor changes. She throws him a scathing look. "What? And let those snoops next door press their blue nosey faces against the window to watch us? Let them criticize how we carve turkey? Spread lies all over town that we blow our noses on our napkins? No sirree, Nels, not on your life."

"Joann, hush! The way you talk. They're nice folks, those Petersons, nice as all get-out. You should meet 'em."

"*Nice?*" Joann fans her irritation, grips the edge of the countertop, and glares at him. "How can you say they're *nice*? I've heard all about them. Don't you ever bring them over here, Nels."

Grimacing, Saffee wipes her hands on her apron and hopes the exchange is not a preview of things to come. She finds it curious that neither parent has mentioned her recent summons to come home. As for her mother meeting neighbors? Fantasy. Joann's disordered thinking has made her unable, or unwilling, to do that since they lived on Second Street. She's heard "all about" the Petersons? From whom? She can't possibly be privy to any information that warrants her mind-set. Nels sits, pinching the bridge of his nose, his eyes closed. There is nothing more to say.

Saffee has avoided looking into the dining room since she came home from school yesterday afternoon. But if the family is going to eat Thanksgiving dinner around the Norway table, as they always do, she had better assess its condition and deal with whatever she finds before the time to set it.

She opens the door to the darkened dining room, switches on the light, and shudders at a hodgepodge of color. Her mother must have had quite a flicking, dribbling frenzy to achieve this random mess. But when it suggests Jackson Pollock's work that she's seen in *Life* magazine, she decides to view it as merely an oddly whimsical mess and tries to forget that it was probably executed during a deranged episode. She opens a china closet drawer to select a suitable tablecloth.

In the afternoon, Saffee mashes potatoes, both white and sweet, drawing only a minimum of correction. But April, Saffee notes, comes under repeated fire.

"April," Joann says, "if that cream is ever going to whip before the cows come home, you'll have to turn the beater like you mean it."

The sisters have long coveted some guise of normalcy within the household, but a clear understanding of what normal is eludes them. So, in spite of a few caustic exchanges, and the usual idiosyncrasies notwithstanding, to their eyes Thanksgiving Day progresses without serious incident. The only noticeable change is Joann's heightened criticism of April, her child who could, at least in the past, do little wrong.

At four o'clock, they sit around a table laden with heaping bowls of holiday fare. Four lime Jell-O trees, topped with stiff peaks of whipped cream, jiggle on salad plates. The feast distracts attention from what they all know: Saffee has covered a white sheet with an ecru lace tablecloth, hoping to hide from sight, if not mind, the splattered paint beneath.

"God is good. God is great. We thank Him for our food. Amen."

It is the same brief prayer that Joann has intoned over every meal since Saffee can remember. Now, as in childhood, she cracks her eyes to watch her mother's face, the uplifted eyebrows above closed lids, as beatific as a Hollywood nun. Saffee does not doubt her mother's sincerity, but its mix with affectation has always been a curiosity.

They all consume large quantities of food. Surely a "normal" American Thanksgiving requires a measure of gluttony. But the eating is only done as ritual. In the absence of conviviality, their eyes do not shine with delight. Instead, intentional carefulness prevails. To be sure, there are no spills of gravy or cranberry sauce on the lace cloth. No one mentions that the rose pleated draperies are pulled at an earlier hour than necessary, covering windows darkened by issues of the *Gazette*. Who knows if lighting by chandelier on a holiday while the sun still shines may also be normal?

Three of them pretend not to notice that Joann holds each forkful slightly aloft for inspection before it enters her mouth. Morsels that do not meet approval are discarded onto a salad plate that overflows by meal's end.

There is no mention of the holiday's origin. Kvaale life mostly senses the present. But no mention either that now there is a college girl in the family. Important matters, such as the food before them and Tuesday's ice storm that caused havoc in the orchard, eclipse other topics. By the time they indulge in slices of pumpkin and pecan pie, Joann has angled her body away from the window and her arms are around her plate.

The next day Joann is reclusive. In the late morning, Saffee catches a glimpse of her in the master bedroom. Wrapped in an old pink chenille robe, she bends over her small desk, intently writing. Not an uncommon posture. Later she hurriedly hobbles by crutch through the living room, abruptly shutting the double dining room doors behind her.

Back to school tomorrow; again Saffee counts the hours. She tries to read assignments for her world history class. Coming upon an unfamiliar word, she takes Joann's new dictionary from its place on a bookshelf. Thumbing through, she is disheartened to see handwritten commentary on page after page. Under *V*, words referring to truth are highlighted: *verify, verisimilitude, veritable*. In the margins are tightly scribbled words. Among them, "truth will liberate you" and "truth without fear." But also "deceiver," "conniver," "hoax," "impostor," "defraud," "sucker." Together, they seem to spell confusion.

Earlier in the day, when she saw Joann writing in a book, it did not appear to be this dictionary. Had it been her Bible? Hadn't April mentioned that in a letter? She remembers how her mother had clobbered her with Sapphira's story. Reinterpreting the dictionary seems foolish enough.

In the late afternoon, Saffee looks out the living room windows toward the orchard. She guesses that her mother has spent considerable time this fall standing here, watching leaves drop from the apple trees, each gust of wind exposing more of the Petersons' blue house, invading more of her privacy.

The weather has reversed itself, turning warm for a Minnesota November. Saffee notices Nels stacking dead branches beneath the apple trees and sees both opportunity and excuse to leave the house. She slips on a windbreaker and knitted gloves with leather palms and goes outside. April soon follows.

Saffee can't remember if she and April have ever helped their dad outdoors. He seems surprised and pleased when they join him.

"The Winesaps got the worst of the storm," he says, as together they pile splintered limbs on the edge of the west bank that overlooks the long, sweeping valley. The orchard is narrow and deep, stretching from the road to the bank, with five rows of apple trees parallel to the house.

April drags a large fallen limb she finds beside the road. As Saffee and Nels carry armloads of brittle branches toward the bank, she broaches the topic of hospitalizing her mother again. "Dad, have you reconsidered taking Mom to see a doctor?"

"Now don't go talkin' that way again. She was fine at Thanksgivin' yesterday, wasn't she? Just fine. See? There's nothin' wrong with her."

Overhearing him, April says, "You call that fine? I guess yesterday could have been worse, but now, one day later, anyone can see she's not fine."

No one has a heart to say more. They continue to gather and lug branches, noting that the sun will soon be down. April scoops up a few rotted apples, recently frozen and now thawed, oozing brown. She flings them into the valley.

"I used to get a royal stomachache from eating green ones," she says.

"I remember seeing you throw apples with some little boys one summer. It looked like fun," Saffee says. "I wanted to do it too."

April gives her a puzzled look. "Well, why didn't you?"

Saffee doesn't answer. April, who lives life exuberantly, not unlike, it seems, the nameless, swirling masses of people on the college campus, would not understand.

With a decisive move, Saffee picks up an apple, reaches back her arm, and flings with all her might. The soggy fruit plops not far from her feet. She is embarrassed, furious with herself.

"It's okay," April says. "Try again. Let your fingers open sooner."

The second toss arches high, streaks across the setting sun, and skitters through brush far below. The sisters' eyes meet. Saffee suppresses a giggle, and then, with impulsiveness, both girls scamper to gather a reserve and begin a competition.

Saffee throws with uncharacteristic abandon, disregarding brown, mushy stains collecting on her jacket and gloves. She wonders if Joann might have made a tiny rip in the newspaper and is watching them, disapprovingly, through the dusk.

Nels joins in. "Let's see who can hit that there willow way down at the bottom." He hurls a missile that flies twenty yards beyond what had been the girls' best shots.

"I can beat that, Daddy!" April challenges. "Just watch!"

They scramble for more ammunition and throw furiously. Unused to such camaraderie, or perhaps solidarity, Saffee's face flushes. Throwing apples, laughing, with April and Dad. At every toss, Saffee's delight is coupled with an inner grief that cries, *Why didn't we do this long ago, Daddy? Why didn't we play? Why didn't we ever, ever have fun together like this?* She is pink from exertion, as well as emotion.

Their diversion is interrupted by a police car. Was there a siren? Afterward, they can't remember. Through the dusk and bare branches, they sense a commotion at the blue house. A man yells; the black Lab barks.

"Wonder what's going on!" April takes off running through the fallen leaves. Nels and Saffee follow until they see a figure in pink chenille, spotlighted by a harsh yard light.

Horrified, Nels shouts, "Joann! Whatcha doin'?"

Disheveled, and with wild-eyed terror, Joann lunges here and there at things invisible in the Petersons' yard, her crutch discarded on the ground. She brandishes a butcher knife, stabbing the air with delusional drama. Brown dormant chrysanthemum plants lie strewn haphazardly at her feet.

# CHAPTER THIRTY-ONE

# ROTTEN APPLES

B lue tares, blue tares," Joann shouts. "The axe comes to lay at the root of blue tares!"

A man and woman, presumably the Petersons, cower on the porch. "Be careful, Officer, she's got a knife," the man calls out.

Joann veers toward the approaching policeman. "The axe is laid . . ." He advances slowly.

"Get back!" Joann screams at him in manic alarm. "Don't come near me. Don't touch me. Leave the blue tares alone. I must get rid of them."

The frenzied dog behind the backyard fence barks and growls.

The officer takes another step. "Mrs. Kvaale, stop right there." He is calm, but firm.

"Joann," Nels shouts, striding across the Petersons' yard.

"Get back! Stay away! Our God is a consuming fire! Get back, Nels." She grips the knife with both hands, bayonet style, pointing it at the policeman's stomach. He darts forward and grabs one of her arms, applies pressure until she drops the knife. The sharp knife. The knife that carved yesterday's turkey.

Saffee's heart pounds. Her feet are rooted to the edge of the

Petersons' yard as if paralyzed. She presses her fists hard against her cheeks, not believing the surreal nightmare unfolding in the glare of the yard light. How can this wild woman be her mother? The woman who bore her, raised her, has gone completely mad. "Mother, stop!" she yells. "Daddy, do something!"

April clings to her sister and cries. Joann struggles with the policeman as he tries to guide her toward the squad car. A second car arrives and another officer hastens to assist.

"Bingo! Quiet!" Mr. Peterson yells.

Nels, breathless and pale, circles his arms around his wife. "I've got 'er," he shouts over the din. "I'll take 'er home now."

"No, Nels," the officer says, trying to still Joann's writhing while his partner clamps cuffs around her wrists, "not this time. I'm sorry. Assaulting an officer, destruction of property—that's criminal offense. I have to take her in. We'll hold her until you get arrangements with one of the hospitals."

With tears in his eyes, Nels looks at his wife already in the squad car, secured behind a black grill that separates the backseat from the front. He sees terror on her face and he stretches his arms toward her. "Oh, Joann," he says, his voice a mixture of grief and helplessness. "Why didja do it, Joann?"

The policeman looks sympathetic. "I'm sorry, Nels. We'll take her to the holding tank at the jail for now and we'll see she gets transportation to some place. Like I told you before, you'll first have to get a court order from a judge to commit her. Too bad it's the weekend."

The officer's voice carries to April and Saffee in the crisp night air. Too horrified to go closer to the police car, closer to their mother, they have not moved. They know their dad is mortified. Keeping Joann's peculiarities out of the public eye has always been imperative. It's obvious now that others know; the policeman called her by name. Saffee's teeth chatter. She feels as if she might vomit.

Mr. Peterson leaves his porch and hurries across the yard. "I'm sorry, Nels. We had to call them, you know. I tried you first, but there was no answer. Look!" He sweeps his arm over the side yard. "She pulled up all Millie's chrysanthemums, right up by the roots. They was growing right over there." He points to the foundation of his house. "When I let Bingo out, he started barking like crazy, and then I saw her slashing that knife around, hacking away at them plants." Mr. Peterson swings his arms back and forth as if he needs to help Nels imagine the scene. "You know, Nels, I couldn't go deal with nobody with a knife. I had to get help. You understand, don'tcha, Nels?"

"Yeah. Sure." Nels shakes his bent head. "I unnerstan' . . . I'll make up the damage to ya, Peterson."

An officer suggests that Nels ride in the other car to the station. As he gets in, he calls over his shoulder, telling his daughters to go home. They needn't be told. Sobbing, adrift in swirling emotion, Saffee and April run back into the dark orchard, toward their empty house, as if pursued. Black low-hanging limbs reach out to scratch them. April trips and falls, face to the cold ground.

"Ick! Yuck!"

"What's the matter, April? Get up."

"It's the rotten apples!" On her knees, April scrapes soft mush from her face in disgust and whimpers, "This is what our life has become, Saffee, rotten apples!"

Looking down at her, never-before-opened floodgates of caring swell within Saffee. Sniffling, she pulls off her gloves, kneels, and wipes away tears and musky apple flesh from April's cheeks. She sinks to the ground and the older cradles the younger in her arms. Tells her not to cry. Tells her everything is going to be okay.

"No, it's not. They took Mom to jail!" April burrows her head in Saffee's chest. "Saffee, I don't get it. Mommy's always treated me . . . sort of special. I always used to feel like, you know, like I was her pet or something. We had good times together. But now she's changed. Now she's so mean, but I don't want her to go to jail. It's so confusing and awful."

Saffee slowly rocks her sister back and forth. Dry leaves, carried in sudden, crazy whirlwinds, pelt their faces. She reminds April that the policeman said something about having their mother committed, and that must mean to a hospital. Perhaps there she will finally get some help. "I know things will be better, April—sometime."

"How do you know?"

"Because God told me."

April looks up. "What do you mean?"

Saffee tells her about the voice she heard on the stairway, saying that her life was going to be different and better than what it had been. Different and better than their parents' lives. "It was a long time ago, and I still believe it. Now, April, I'll believe it for you too."

## CHAPTER THIRTY-TWO

# TASTE AND SEE

1960

January 1, 1960

Dear Saffee,

Happy New Year! And hope it's happier than the last one. Seems an odd beginning, though—me at Marilyn's and Mom still in the hospital. Thanks for your letter. I'm glad you had a good time at Gloria's for Christmas, in spite of the circumstances. I talked to Daddy on the phone after he visited Mother on Christmas Day. He sounded discouraged.

Mrs. Johnson, Marilyn's mom, is a great cook—couldn't leave her Christmas cookies alone. She even gave me presents, a red sweater and a charm bracelet. And Marilyn gave me a jewelry box and a game called Password. I pretended I was part of the family. I think Daddy's paying them to let me stay here until Mother gets out of the hospital.

Some people named Franken live next door to Marilyn. They

have twin girls, two years old. So cute! Marilyn and I babysat for them on New Year's Eve—it took two of us!

Love,
April

Over the next months, Joann has multiple "visits" of varying length to a state mental hospital. Each time she is treated with a different high-powered, experimental drug, each one producing intolerable side effects when she returns home. She alternates between lethargy and agitation, weight loss and weight gain, dry mouth and drooling. She has little choice but to conceal the hated pills under her tongue and spit them out when Nels is not looking. Invariably, irrationality returns.

More than once, when Nels is at work, Joann wanders through the neighborhood knocking on doors, warning of coming apocalypse. And once, just about dawn, a policeman finds her scantily dressed crossing the Blue River bridge, a great distance from home. One Saturday night, she orders April, now a high school sophomore, to go to bed at seven o'clock. When April refuses, Joann strikes her legs several times with a broom handle.

In response to such behavior, Nels has little recourse but to secure another court order to have his wife once again "treated" in confinement.

"The rings, Joann. I forgot to take off your rings." He'd remembered as he drove the fifty miles following the police car. The police car in which his wife, his beloved, deranged wife, was again seated, restrained in the backseat behind the black metal grate. Aching, for almost an hour, he'd watched the back of her head, bobbing indignantly back and forth.

"No!" she howls. "No! You can't have them!"

"Come on, Joann. Don't make no trouble. I always keep 'em at home, but I'll put 'em in the bank if ya want. Now give 'em to me."

She lunges at him, pummels his chest, yelling, "I am a married woman! I should wear my rings. You gave them to me, Nels. What is it? You want to give them to somebody else?"

Nels controls her flailing arms. "It's the rules, Joann. Ya gotta follow the rules! Be good now, so you don't hafta stay so long this time."

"Abandonment! That's what it is, abandonment!"

An orderly appears with the garment. Straps and ties.

"Don't worry, Mr. Kvaale. We know how to do this." His voice is brusque, not sympathetic. Joann Kvaale is part of his day's work.

Nels usually makes it back to the car before he breaks down, but not today. He leaves the tiny room, heads for the exit, and crumples against a door frame in the entry. Sobs of grief and guilt.

April's letters continue to keep Saffee informed about ups and downs on the home front. She writes that she spends more and more time in their old neighborhood with Marilyn Johnson's "normal" family, and she continues to babysit the young twins next door to them. Nels only summons her home whenever he has some confidence that Joann's latest treatment will this time bring them peace.

Although Saffee still feels like "a fish out of water" at school, she too gets a taste of normal family life when roommate Gloria invites her home some weekends. She writes to April how strange it is to experience a household "full of little brothers that make noise and mess, while the family takes it all in stride." Gloria is teaching her how to play a few board games, something Saffee has been embarrassed to know nothing about.

She surprises herself by going to Friday night mixers at the student union to learn the lindy and cha-cha. She writes, "It's not exactly 'tripping the light fantastic,' like Mother used to do, but still lots of fun. And get this, you know how only classical music used to interest me? I've found out that rock 'n' roll is okay too!"

Saffee is quite sure her parents expect her to return home during the summer break. But by February, she knows that she will not. She can never go back "home." Academics and a fledgling social life have ushered her into a different world. She refuses to consider that by staying away she is abandoning April.

During Saffee's second year at school, April writes:

Life here is crazier than ever. You won't believe what happened now— Mother and Daddy went up to the church and signed some papers to withdraw membership from the Methodist church! They say I can't go to Sunday school or youth meetings.

Here's what happened. Daddy was out of town (I hate it when he's gone), and when I came home from school, Rev. Blakley was here arguing with Mother. She told me to go to my room and shut the door, so I did, but their voices were loud so I could still hear. Mother insisted that the end of the world is coming soon and Rev. Blakley had better do his part to warn the congregation. She said she hears information from "those who know" and that she's a messenger to warn people, especially him. Rev. B. told her that she's just an ordinary person and not a prophet, and she shouldn't listen to voices, and the Bible says only God knows when the end of the world is coming.

Then he read her some verses out of the Bible. I only remember a little of the one that made her the maddest. It was something about when she dies she's going to fade away and wither just like flowers and grass, but that God's Word will still be around. She shouted that she will never be dead grass because dead grass is for burning and God told her she won't burn and he better leave the house FAST! Which he did. She probably chased him out with her crutch. I stayed in the bedroom 'til suppertime. That's when she told me none of us will be going to the church anymore.

When Daddy came home she made Rev. B. sound really bad and he believed her. Now he's mad at the minister too!

Saffee, it was so upsetting. Write to me—at Marilyn's.

Saffee writes back, "Hang on, little sister, your life will get better too before long. College in just three years." That must seem like an eternity to April, but what else can she say? She encourages her to attend a different church.

Even though their mother has never embraced much that is offered by the organized church, and often distorts truth, Saffee wants to believe that her trust in Jesus Christ is genuine. Saffee rarely thinks to spend much time talking to God, but the mounting tensions at home that April writes about remind her that He is available. She begins to pray regularly for both parents and April, chastising herself that this has not been her habit.

Saffee checks the clock and scans her biology notes one more time. "Evolution is the cornerstone of modern biology"—a quote from her professor the first day of class. She glances at a few underlined words: *mutation, natural selection, genetic drift, evolutionary lineage.* The last term is underlined twice. Some things about biology puzzle her. She entered college not doubting, "In the beginning God . . ." But how does *He* fit into all of *this*? In particular, does "evolutionary lineage" mean that she is trapped by a predestined genetic makeup to be like her mentally ill mother? What about "Your life will be different"? In spite of this promise, she'll have to write a test the professor agrees with.

The last Sunday morning in November is clear and cold. Bare tree branches and street signs look as brittle as icicles. Saffee and Gloria hurry along neighborhood streets wondering why they had thought sheer hose would keep their legs warm and they didn't need boots. Their black pumps skirt drifted snow. What was it that Joann had said when they shopped for school clothes? Something about womanhood succumbing to outrageous whims of fashion. Saffee chuckles to herself.

In her fourteen months away from parental expectation, Saffee has never accompanied her roommate to church, enjoying instead Sunday morning slumber, completely alone in the dorm room they now share for a second year. But after receiving April's letter about the sisters' involuntary excommunication from their Miller's Ford church, today it seemed important to join her roommate on this frigid hike.

She's never shared with Gloria, or anyone at school, for that matter, that her mother has psychiatric problems. Wouldn't they look at her through different eyes, perhaps attribute every mannerism, maybe every word, to the possibility that she too must be . . . crazy? Other parents visit their offspring at school once in a while. Saffee is good at making excuses for hers—obligations, terribly busy all the time, you know.

Inside the chilly sanctuary, congregants wear their coats. Saffee heads for a back pew, but Gloria prods her halfway down to the front. Unfamiliar with Lutheran liturgy, Saffee mimics her roommate, like she still does concerning many aspects of life.

When the robed minister, Dr. Price, ascends the pulpit, Saffee takes it as a signal to daydream, but within moments she is arrested by his eloquence and resonant baritone voice.

". . . He could have made us into lumps of stone to line up and admire. But He chooses to give us the breath of humanity.

"He fashions ears to hear, not merely for self-defense, but to welcome the patter of rain, the trill of a robin.

"He could give us noses with which to merely draw air, but He gifts us with the exquisite perfume of blossoms.

"He could give us skin sensitive only to pain, but He accommodates our desire to receive a loved one's tender caress."

*Oh, Mother, how could you misunderstand and distort such a God?*

"He could have made eyes that see only light or dark, but He created a world with an immensity of color.

"And taste. Are we bored by flavorless nourishment? No! He made tiny taste buds that differentiate exquisite delicacies from land and sea!

"Beloved! *Taste* and *see* that our Creator God is good! Drink from His river of life . . ."

Soft light filters through the stained glass windows and hovers overhead. Saffee is comfortably warmed. In her heart, she thanks God for His creative goodness. She resolves to trust Him to teach her more than the professors she esteems.

At the same time, she is saddened that her mother, who would have once loved this sermon, has perhaps banished herself from ever hearing another.

That night, as Saffee lies awake in bed, three words from the sermon replay in her head: *Taste and see, taste and see.* Isn't this the opposite of how she lives? In spite of Gloria's tutoring on campus social skills (Gloria even arranged a couple double dates), Saffee still prefers cautious anonymity, devising excuses why she can't do various things that others seem to do so easily, such as ask a professor a question or learn to play bridge. Gloria, on the other hand, is running for student council and has planned a trip to New York City with friends over spring break.

God's directives—*Watch. Listen. Learn*—have been instructive, but they are passive assignments, requiring only observation and thought. Now it seems He's added a fourth instruction, one that will call for involvement, expecting her to abandon her familiar role as left-out child.

For her Shakespeare class, she's memorized a sonnet. What is that line? Something about killing the spirit of life (or is it love?) with perpetual dullness. She's tired of dullness.

*Taste and see.* A new mandate.

After forty minutes in the phone booth down the hall, Gloria twirls into the room. "Saffee, it's going to be such a great party. I hope you decide to come."

*Taste and see.*

"I'll be there," Saffee says.

She combs her straight, wet hair, conscious of her roommate's exuberant countenance beside her own more sober expression in the mirror. Gloria shares the plans for a surprise birthday party she and various friends and relatives are to give her mother. As she talks about cakes and decorations and entertainment, Gloria's joyful face sometimes comes a little too close, invading space, and contributing to Saffee's envy of porcelain skin.

"That's nice," Saffee says, moving a few inches away to reach into her bag of prickly brush rollers. "How old is your mom going to be?"

*"Forty-six."* Gloria's natural red hair bounces without the benefit of rollers. "She's ancient."

"Yeah. Same as my mom." It's a slip. Saffee, to avoid questions, makes a point not to ever mention that she even has a mother. She's relieved when Gloria bubbles on.

"I made Dad promise to keep everything secret from the brothers. If they told, I'd . . ."

Gloria says she expects at least thirty people to attend.

*Thirty!* Saffee doesn't think she even knows that many people.

"Gloria, why are you doing this?"

"Why? Because it's her birthday! And to honor her, of course, for being such a great mom."

Saffee looks into the mirror, unseeing, while Gloria itemizes the menu for the buffet dinner. Saffee interrupts, "Would you do this if she weren't? A great mom, I mean." Now she's really said too much.

Gloria raises her eyebrows. "Well," she says slowly, "the commandment isn't to honor *great* mothers and *great* fathers, it's just—"

"Yeah, I know. You're right." Saffee selects another roller and wishes she could stuff the question back into her mouth.

Gloria doesn't let it drop. "I mean, well, if my mom were"—she says the next word delicately—"incarcerated, or something, I'd have to find some different way to honor her." She takes a package of party invitations and an address book from a drawer and prepares to write. Saffee detects embarrassment.

*Incarcerated.* Has Gloria assumed that Saffee's reticence is because her mother is in prison? Stunned, she winds a too-large section of brown hair around a roller and anchors it firmly with a plastic pick. Incarcerated.

Well, yes, Joann *is* in a sort of prison, not physically—although Saffee imagines that the state hospital is much like one—but emotionally for sure. For a long time Joann has been in a sort of prison, not entirely of her own making. Saffee doesn't have any more insight into mental illness than her dad does and, if she were honest about it, she doesn't want to know more. At any rate, Saffee will have to find a different way to keep the commandment about honoring one's mother. It is unlikely that prisons of any kind cater to birthday parties. She won't set Gloria straight on the facts. Her roommate can think what she wants.

"Oh! One more thing—a present," Gloria says, reaching for her to-do list.

"Isn't giving a party enough of a present?" Saffee asks.

"Oh no, I want to give her a gift too. At Dayton's I saw a manicure set with oodles of nifty tools . . ."

*No!* Saffee wants to shout. *Not a manicure set!* She remembers the scene in Technicolor. *Anything but that. Mothers don't like them.*

She winds the last roller extra tight and jabs it with a pick.

# CHAPTER THIRTY-THREE

# JACK

1961

"You're going to *Paris*? April, that's amazing."

April's phone call catches Saffee by surprise. Europe. Saffee wouldn't even consider something so daring. April's capricious tendencies have always served to liberate her from various restraints. Now, since the latest shred of Joann's stability has again disappeared, she no longer tolerates any independence in April, and April's creativity resists a harness. Her only recourse is to flee; to remain would be to break.

April explains that Mr. Franken, the father of the twins she babysits, is Miller's Ford's city planner. He and his family have been invited to a small French city as part of a six-month exchange program and have asked April to accompany them as their nanny. Mr. Franken is arranging a correspondence course for her to keep up with school.

"It's not Paris exactly," she says. "I think it's a little town south of there, or maybe north. I don't know. I don't really care. Saffee, I've been hoping and hoping for some miraculous opportunity like this, and now it's come. For six whole months I'll be away from all the nonsense at home."

"But, April, how about Mom and Dad . . . ?"

"That's the biggest shock. Dad says I can go. I guess he thinks if I'm gone I'm one less thing for him to worry about. Mom's in the hospital again, and I get the idea she doesn't comprehend much right now. I think Dad will just tell her later. Saffee, it's going to be a blast!"

Saffee gives her red scarf a toss over her shoulder as she and her friend Kathy meet on the campus mall. They hug hello, then head toward a costume jewelry store they both love. "So, Saffee, I'm so excited to tell you that I have a really nice guy to set you up with . . ."

Saffee laughs. "No way, Kathy, no more matchmaking. I'll never forget that last weirdo. You told me he was, what did you say, sensitive? Yeah, like a gorilla is sensitive! That one made me swear off blind dates forever."

"Yeah, I'm sorry about him, but I know, I really know you'd like Jack. He's just like you, serious about stuff, but interesting, and fun too. I think he likes to go to the theater. I have this feeling you were made for each other!"

"And why do you think I'd like to go out with someone like *me*? Is this the same Jack you told me about months ago? I thought he graduated."

"Yeah, Jack Andrews, he did graduate. So what?"

"Sorry, Kathy, not interested. I'm still trying to fit in with college age, don't care anything about older men out of school. Fix him up with one of your sorority sisters if he's so wonderful."

"He's not an 'older man.' He just graduated at the end of last quarter. And I would fix him up with a Tri Delt in a heartbeat, except for one thing."

"So, what's that?"

Kathy grins in her impish way. "I think he's meant for you."

They walk in silence for a while.

"Kathy?"

"Yeah?"

"This Jack Andrews. Is he a good dancer?"

She's just making sure. Joann had told her never to marry a man who can't dance.

When he calls, they talk for half an hour. Small talk. Investigating. He sounds polite. He works for a St. Paul insurance company in their work/study actuarial program—whatever that is. He explains, but she still isn't sure. "Okay," he says, "just think that an actuary is a place where they bury dead actors." She laughs.

He serves in the National Guard. His favorite movie is *High Noon*. His favorite activity? Playing football in the snow with buddies from high school.

He asks if she plays golf. "No? Too bad," he says. "Putting green underfoot is the best feeling on earth."

She doesn't see that they have anything in common and wonders why he hasn't already ended the conversation.

"What's your favorite food?" she asks, hating herself for the dumb question.

"Steak," he says. "Sirloin, of course."

"Of course," she says.

"And yours?"

"Vanilla pudding."

"Vanilla pudding?" He sounds amused. "Of all the food in the world, don't you like anything better than that?"

Now she's stupidly given him a clue about her life. Her vanilla life. "Well," she hastens to add, "I mean, it's white, and Norwegians eat a lot of white food and I'm Norwegian, second generation, or, I guess third . . . white potatoes, white gravy, creamed vegetables . . . and, of course, if you mix strawberries into the pudding . . . Doesn't that sound good?"

"Mmm," he says. "I'd rather have ice cream."

"Vanilla?"

"Chocolate."

"Of course."

She avoids asking about his family for fear he'd ask about hers. She chatters on about being a small-town escapee who loves college and the big city and has never missed a performance of the university's theater company. An ideal afternoon might be a walk in a park or exploring an art gallery. He says he likes those things too. How about a movie Friday night?

Suddenly she feels bold—how about the mixer at the Union instead? No? Well, okay, movie it is.

Wearing a new red angora sweater and gray pleated skirt, Saffee goes to the dorm lobby at the appointed time. She looks for someone of football player girth. Didn't Jack say that playing football is his favorite activity? But even with an overcoat, the dark-haired young man who approaches her appears to be slender. She doesn't miss his look of approval as he helps her with her coat.

They head toward his Volkswagen and then decide instead to walk the four blocks to the Varsity theater. Speaking only when necessary, they crunch through an inch of new snow in winter night stillness. Saffee continues to size him up: nice-looking, well-groomed, and mannerly—intentional about walking on the street side of the sidewalk. Best of all, and most telling, he laughs easily, not nervously or inappropriately, but comfortably.

No sooner do they sit down in the darkness, popcorn in hand, than one of Jack's new contact lenses pops out and falls somewhere at their feet. They spend ten minutes on hands and knees gingerly feeling the cement until they find the hard, no-longer-clean lens. He had not brought his glasses. Since Jack now has clear vision in only one eye and they've missed the beginning of the movie, they go to the box office and request a refund. *Gone with the Wind*. She quickly pushes the memory aside.

Jack seems to accept the awkward situation with aplomb; Saffee is impressed. They walk back toward campus under a cold, starry sky. He is witty, self-deprecating.

"'My contacts fell out!' Tom said *ex-sightedly*."

"What?"

Jack repeats the pun. She still doesn't get it.

"What are you talking about?"

"Haven't you heard of Tom Swifties?"

"No. Who's he?"

Jack laughs. "It's a kind of joke that links an adverb to a quote in an unusual way."

He tells her that Tom is a character in a book and that there is a Tom Swiftie contest running in the newspaper. He says he makes them up, even when he doesn't want to.

Saffee tries to decide if this makes Jack wonderfully clever or a little strange. Whichever it is, for a date, she is uncharacteristically comfortable.

"So, you like living in the dorm?" He asks, as it turns out, not because he wants to know, but so he can follow her answer with: "I could never live in one. 'I need accommodations that will accept Rover,' Tom said *dogmatically*."

She groans, but at the same time leans slightly toward clever.

The night is beautiful, the air is mild, tall lamps illumine the wide campus mall. When they reach the end, they decide to double back.

When he asks about her family, she tells him she has one sister named April and turns the inquiry onto him. He has a married older brother, Danny, who lives in Michigan with his wife and two children.

Jack tells her about his new job and offers opinions on sports and politics. It must be obvious she knows little about either one. He answers her questions, never giving her the idea that he finds her stupid. With his range of interests and knowledge, could he ever be interested in *her*? A nobody, from a strange family? Kathy seems to think so, but Saffee doesn't dare hope.

Later, at the dorm door, she says sincerely, "I've really enjoyed the evening. You know so much about so many interesting things."

"I like the way you laugh at my jokes," he says. Would she like to try the movie again the next night?

On Saturday, another pesky contact lens falls out onto the carpeted aisle, even before they are seated. Again unruffled, Jack guides her into a row, pops out the other lens, and reaches for his glasses. They laugh throughout the comedy until the house lights come on. When the crowd thins, Saffee insists they again search on hands and knees. This time the lens they find is shattered. Like the night before, Saffee notices that Jack is matter-of-fact, does not get mad or seem embarrassed, does not blame his eye doctor or optician. This is not the way she is used to handling the unexpected.

In the middle of the next week, they go to a Minnesota/Michigan hockey game. She's never watched a hockey game, or any kind of athletic contest, long enough to catch on to how it's played. Pleased to be with him, she feigns interest as he explains game strategy; he's played hockey most of his life.

"On your high school team?" she asks.

"No," he says, seeming flattered to be asked, "just pickup games."

"I love to skate," she tells him, happy there is something to mention that she does fairly well.

He suggests they return to the rink Saturday afternoon during open skating.

On Saturday, in spite of her still-too-large size-nine figure skates, she takes secret satisfaction that she's more graceful on ice than Jack. Grace obviously isn't necessary to chase a hockey puck. He compliments her skill.

Later, with two plastic spoons, they share an entire pint of chocolate ice cream in the Union lounge, laughing, talking with their heads together. His good humor makes her laugh from a deep place unfamiliar with laughter. It seems even his slightest phrase brings her an overflow of spirit. In return, yet unaware, she gives him a wisp of her heart.

He asks her if she believes in God.

"I do," she says.

He suggests they go to church together on Sunday.

## CHAPTER THIRTY-FOUR

# THE VALENTINE

affee's cheeks flame. She leans against the drugstore card display and reads the simple, romantic words again . . .

> *When you entered my life*
> *My world became more beautiful.*
> *You gave me your friendship*
> *And now I know what it is like to be truly happy.*

Inside . . .

> *I Think You're Wonderful!*
> *Happy Valentine's Day*

This is how she feels about Jack. This is the card she wants to give him. But how can she? It seems unbelievable that Kathy might be right, that they are "made for each other." And these words that coax tears, aren't they too forward? Jack hasn't suggested he has a romantic interest in her. All she knows is that she's never felt more comfortable, or happier, around any other male. Not that she's been acquainted with that many. Steady, purposeful, so . . . so . . . gentle-manly Jack. All right, he doesn't dance at all, but his sense of humor, sometimes witty, sometimes dry, makes her laugh. Laugh! What a wonderful thing, in which she has had way too little practice. He *has* painted her world with beauty.

With her finger she traces the card's two red intertwining hearts. Is it *proper* to give a Valentine to someone she's only known for *two weeks*? Two weeks, yes, but *five* dates—if going to church counts. But what if he never asks her out again? And if he does, maybe he won't give her a card at all. But if he does, shouldn't she be prepared? With a sigh, she reads the dreamy sentiment again, replaces it on the rack, and searches for something . . . safer.

On the phone, Jack learns that Saffee has never had Chinese food. He says chow mein from a can doesn't count. He suggests that their next date ("How about Valentine's Day?") should be downtown at the Nankin restaurant.

They indulge in generous quantities of crab Rangoon, sweet-and-sour pork, and steamed rice (for a while they fumble with chopsticks), and drink green tea. The unfamiliar exotic flavors, décor, and tonal music spur an adventurous side Saffee didn't know she had.

Jack tells her about Kenny, an ingenious friend from high school days who has worked for months constructing a hot-air balloon. After sewing silk parachutes together and rigging up a propane burner, he's spent several weeks perfecting flights, tethered in a meadow behind Jack's parents' home.

"So far he's been carried along beneath the balloon and the burner in a lawn chair," Jack tells Saffee. "Now he's working on a basket to hold the burner and he says there will be room for two passengers."

"It sounds so dangerous!" Saffee says.

"Probably not as dangerous as sky diving."

"You mean, jumping out of a plane? Don't tell me you've done that."

"A couple times," he says.

"Why?"

"Just to see if I could do it. I admit, it was a little scary, but fun."

Saffee is amazed. Risk avoidance has always been one of her priorities. She's overwhelmed by the thought that she doesn't know a blasted thing about what people call fun. For others, fun just seems to naturally happen.

On sudden impulse she says, "'How high can the balloon go?' Tom asked *loftily*!"

Jack laughs; she loves his laugh. "Bravo!" he says. "Good one!"

Saffee blushes and self-consciously glides her fork around the edge of her plate, capturing the last tangy morsels. After they compare suspect fortunes from odd little cookies, Jack removes an envelope from a pocket of his sport coat. "Read it out loud," he says.

"Out loud?" Nervous, she makes a ragged mess of the envelope. She's flabbergasted. It's the same card she wanted to buy for him.

"Read it," he prompts, leaning forward, watching her.

Turning a deeper shade of red, she reads . . .

> *When you entered my life*
> *My world became more beautiful.*

When she stops, he says, "Go on."

> *You gave me your friendship*
> *And now I know what it is like to be truly happy.*

She doesn't dare look up.

"Read inside," he says.

She already knows what is there.

> *I Think You're Wonderful!*

*Happy Valentine's Day*
*Love, Jack*

She meets his eyes. His expression says he intends the sentiment to speak for him. She remembers the card tucked in her purse and is furious with herself. She has misjudged his feelings and now will miss an opportunity to express her own. Presumably he is hoping she will also reveal romantic interest. She struggles not to show embarrassment as she hands him his card. What else can she do?

Jack opens the envelope to find a cartoonish picture of a towering ice-cream sundae. Saffee squints, wishing she were elsewhere. "'I like you better than ice cream,'" he reads. Is that a look of disappointment? She quickly attempts to defend her choice.

"Because we bought that pint of chocolate and shared it at the Union, remember?"

"Sure," Jack says.

"Well, you saw how *much* I like *ice cream*!" Saffee says.

She drops her eyes to the gift of poetry he gave her. "I just didn't expect such a beautiful, I mean, well, romantic card from you, Jack." She smiles at him. "Thank you."

"'I like yours too,' Tom said *sweetly*."

She grins and sighs with relief. After a childhood where nothing emotional, good or bad, was handled well, maybe she's learning a thing or two from Jack.

## CHAPTER THIRTY-FIVE

# THE COCOON

I can hardly believe it, Jack. I was skiing! Buck Hill isn't the Rockies, but I was actually skiing."

Saffee is rarely this pleased with herself. She lifts her sock-feet up onto the dashboard and rubs sore ankles, chafed by ill-fitting rental boots. The pain is worth it. "I need more work on traversing, but don't you think I pretty much mastered the snowplow?" she says, angling for a compliment.

Jack turns on the headlights as the brief twilight gives way to a cloudy darkness releasing buckets of snow held back all afternoon. He tells her she did great and sounds like he means it. The windshield wipers swish and scrape. Jack boosts the blades to their dizzying limit.

They pull onto the highway and pick up speed. Hypnotic flakes rush like pinpoints of light pelting the windshield, pulling Saffee into reflection. Today she did not shrink from challenge, in spite of repeatedly falling off the T-bar lift while small children around her had little trouble. She had persevered. Too many times she has said, "I can't." Today was different.

"Who would ever think that I could ski?" she says, more to herself than Jack.

"Seems to me you're naturally coordinated," he says.

She steals a glance at him. "Really? Do you mean that?"

"I think you could learn any sport you set your mind to." Her heart swells and she sucks in her breath. She's not used to such a thought.

Keeping his eyes on the road, he says, "Sometimes I get the idea you've been in a cocoon most of your life." Whether Jack means it to be an observation or a question, it exposes her reality. She swings from the warmth of his compliment to embarrassment. She pulls her feet down from the dashboard. Cocky posture no longer seems appropriate. It is true. Most of her life she has lived in a stifling cocoon where normal things didn't happen. Things like learning to play.

Saffee used to reason that if she didn't try new things, technically she wouldn't fail. Now, with Jack, she has begun to try a little, but her lifelong reality has been found out—her cocoon. The word makes her squirm and threatens to ruin a good day. Neither one speaks for several moments.

"I didn't mean to be rude or critical," he says. "Cocoons are good things, you know."

"No. I don't know." She is curt. "Why?"

He gives her the unself-conscious smile she's come to love. "Because from cocoons come lovely butterflies."

If she had been frozen to the bone on Buck Hill, his fact-become-poetry would have melted her entire being.

Inspired by what sounds like approval, she dares ask, "The cocoon is opening a little, don't you think, Jack?"

"Yes," he says, "I think so."

A few weeks later, after several more dates, Jack says he won't be seeing her during the month of April because of an intense study schedule prior to his May actuarial exam. Throughout the month she misses him terribly and worries he'll forget her. But when the exam is over, and the trees are beginning to show spring buds, he calls. They go biking along trails bordering Minnehaha Creek. She doesn't tell him that she didn't learn to ride a bike until after sixth grade.

The summer before her senior year, Saffee again doesn't consider going home to Miller's Ford. Even another summer of typing catalogue cards sounds more appealing.

## CHAPTER THIRTY-SIX

# LOYALTY

1963

Saffee and Nels sit in a back booth of a Dinky Town hamburger joint. This is the first time Nels has visited his daughter at college, even though the hospital Joann frequents is only about an hour from the university. During infrequent telephone calls, Saffee has sensed it is even harder than before for him to communicate with her, a college girl. When he's not telling jokes, he has never had much to say. It was a surprise when he called to take her out to eat.

She will inquire about her mother first—because that's the right thing to do—then she'll tell her dad about Jack. She reaches for the ketchup. "What's going on with Mom, Daddy?"

Until April went to France, she had supplied Saffee's only updates on her mother. Saffee has not been back to Miller's Ford since the disastrous Thanksgiving her freshman year, more than three years ago. She almost never has taken the initiative to inquire about Joann by phone. To her, her mother is dead. No one asks about the dead. By extension, neither has her father occupied much room in her thoughts. She rarely remembered her past resolve to pray for them.

Instead of answering her question, Nels eats his coleslaw. He looks downcast. His left arm is deeply tanned from hours out the open window as he drives day in and day out for his job.

"Daddy?" she repeats.

"Ahh," he says, shaking his head. He puts down his fork and crumples a paper napkin. "She's back in the hospital. She was doin' more awful stuff."

"Like what?"

Nels takes a deep breath and glances at the ceiling, the way he does when pushed to confide and doesn't want to. "She was throwin' stuff away."

"What stuff?"

"Stuff that shoulda been saved, important papers, like insurance policies, bills . . . the pitures."

"What pictures? Our baby pictures?" Other than a box full of photos of April and Saffee when they were very young, she recalls few pictures in the house.

He nods. "Plus other things," he says. "The toaster, the radio, perfectly good lamps, anything she thought might be dangerous to her." He sighs heavily. "I'll never understand her. When she don't take her medicine, she talks to things, listens to things." He drops the shredded napkin onto his plate and drums the table. "It's good April's gone. Home ain't no place for her no more."

In July, Saffee had received a postcard from April. "I've decided to celebrate my seventeenth birthday in Switzerland!" Later she wrote that with the money she had earned during the nanny stint, she planned to backpack through Europe. She saw no reason to return home for school. "What could be more educational than climbing the Alps?" she wrote.

"How did you find out about her throwing things away, Daddy?" More pain crosses his face. He tells her that he realized various things were missing, and eventually the garbage collectors noticed and started saving "the garbage" for him. And now, he laments, the whole town knows and that was the last straw.

"So I come here to tell you—we ain't gonna live in Miller's Ford no more. I can't take this kinda embarrassment."

He seems to be imploring her to understand. It stings that her mother would throw away baby pictures, but their loss is of little consequence in the face of the shame and frustration her dad carries. It seems he is sharing the news of moving because he considers the Miller's Ford house to still be her home, but it is not.

"Oh, Daddy." Her compassion triggers anger. It rises up, overflows. She knows she shouldn't say it, in this public place or anywhere, but she does. She leans forward and hits the table with an open hand. "Daddy!" She doesn't care if others hear. "Why don't you just leave her?"

It is as if she slapped him. His stricken face turns deeper red and he glares at her. Placing both hands on the table, he leans forward and declares, "When I married your mother, I promised to stick with her through thick and thin, and I will."

It is a defining moment that Saffee will never forget. She is ashamed of herself, saying what she had no right to say.

She has never been prouder of her father.

*Oh, God, in spite of me, redeem the time for my family.*

A few moments pass as both struggle to regain composure. In those moments, she sees him as more than her teasing but sometimes stern father. More than the back-slapping, extroverted, good-old-boy he shows the world. Beyond his simple ways, he is both tragic and noble. He will not chuck his burden, he will shoulder it.

Finally, she says, "You've been 'batching' it for a long time, haven't you, Daddy?"

"I get by," he says.

Saffee once heard when a classmate's mother was dying of cancer that for weeks friends and neighbors brought the family casseroles and home-baked bread and desserts, showing love and support. Various afflictions seem to merit this kindness, but not mental illness. Secrecy doesn't lay groundwork for others to reach out.

Saffee pushes her hamburger aside and circles a french fry in a blob of ketchup. Memories flash. Vivid is the day her father returned from the navy and he and her mother needlessly argued about April's paternity. Saffee has long suspected that Joann naively planted the suspicion with unfounded innuendo. Now Saffee sees that those hot words in San Francisco, that branded her earliest remembrance of him, had come from his hurt, and hurt had come from his love.

Until this moment, youth's capacity for ingratitude had hidden that it was out of love and duty that Nels worked so diligently to provide a comfortable material life for his disabled family. She also sees that, wise or unwise, his denial of Joann's need for psychiatric help, allowing skepticism of the treatment she might receive, had also stemmed from love. He had only been trying to protect her.

What unfulfilled expectations had her dad brought to marriage? What were his dreams? She had never thought to ask or even wonder. But here, across the table, his impassioned declaration of loyalty has shown her what she did not understand in her youth—that his love for her mother superseded any dream.

Conviction stabs her. How much greater is this love from husband than has been from daughter? Daughter, who tries to hide the very existence of an unfortunate mother.

Nels interrupts her reflections. "Actually," he says, "I've been thinkin' for some time we better move. Last summer, when Mother was doin' good, we picked out a trailer in Red Bridge."

A french fry stops midway to Saffee's mouth. "A trailer?"

"Guess they don't call 'em trailers no more—mobile home, I mean."

Nels tells her that the house is jointly owned and Joann, in her current state, refuses to sign over the papers. He'll move to Red Bridge anyway and sell the house later. It will be more convenient because the mobile home park is only eight miles from the state hospital.

The conversation has drained them both. It is clear that Saffee won't be telling her dad about Jack today. It doesn't seem to be the right time to bring up a boyfriend. A boyfriend she really cares about, who has hinted at marriage. Anyway, how could anyone marry Sapphire Kvaale, the girl with the deranged mother? If Jack knew about her, he might run the other way. Her dad has been the epitome of loyalty to a demented wife. If need be, could she expect that of Jack? Or any man?

## CHAPTER THIRTY-SEVEN

# FLOATING FREE

More than once Jack has said that he'd like to meet Saffee's parents. She's been to his home several times—James and Harriet Andrews are gracious and lovely. Shouldn't he know that her family members, now more like acquaintances than intimates, are not like his? Not like his at all. Saffee is longing to be known, yet frightened to be known. Finally, she resolves to quit sidestepping her family credentials and tell him all.

After their next movie date, they sit in the VW in front of the dormitory, idly chatting, watching light snow fall. It's an hour and a half until curfew.

Saffee takes a deep breath and begins. "From the day we met, you've shared your good life with me, but I've, well, I'm sure you've noticed, I'm evasive sometimes."

"I figured you'd tell me what you want me to know when the time is right," Jack says.

She suddenly sees a measure of absurdity in her reticence. Does he think she might have a sinister past, raised by the Mafia or something? Just as Gloria believed her mother . . . For a moment, the humor of the situation eases her discomfort.

She begins by telling him that her mother is mentally ill, and although she understands little about her condition, a childhood trauma, a prairie fire, seems to have been a contributing factor. Trying to be light on details, but not completely succeeding, she tells him what she knows about her mother's nightmares and how for years Joann obsessively painted a table she had hidden beneath during the fire. She recounts her mother's temper tantrums and some of the aberrant episodes that finally led to repeated hospitalizations.

Summoning such scenes from the past puts Saffee's stomach in knots. Her mouth is dry and she feels like a traitor. Even though most of her hometown probably knows about Joann's unfortunate condition, Saffee, until now, has guarded the "family secrets."

Jack listens, takes her hand when she falters, wipes a tear.

She tells him about some of the by-products of living in close quarters with mental illness—her own inadequacies and fears, both perceived and real; her sister essentially running away at the first opportunity; and her father's denial and inability to help his very troubled wife. She is quick to add her admiration for his fidelity.

After several minutes of monologue, Saffee's head tells her to stop. But once unbridled, she continues at a gallop, launching into the similarities she often notes between herself and her mother. Her mother imagines things. Saffee confesses she used to imagine herself to be every female character she met in books and movies. It's, well, crazy. (Why did she use that word?) She tells him how, like her mother, she has always preferred a life hidden away. And also, like her mother, she is critical and negative. Her self-condemning litany goes on and on.

Finally, out of breath, she drops her tense shoulders and quits. She has finally exposed her troubled mother. And herself. She threads her long wool scarf in and out around her fingers and waits for him to respond, dreading what he might say.

He says nothing. In the silence, an ugly, condemning word throbs. *Stigma.* Association with mental illness always carries stigma.

Jack continues to look out the window while silence continues to crash the hated word.

A hand-holding couple walks by headed for the front door. The door opens. The young man returns to his car and drives away.

"Let's get out and walk," Jack says. "Shouldn't waste this snowfall."

She wraps the scarf loosely around her head and begins to open the car door, but Jack has already come around. Perhaps this will be their final walk together.

"Looks like we'll have a white Christmas," he says as they walk through gentle mounds that powder the sidewalk.

"Jack"—she can't help but sound impatient—"I thought you might have something to say about what I've just told you. It was very hard for me to share those things."

"Well. Okay. First of all, what's wrong with dreaming about being someone else?" he says. "Imagination spurs achievement. And second, *you* weren't in your mother's prairie fire."

She's taken aback. He's so dismissive. Doesn't he realize that she just spilled her guts, her entire emotional being? "Of course *I* was not in the fire, but I grew up in a house contaminated with the memory of its trauma. It was not a good place, Jack."

"I heard that. So what are you going to do about it?"

"*Do?* I don't know. All I *do* is try to hide our family secrets and their influence on me and April and Dad. But I thought"—she whips around to face him—"I *thought* you'd want to know. In fact, I thought you had a *right* to know, because it seems to me"—she takes a softer tone mid-sentence—"it seems to me that we've become more than just two friends having fun times. I guess it all boils down to this: I've been hoping that our friendship will continue, even though now you know that I come from an odd family and I have . . . some hang-ups."

She's weak from being so bold. She's afraid he will say something meaningless, like he understands, and then disappear.

Guilt rolls in. "Jack," she begins again, "I never tell anyone about my family, and now I feel terrible that I told you. Especially about

Mother. She doesn't deserve my talking about her like she's some kind of freak or something. As her daughter, I'm supposed to honor her, not disparage her."

Again, Jack doesn't respond quickly. His silence convinces her that they will never again be together on a beautiful snowy night. Disappointment, anger, and guilt collide. She feels ill.

Finally, he says, "It seems to me . . ."

She waits.

"It seems to me that maybe the best way to honor your mother is not to become like her."

"But isn't it a little late? I lived at home under Mother's influence for seventeen years. I see her when I look in the mirror. Her tense expression, her narrowed eyes."

Jack looks at her face and grins. "Mmm, you mean the way you look right now?"

She's infuriated. "Jack! I'm telling you serious stuff. Of course I look tense now. And I even talk like her. I open my mouth, my mother comes out. Her emotions, even her vocabulary."

Once again the words tumble—about funny looks she receives when she innocently uses pretentious words learned at her mother's knee.

Why does she keep blabbing in this argumentative way? Why stupidly try to convince him that she is strange? At the moment, she does sound like Joann, Joann who always has to win an argument. But this is an argument Saffee should not want to win. She again gentles her voice, but continues the self-incrimination.

Finally, Jack takes charge, ropes her in. "What's so hard about changing facial expressions and choosing words more carefully if you think you need to?" he says. "Shouldn't be hard. Your fault, Saffee, is that you run yourself down. Sounds like you've rehearsed saying negative things about yourself for so long that you believe them. But if you have your mom's bad temper, I haven't seen it. Well, not much, until tonight."

"I do have a temper, just not as volatile as hers. And you know very well that I'm pretty opinionated and . . ." She's about to launch into another list of faults.

"Saffee"—he lightly touches two fingers to her lips—"stop." He takes her mittened hand.

"The question is *how* to honor your mother. Obviously she has, or at one time had, lots of good qualities that you'd be wise to retain."

"How can you say that? You haven't even met her."

"No." Jack looks full into her face. "But I've seen them in you since the day we met."

She reddens. She will not put him on the spot by asking what he has seen. She only hopes it's true. For an hour she's been babbling about her family and her burdens. But Jack, with his customary few words, has again pronounced a compliment that soothes her pain and washes her with happiness.

The streetlights showcase a sidewalk scattered over with glistening gems. They walk hand in hand in the white silence.

*How long have I made huge mountains out of molehills,* she wonders, *and missed gemstones at my feet?*

Jack looks high into the dizzying flakes. "Hey," he says, "it's coming down pretty good. You know what we should do tomorrow? I've got an old toboggan . . ."

*Click-click-click.* Kathy's oversized knitting needles gobble up lumpy red Scandia yarn. Kathy dates a hockey player who is huge even without his game pads. She's been working on a sweater for him for over two weeks.

"You make it look easy," Saffee says. "How about teaching me?"

"Sure. You want to make a sweater for Jack?"

"Well, if I can do it, it would solve the gift dilemma." She doesn't mention that Christmas giving in her family always triggered tension.

Saffee buys a simple pattern for a man's pullover, large needles like Kathy's, and skeins of bright blue Scandia yarn. Soon her needles click in concert with her friend's. Since Jack seems half the size around as Kathy's friend, it shouldn't take long. His arms are pretty long, though.

"I sure hope he likes this," Saffee says for the third time.

"If he doesn't, it's *'Hit the road, Jack'*"—Kathy breaks into a zany rendition of the popular song—"*'and don'tcha come back no more, no more . . .'*"

"Stop!" Saffee laughs. "You made me drop a stitch! Sweater or no sweater, I don't want him to go away." Then she adds, "But . . ."

"But what?"

"But I can't figure out what he sees in me. Really, I can't."

"Well, why don't you ask him?"

"Oh sure, and risk embarrassment when he can't tell me?" She remembers Jack's comment about cocoons. She's not sure if Kathy would appreciate the poetry of what Jack said, but she blurts it anyway.

"He said it seems like I was raised in a cocoon, but that was okay because, get this, from cocoons come butterflies." She sighs. "Wasn't that lovely?"

Kathy rolls her eyes and says, "Oh brother! So why didn't he just say he thinks you have potential?"

"Potential! That sounds clinical. Jack obviously knows the right thing to say to an English lit major."

During the next days, Saffee fills every available minute coaxing the blue yarn into the shape of a wearable garment. As she knits, she gives serious thought to Jack's advice that she honor her mother by not becoming her. As they had parted at the door that night, seconds before curfew, he added, "God knows the ways you should be like her and the ways to avoid. Let Him help you."

*Yes, God, help me,* she breathes as her needles click.

She had often tried to please her mother by copying ways she did things. Little things, like folding laundry with precision, ordering her world, as much as possible, with neatness and cleanliness. Wouldn't it be dishonoring not to be like her in these ways? But to Joann, simple tasks often became obsessions. Saffee thinks about other, more vital qualities that might put her on the right path.

She must make an effort to shed her mother-like aloofness. It's good to have friends—why scare them away? And she must temper her critical nature. What was that her dad used to say? Something about her mother never being happy unless she was complaining. She gives the yarn a tug, unwinding the ball, and adds becoming generous and courageous to the list. It will take a lifetime of amends. Yes, she will need God's help to make His promise of a "different" life a reality. She dares to hope that Jack is not only a heaven-sent reminder of God's promise but also part of its fulfillment.

Saffee and Kathy continue to knit, sometimes laughing with nearly every stitch. Knitting is giving. Giving to Jack. He has given her priceless gifts of friendship, approval, encouragement, and happiness. These have planted a desire to give in return: appreciation, admiration, affection—knit together into a tangible gift, right here in her hands.

Saffee finishes the sweater by Christmas. When Jack tries it on, the sleeves dangle almost to his knees.

"I was trying to adjust for your long arms," she moans.

"'I don't know where all this wool could have come from,' Tom said *sheepishly.*"

"Jack! How can you make jokes when I've ruined your Christmas present?"

"It's not ruined, it feels nice and warm," he says, grinning, trying to roll the sleeves into thick cuffs. "Maybe I'll grow into it."

Gratefulness warms Saffee to the core.

❖

The day finally comes (Saffee had hoped it wouldn't) that Jack's friend Kenny invites them to go up in his homemade balloon.

"I'm sure it's safe," Jack assures Saffee when she questions him. "My pesky vertigo wouldn't like riding in that flimsy lawn chair of his, but in the basket I think we'll feel contained."

"Wait a minute. If you have vertigo, why do you want to go way up in the air, hanging under a balloon?"

Jack grins. "Life's too short not to enjoy it."

Saffee is quick to jump on that one. "Yes," she says with a smile, "life is short; why make it shorter?"

"Without a few risks, it would be downright boring."

*Boring?* Saffee hates the word that has typified her life. And she wishes she had more courage.

*Not a single sparrow can fall to the ground without your Father knowing . . . Don't be afraid; you are more valuable to God than a whole flock of sparrows . . .*

How many times has she been grateful that she read the Psalms and New Testament during her freshman and sophomore years? Although at the time her motivation was to receive approval from her roommate, nevertheless, the wisdom of the Scriptures made a lasting impression.

"All right. I'll go," she says. *With the sparrows.*

The white parachutes Kenny has sewn together mushroom like a silken cloud, then rise plump and firm sixty feet above them. To control altitude, the enterprising pilot regulates propane from a tank in the center of the basket. Standing arm in arm, Saffee and Jack cautiously look down over the side. The trees and snow-covered fields are a startling distance away and rapidly getting farther.

"Kenny, where's the rope? You know, the whatcha call it, the tether." Saffee tries not to sound alarmed.

He tells her he only used a tether while perfecting the burner regulator, but not anymore. The three are cramped for space. When he's licensed, Kenny says, the FAA will probably limit him to one passenger. The information does not give comfort.

Saffee grips Jack's hand more tightly. The January air is cold; the silence is startling. She tugs the hood of her oversized, fake fur parka more tightly around her head.

"What are we, Kenny, about three thousand feet?" Jack asks. Saffee notices that Jack's glances to the ground are brief. *He's doing this, even though he's afraid.* Kenny agrees with Jack's estimate.

In the past, Saffee's fears have generally been about silly things—speaking to teachers, dogs yipping at her heels. She used to be afraid of the cavernous university library—and now she works there. Progress. But free-floating in a hot-air balloon? Her heart beats quickly—strangely, she senses that exhilaration is ruling over fear.

When Saffee asks if Kenny has had any close calls, he is dismissive. "The basket touched power lines once," he says. "They arced, but it was no big deal." Saffee and Jack squint at the ground below, looking for telephone lines.

There is a singey smell and a flicker of sparks on Saffee's shoulder.

"Oh no!" she yelps. Jack and Kenny slap her parka several times with their leather gloves. It happens quickly, and then is over.

"No worry—just sparks from the burner," Kenny says.

There are two quarter-sized black spots where the "fur" has burned away. She doesn't miss that Jack looks relieved. So is she.

"As if dangling from a balloon under a winter sky isn't thrill enough, *now* this adventure will be even more exciting to tell my grandchildren," she says, then gulps, mortified. Her face turns hot, not because she imagined falling in flames three thousand feet, but at the thought of grandchildren. She is careful not to look at Jack. She's never thought of herself with children, and certainly not grandchildren. Anyway, one story of fire in a family is enough.

Thirty minutes later they touch down on the frozen ground and help Kenny coax air out of the collapsing billows, until a friend, his spotter, arrives with a pickup truck to assist with the loading. Saffee and Jack thank their trusty pilot; Jack thumps him on the back. Saffee can tell he's as happy as she to be on the ground. Hand in hand, they begin the mile trek back to Jack's car, walking over lumpy black furrows of earth spotted with light snow.

"I'm proud of you, Saffee," he says. "That was a challenge. And you did it."

Saffee bubbles over. "Well, you did too. Today will always be a special memory."

He gives her a significant look and then says he's disappointed about one thing. He had wanted Kenny to let them go up in the air alone.

"*Alone?* Are you kidding? We wouldn't have known how to fly that thing!"

"I wanted him to show us and then just let us go. Wouldn't that have been more romantic, just the two of us? The silence. The view." Jack stops walking. "You see, well, I mean, up there I wanted to give you this"—he reaches into an inside pocket of his jacket—"instead of in the middle of some farmer's field of dirt. But I guess it is better to propose with both feet on the ground."

Her breath catches. Jack hands her a small white drawstring bag made from kidskin and closed with a satin ribbon. She takes off her gloves and opens it with shaking hands. Inside is the most beautiful diamond ring she has ever seen.

"It was my grandmother's wedding ring," he says. "I hope you don't mind."

"Mind? It's *so* beautiful."

"My mother inherited it when Grandmother died about three years ago. I bought it from Mother. For you."

He slips it on her finger. Saffee's feet are *not* on the ground. The field around them spins. Is this too good to be true?

"Why, Jack?" she demands. "Tell me, why in the world would you want to marry me?"

"Because I love you, of course."

"And I love you, more than you could ever know. And I'd love to marry you. But why in the world would you want to marry me after all I've told you?"

"Well, let's see." He pretends to be deep in thought. "I guess, like I've told you before, I like the way you laugh at my jokes."

"Be serious! You're the one who taught me how to laugh and how to have fun, but marriage is more than jokes and fun. I hope there's more reason that that." She smiles. "You better not be counting on my cooking, because I don't know how."

He momentarily feigns alarm, then says, "I've admired how you strive to learn new things. I'm not worried."

She looks down in disbelief at the sparkling diamond.

"Saffee." Jack takes her face in his hands. "You are everything I want in a wife. You're smart. You're sensible. You're honest. You're real. You're responsible. And not last, and not least, you're beautiful."

His kiss rules out rebuttal.

## Chapter Thirty-Eight

# The Wedding

Reverend Price raises his shaggy eyebrows and looks over his glasses. "Which one of you will be taking care of the finances?" he asks.

They answer together, "I will," and exchange looks of surprise.

"*I* will," Jack repeats.

"But I'd be happy to," Saffee insists, not because she's given it any thought or is qualified (she's not), but just because she wants to be agreeable to do her part.

Jack, the math whiz and business major, looks slightly perturbed. Reverend Price, senior minister of the Lutheran church Saffee had attended with Gloria, is familiar with naive young lovers on their way to the altar. He smiles a bit wearily.

"How about children?" he continues. "How large of a family do you plan to have?"

Neither one answers. *None* goes through Saffee's mind. They haven't talked about this either. Not that Jack was unwilling to talk about it, but because she found ways to change the subject.

"Mmm." Reverend Price taps his fingertips together. "Perhaps you two have a few things to discuss before we meet again next week."

They planned to eat out after the counseling session, but when they get into the car, Jack doesn't even start the motor. They both feel impressed to immediately discuss the matters Reverend Price brought up.

Saffee apologizes about her presumption to take care of their finances and assures him that she knows he can do it better than she. Saffee's dad sent her signed checks throughout college and she's never even balanced a checkbook.

"How about children?" Jack asks.

Children? Saffee become a mother? Unimaginable. She looks down at the diamond engagement ring. A lump rises in her throat. It seems that children often do go along with marriage. What is she getting into? She decides to be noncommittal but is curious to know what Jack's view is.

"Well, um. What do you think?"

He tells her that it would be unwise to have children until he is finished with actuarial exams. "I couldn't study after work all the time and be a good father too," he says. For his age, Jack is ahead in the program. Of the ten examinations, he has five to go, which, if he passes each one as it comes, will take two and a half years. She is relieved; that sounds like a long way off.

"So, after that, just for conversation, how about one?" he suggests.

"One? An only child might be pretty lonesome, don't you think?" She wants to sound open to possibilities. "If we ever have one, maybe there should be two," she says recklessly. "I've never liked uneven numbers."

"So then, two? And what if there's a number three?"

"Oh no. Then we'd have to have four. That's way too many." She looks him squarely in the face. "Actually, Jack, don't you think *no* children would be best? Why do we need more than just you and me?"

"I guess that sounds okay with me too," Jack says, pulling her close. "We can always change our minds."

It doesn't seem necessary to tell him that her mind is already made up.

They move on to another topic—handling disagreements. Neither one imagines they will have any.

*My life will be different.*

Supporting themselves? Jack's job is going well; Saffee plans to continue working at the university library. She's switched from typing cards to locating items in the stacks and checking out materials at the front desk. They were both raised to be frugal; financially, they'll get by.

Getting along with in-laws? Mr. and Mrs. Andrews have embraced Saffee with cordiality. After the engagement was announced, they invited Nels to come to their home in Minneapolis and they all had an enjoyable dinner together. Jack has not met her mother. Saffee hopes to forestall that until the wedding.

At the second meeting with Reverend Price, Jack and Saffee clarify their decisions, making an effort to cover their former naiveté. The hour passes quickly. Reverend Price prays over them and they prepare to leave. He motions them to wait.

"On your wedding night," he says, "before you get into bed, get down on your knees. Thank God for each other. Thank Him for your marriage. Ask Him to bless it."

At the back of the sanctuary during the rehearsal, Reverend Price gives instructions to Jack, bridesmaids Gloria and Kathy (vagabond April could not be located), and groomsmen, Jack's brother, Danny, and Kenny. Saffee and Nels stand in the vestibule, her arm encircling his, waiting for their cue to walk the aisle.

The organist runs through pieces she has chosen to play. Saffee, not knowing the names of traditional wedding music, has given her free rein, only specifying classical. She has only attended a couple of weddings in her life and, unlike her friends in the dormitory, never tried to imagine her own.

The mother of the bride sits alone in a pew down in front, to the right of the aisle. From time to time, Saffee casts a worried look in her direction.

"Daddy, I'm so nervous I can hardly stand up."

"Why? Jack is a good man." He pats her hand. He has misunderstood her, but the unusual, small gesture makes her feel close to him.

"Not nervous about being married, but about getting married. Mostly I'm worried Mother will do something to ruin the ceremony."

"Don't worry. She's doin' fine. I'm makin' sure she's takin' her medicine." He sounds matter-of-fact, then becomes more serious, his voice husky. "Anyway, a weddin' ceremony's short. It's the marriage that's . . ." He doesn't finish. The reference to his own experience is obvious. Was it an attempt to caution her? Counsel her? If so, it would have been a first.

Since the last hospitalization, Joann has rallied, enabling her to be present at this first family wedding. The hiatus has allowed her and Nels to move into a double-wide mobile home in Red Bridge, leaving wagging tongues behind. The Miller's Ford house sold two weeks ago.

When they arrived at the church a half hour earlier, Saffee immediately introduced Jack to her mother. Joann's pale countenance bore the marks of illness. She extended her hand, laughed nervously, turning her head to the side. Saffee sensed that she might be pleased about the marriage but was too self-conscious to say anything appropriate to her almost-son-in-law. Perhaps it had been unfair that Saffee had not arranged for them to meet earlier.

She looks down the long center aisle, flanked by empty pews. Tomorrow evening most of the guests will be Andrews family friends and relatives, people Saffee doesn't know. The ushers, Jack's cousins, have been instructed to seat guests on either side of the aisle.

Following instructions, the attendants move to the front of the church. Saffee continues to wait at the back beside the man she has always called "Daddy." Years ago, didn't Joann often refer to her as

"Daddy's little girl"? He has been a long-distance father, preoccupied with necessary matters, but as her daddy, he has been the most important man in her life. Tomorrow, a different man will claim that place. In spite of her eagerness, her hands are clammy. She wipes them on her linen skirt.

"We've already took everythin' we're gonna need outta the house," Nels tells her. "We give possession in about ten days. You and Jack should drive over to Miller's Ford, see if there's anythin' there you want. 'Fraid we din't leave much. What you don't take, I'll try to sell."

"Thanks, Daddy. We've taken a week off work, you know. Going to spend three or four days at a place near Wisconsin Dells," she says. "We'll try to drive over when we get back." Saffee has no intention of dragging any reminders of her childhood into her new life.

"Did you take the Norway table with you?" She could have asked about any number of items, why does she wonder about this one?

"No," he says. "Way too big. The new place is pretty small."

Saffee survives the wedding. Barely. The mother of the bride shows little interest in the groom and has a vehement temper tantrum about her corsage in the bridal dressing room moments before the ceremony. Saffee had no idea that certain flowers have a snoot factor and those she had selected for Joann were "low class." The altercation makes Saffee's nose run and tears stream as she walks down the aisle on her father's arm, devastated. By the time she joins Jack at the altar she is still sniffling, but wears a smile that says she has never been happier.

At the reception in the church parlor she stands dazed and as close to her new husband as possible. She does her best to greet each guest, cut the cake, and pose for pictures. Terribly uncomfortable being the center of attention, and on impulse after forty minutes, she whispers to Jack, "Let's go."

"You mean leave? Already?"

"Yes, really."

Jack is all for it. They duck out a side entrance.

In the bridal suite at the Holiday Inn, Saffee reaches to turn back the sheets. Jack takes her hand.

"We told Reverend Price that we'd pray," he says. Saffee has forgotten. She is amazed and impressed that Jack has not. They kneel, as self-conscious as they will ever be.

"Lord Jesus, thank You for Saffee, my wonderful, beautiful wife. May we always love each other and please You in our marriage."

Her heart swells. All she can say is, "Thank You, God."

## CHAPTER THIRTY-NINE

# LEGACY

Jack guides the borrowed pickup through countryside dotted with tidy farms. God has gone before them, embroidering His early-morning beauty all around. Diaphanous ribbons of fog silently disperse to reveal a rosy dawn. Their spirits are high and banter comes easily. Jack's laughter is Saffee's favorite sound.

Although she has dreaded this trip back to Miller's Ford, here she is, sitting next to her husband of one week, wishing the drive would never end. She'd watched the clock most of the night. At 5:00 a.m. she woke him. "Let's go," she said. "If we get an early start, we can get back and still enjoy the afternoon. It's a three-hour trip each way."

Thirty minutes later they left the modest duplex that became their home after a brief honeymoon at the Dells. At first, Saffee was doubtful about renting a duplex. Would she like sharing a house with neighbors? Because the two single garages make a separation between the units, and the rent is reasonable for a two-bedroom place, she agreed.

She had looked forward to shopping with Jack for furniture, but, as keeper of the budget, he sees no possibility of that for some time. They will get by with basics from his parents' attic until there is some reserve in the bank, he says. There they found a double bed frame, a love seat in need of a slipcover, two mismatched Danish modern chairs, and a small Formica table with tubular aluminum legs. Their only major purchase was a mattress for the bed. Various household items from Kmart filled in where the attic and wedding gifts left off.

"I don't think my parents left much in the house," she says as they draw near the town she has avoided for four years. "We can probably check it out pretty quickly." Maybe there are some dishes, she says. They could use cereal bowls and maybe a chair for the bedroom. She wants to sound as if she's open to taking away something. After all, Jack borrowed the truck.

When the Miller's Ford water tower appears on the horizon, Jack is more eager than Saffee. "I want to see where my wife grew up," he says.

As they cross the bridge over Blue River, she tells him it is where she used to roller-skate in summer and ice-skate below in winter. She directs him to turn right, then left onto Second Street, and points out a large white house on the corner.

"That's where we lived until I was in ninth grade." Any number of memories could have come to Saffee as they drive by the house, but the one that comes is of her mother vigorously sanding the Norway table. Saffee's been trying to figure out how they can avoid seeing it when they get to the "new" house.

The pickup ascends Second Street hill—she marvels that it no longer seems particularly steep. She guides him through the uptown business district, with its familiar storefronts she hurried by for years on her way to school, yet felt like a stranger if ever she entered. She points out the library and, around the corner, the aging Methodist church with its splendid pipe organ. The church where her family no longer holds membership. This guided tour has been a delaying tactic.

They drive along Cottonwood Point Road and turn into the small subdivision with its valley view that so captivated Joann years ago. Saffee eyes the Peterson house. It appears to have a new coat of blue paint. Carefree daffodils bloom along the foundation.

On the adjacent lot, leaves on the ancient apple trees are sparse. Beyond, the redbrick house and yard her parents had once taken pride in looks unkempt. They pull into the driveway. Saffee can't name her emotion, but it is not a sense of homeness. The garage door needs paint. Nels had been so meticulous. She is glad the house has sold.

"Looks like the new owners will have some work to do," she says as they walk toward the back entry door. She takes a deep breath and turns the key. Inside, the air is stale and chilly. Saffee pulls back the faded, sun-damaged kitchen curtains to let in light. She remembers Joann sewing them, red-checkered with rickrack trim.

They open cupboards and find most of them empty, other than a dozen or more jelly jars.

She explains that they were used for "everyday" drinking and that, of course, her mother also had nice goblets for guests. Meaning the jelly jars were used every day.

Jack wanders into the living room and pulls cords to open the heavy, rose-colored draperies along the wall of windows. In several places the aging *peau de soie* fabric hangs fragmented by vertical splits.

"Wow," he says. "What a beautiful view down in the valley." Saffee stands close to him. It is beautiful. But she doesn't miss it. The dirty windows are stuck with tape residue, but Jack doesn't seem to notice.

*Poor Daddy.*

She remembers to add, *Poor Mother.*

The double doors to the dining room behind them are closed. Let them be. She has told him about the table, that should be enough. He doesn't have to know that being in the house with this element of her mother's aberrations is making her heart race.

The only item in the living room is the piano. "It's always been considered April's," she tells Jack.

"You girls shoulda taken accordeen lessons instead of piano," Nels had said to Saffee when he gave her the house key. "An accordeen, now, you can take that around with you easy. What am I s'posed to do with April's piano? Can't send it to her." There has been no word from April for several months.

Saffee pulls Jack toward the hallway. "This was Daddy's den," she says, opening more drapes. She doesn't mention that for years it was here her father slept. It was not to spite her mother, Saffee has come to realize; it was one of the sacrifices he had made for her.

The master bedroom is empty except for a bedside table. "Maybe this would be handy in our bedroom?" Jack asks.

"No," she says quickly, "they'll probably come back for it. It matches their bedroom set."

They cross the hall to the bedroom she had shared with April. She surveys the white twin beds and the bureau that once had been a dining room piece, until Joann saw its bedroom possibilities.

"I guess we don't need more old furniture," he says, "but maybe we could find a place for the matching lamps." To be reasonable, she agrees.

Saffee slides open the closet door and finds two cardboard cartons. One is labeled "Saffee," the other "April." Uncovering the first, she sees school mementos. She shows Jack her senior picture in her high school yearbook.

"Why the solemn face?"

She mugs a frown. "I'm a sober person, you know that."

Saffee suggests they put both boxes into the pickup; she'll sort through hers at home and save April's. *Home!* She already calls their duplex *home*. The word has taken on a new, positive meaning.

Minutes later, as they venture to the basement, Jack stops. "Is this where God spoke to you?" On their honeymoon trip she told him about God's promise, *Your life will be different.*

"No," she says, wrapping her arm around his, "that was when I was younger, in the house on Second Street." She grins. "And now I know He had you in my mind, way back then." He grins back.

In the first room below, a row of high, glass-block windows gives filtered light. "We called this room the family room," Saffee says. "But I can't remember one time when all the family was together here."

"Was it the TV room?" Jack asks.

*"Mom, who's Elvis Presley? Everyone at school is talking about him. I think he's on TV."*

*"Don't worry about it. With a name like that, he'll never amount to anything. And, no, we don't need a TV."*

"No," she says.

In the unfinished half of the basement, the Maytag wringer washer still stands near the laundry tubs. One of the lines sags, supporting the weight of a full bag of clothespins.

In Nels's workshop, Jack picks up pieces of lumber. "Think he'd mind?" he asks. "Never know when a man needs some wood."

She is amused and tells him to take all he wants. *You never know what will interest a man.* Jack sets aside a few two-by-fours and miscellaneous pieces of plywood and looks pleased. He sees a wooden box on a shelf, lifts it down, and slides off the lid. "This would be just the thing for small tools," he says. "Looks like some old documents inside."

"Take it," she says. "Daddy said anything we want is ours."

In a far corner he sees a child's high chair and asks if they should put it in the truck.

"You've got to be kidding. What for?"

"Suit yourself," he says. She can see that he was teasing her.

They carry up the wood and the box and put them in the pickup. Maybe they can leave now, without either of them seeing the Norway table. If she can avoid it today, chances are she will never have to see it again.

"We should shut all the curtains like we found them," Saffee says. "Will you check the rooms down the hall, Jack? I'll do the living room." It is a mistake.

In her haste, the drapery cords tangle. Jack finishes in the bedrooms and den and comes to help her. He gestures toward the double doors. "The dining room?"

"Oh. Yeah," she says. "But it's probably empty. Jack, um, I think we could use some extra spoons. Should we look through the kitchen drawers again?" She reaches for his hand as if to lead him there but is too late. He crosses the room and opens the dining room doors.

"Saffee. Look at this table. I've never seen anything like it."

She continues to walk away. "Right. Come on, Jack, let's get going."

"No. Come here, Saffee."

"Jack, I . . ." Reluctantly she joins him. The Norway table still wears the multicolored splatter of four years ago, when she had compared it to a Jackson Pollock. Today it seems closer to some putrid disease.

"Oh, you told me," he says. "This must be the table your mother—"

"Yes." She tries to sound dismissive. "Let's get going."

Jack, not listening, is down on one knee. "Saffee, I can't believe they left this unusual table. Look at the carving on the side."

His interest irritates her. Does he think she has never seen it before? She tries to sound offhanded. "Well, it's big. They moved into a trailer, you know." She suggests they get back on the road in time to do something special with the afternoon.

"If your parents don't want it, our dining room is completely empty. We could take this leaf out—"

"No!" She stamps her foot. "I don't want this table."

He looks up, startled by her change in tone. "Why not?"

"It's ugly, Jack. Really ugly."

"Well, I don't think so." He crawls under. "There's no paint on the underside," he calls, as if she is far away. "It's beautiful wood! Light-colored. Ash, or maybe birch. Hey! Here are some words burned into the back of this side piece, but they're not English. Norwegian maybe?" He begins to read, laughing as he guesses the pronunciation. *"'Din hustru er som et frukbart vintre der inne i ditt hus . . .'"*

Saffee stands with knees locked and arms crossed over her chest. Why is she so tense? It's just a table, an inanimate object with history . . . lots of history.

Jack continues to muddle through the inscription. *"'. . . dine barn som oljekvister rundt om ditt bord. Salmenes 128:3.'"*

Why is he reading those funny words? When he finally finishes, she thrusts her hands into her pockets and takes a deep breath. "Jack," she says deliberately, trying to contain rising impatience, "I have bad memories associated with this old table. I never realized the extent of how much it affected me until now. Listen to me. *I don't want it.*"

He backs out and stands up, giving her a questioning look.

She struggles to find the right words, tries to explain how it had been frightening to see her mother obsessed with painting. That it seemed as if someone or something compelled her. She laments that her family was baffled by Joann's irrational mind. Was she trying to cover over her trauma? Some secret sins? Pain that was never shared?

"I never understood her, Jack. All I know is that I hated to come home from school and smell paint."

"So, if this table caused her so much grief, why didn't she just get rid of it?"

"Good question. And I don't know the answer. It seemed to have some kind of power over her. At times it seemed something to fear. At other times she treated it as if it were a gift from God that had sheltered her during that fire."

She takes his arm as she speaks, gently trying to pull him out of the room, but he resists. "At any rate," she continues, "painting was probably her attempt to expunge bad memories, real or imagined, and I have bad memories too—of being surrounded by her misery. Frankly, it was sometimes scary in this house."

She leans against a wall, scans the room, then looks at him imploringly. "Now can you see why I don't want it around? Let's

leave it here for my dad to take care of. Please. It's not my problem."
The lump in her throat can no longer be put down. The dam bursts.
Hating herself, she burrows her head in that comfortable place just
below his right shoulder and cries. He holds her close and rubs her
back.

"Saffee. Look at me." He tilts her chin. "All this emotion says
that it *is* your problem. I think the best thing to do is to take the table
home with us . . . and conquer it."

She pulls away. "Jack, surely, now you understand why we've got
to leave it. I don't want to ever see it again!"

Jack is not deterred. "What I mean is, what if you would strip
off all the paint, Saffee? Every layer. Strip it away, scrape it off, right
down to the raw wood." He runs a hand over the speckled top. "It
would be a really big job, of course, but as you did it, I bet you'd get
a fresh perspective. You'd be an overcomer. It would be a sort of, well,
cleansing."

Now she is furious. "There you go with your psychology." She
usually appreciates his analytical comments, but this is going too far.
"I told you, I just want to walk—"

As he has done before, Jack gently touches her lips with two fingers. "But that's not victory, Saffee. Don't you see? That's letting a
wooden table haunt you like it haunted your mother. Right now it *is*
ugly, covered over by your mother's agony. But underneath, judging
by what I saw, there lies a piece of beautiful, redeemable work. By
restoring it, I have an idea there will be benefits for you too."

He talks as if she has agreed to do this harebrained thing. Slave
over this table? That is the last thing she wants to do. However, a
degree of release has accompanied her outburst, and because of it,
and because of her trusting love for Jack, she melts. She agrees to take
the troublesome table home. Perhaps they can store it in the garage.

Together, they force apart the tabletop to release the extra leaf. It
is obvious that they will be unable to load the table into the pickup
themselves. To Saffee's chagrin, Jack says he will go to the house next

door, that blue house, he says, to enlist help. Saffee is too disconcerted to object.

While he is gone she leans against a wall, staring at the table in disbelief. How could she have agreed to take it home to their honeymoon cottage? What peculiar hold does it have over people? Over her to make her so emotional, and now, over Jack, that he would be so drawn to it he would even knock on a stranger's door in order to move it?

As they drive back to Minneapolis, Saffee is silent in disbelief. Here they are, rolling down the highway with the paint-splattered Norway table, of all things, in the truck bed. She had not expected to be dogged in marriage by anything so painfully tangible from the past.

Ten miles from Miller's Ford, Saffee blurts, "Jack, can't we turn around and put it back in the house?"

Jack says he loves her so much that he doesn't want her to carry around "memory baggage" for the rest of her life. "Don't you think everyone has something they want to forget?" he asks. "No one can completely unplug unpleasantness of the past, but sometimes actions help deal with it."

Her temper flares. "And how would you know?" Their first week of marriage not over and she sounds ugly. "You, with the perfect childhood and natural abilities and talents galore, you're lecturing me about memories!" She glares out the window, sickened that she yelled, yet not willing to retract her words.

Jack says something about as a young boy not being good in sports, having a bodybuilding regimen, compensating his inadequacies with good academic habits. She hardly listens. How can he compare her upbringing to some mere struggle with male ego—even if male ego is something she knows little about?

"I don't know about your, well, challenges," she says, "but I can't see how they compare to growing up in a home as crazy as mine and wanting to forget about it, and certainly not wanting symbols around like that old table."

"I am sympathetic, Saffee, really I am, and of course I can't completely identify. But I'll just say again that running away from memories doesn't leave them behind."

Inwardly she huffs.

# Chapter Forty

# Weeds

The next day Jack tinkers with the lawn mower Nels had left behind in the Miller's Ford garage. Mrs. Corbet, the duplex owner, had made it clear that both tenants were to care for half of the yard. Saffee leans against the Volkswagen parked in the driveway and watches him fill the mower with gas. She looks askance at the Norway table's disassembled parts taking up most of the floor space of the single-car garage. There is no other place to put them. She wonders how long Jack will be happy to leave the car outdoors. Maybe by the time winter comes he will agree to throw the table away.

The spring grass is hardly long enough to cut, but Jack is eager to try. "Mowing might become a chore someday," he says, "so right now I think I'll enjoy it." He pulls the starter cord and roars off. She lowers the garage door.

Enjoying the warm sun, Saffee surveys their new neighborhood. She notices that the yard fronting the other side of the duplex is perfectly groomed. The tenants have yet to be seen. Across the street is a dense wooded area that runs the length of three blocks. She admires a stand of white-barked birch trees exactly opposite the duplex. They bend and mingle like whispering old women, then shake with laughter in the breeze. Jack thinks the Norway table might be birch. It is hard to believe that the table she has grown to despise in its ugliness was once a lovely tree, or, more likely, trees free to yield their branches to the wind, free to shake their leaves.

She catches a glimpse of Jack as he heads around the corner of the house. Already, streaks of sweat on his shirt validate his effort. In the Kvaale household, she was a spectator to domestic life, rarely doing, certainly never sweating. Not knowing how to share responsibility, she has little confidence she can contribute acceptably to any task, but it seems important that she try.

Making a quick tour of the yard, she notices an unsightly brown brush along the entire east side of the house. It wouldn't require any expertise to rid the area of last year's weeds. With bare hands—she has no work gloves—she begins to remove tangles of debris. The roots are fairly deep and the stems dry and rough, but hard work feels good. Maybe they can plant some petunias here. Or geraniums? The thought energizes her. She gives Jack a wave as he roars past; he gives her a thumbs-up.

After about thirty minutes of work, a two-foot strip of brown earth is freed along the house between the lawn and the cement block foundation. Her burning hands and damp shirt give satisfaction, and she knows that Jack will approve her minor accomplishment. She jauntily heads toward the garage for a rake, stopping when she hears voices and laughter. Who could Jack be talking to? She has a familiar but unwelcome mental flash of her mother's slightly bent listening posture. Determinedly, Saffee rounds the corner. Jack is on the shared driveway shaking hands with a smiling young couple and a little girl.

"Honey," he calls, "come meet the neighbors!"

With an arm Saffee wipes perspiration from her forehead. She is relieved the garage door is still down, concealing a peculiar pile of spotted wood.

"Saffee, this is Gail and Bill." Gail holds the hand of dark-haired Jenny Rose, who, her proud mother says, is four years old. Saffee notes immediately how jovial they are.

"I'm awmost five!" Jenny Rose declares. "An' I'm gonna have a brudder! Oh, or maybe a sister!" Gail's round middle confirms the fact.

"Not due until the end of August," Gail pretends to lament, "and it's only May."

Saffee slaps her grimy hands on her jeans and apologizes for not shaking hands. She tells them she's just pulled up all the weeds on the side of the house and is about to rake.

Gail's dark eyebrows go up. "Weeds?" she says.

"Yeah. Lots. Want to see?" Saffee is pleased she can share her first visible contribution to their household.

The two young neighbors go around to the side of the house, Jenny Rose in tow.

"Oh dear," Gail says, then hesitates, eyebrows up again. "Saffee, I hate to tell you, but those weren't weeds, they were chrysanthemums. They did need cutting back, but not pulling up. I think Mrs. Corbett, the owner, was sort of proud of them."

*Chrysanthemums?* Any plant pulled in error would be bad, but *chrysanthemums?*

*. . . the butcher knife . . . the blue house . . . the police . . .*

Later that night Saffee lies awake. Her intentions to do a bit of honest labor had been innocent. She jerks over onto her side and pulls the pillow tightly around her head. *Think about things that are good. Think about ways I am not like her. Think . . . Think . . .*

# CHAPTER FORTY-ONE

# SOFTBALL RELIGION

"What do you want on your waffles?' Tom whispered *syrup-titiously*."

"Oh, Jack, now *that's* a funny one," Saffee says, throwing her arms around him.

Looking pleased, he says, "I'll scramble the eggs."

Having been married for a week, they celebrate with a late Sunday morning brunch. The waffles drip with melted butter and maple syrup. Happy, they sit in the kitchen at the little red Formica table, knees bumping. With second cups of coffee, they move to the love seat that faces a small alcove meant to serve as dining room.

"When are you going to start taking paint off that old table in the garage?" he asks.

"Jack," Saffee sighs, "we're having a lovely morning, let's not break the mood." She pulls her legs up under her. Honeymoon contentment, other than their trip to Miller's Ford, has made her feel as if they are the only people in a world that has stopped. Nothing else, especially issues of the past, could possibly be important.

Not reading her, he says that if their neighbor, Bill, is around this afternoon, he will ask him to help assemble the parts. "It will be easier to work on if it's upright," he says.

"I'd guess the scraping is going to take some time." He catches her expression. "Just hoping there'll be room in the garage for the car by winter, that's all."

"I don't know, Jack. Maybe later, when summer comes."

"Are you saying you want to *table* the project?"

She grins.

He doesn't wheedle, cajole, or manipulate. In return, she does not argue.

On Monday morning, Saffee walks two blocks to a neighborhood shopping center where she has noticed a hardware store and buys the supplies she'll need for stripping the table. For when she gets around to it.

Back home, she pulls up the garage door and dumps her purchases onto the offending piece. She stands for several moments, arms crossed, staring at it, then brings down the door and goes into the house.

She's never been fond of talking on the telephone.

She doesn't want to call. She must call.

"Hello, Mrs. Corbett? Hi, this is Saffee Andrews . . . Saffee— Mrs. Jack Andrews . . . We rented your duplex on . . . Yes, that's right, it is Sapphire, but I don't use . . . Yes, the duplex . . . Oh no, uh, there's nothing wrong . . . No, it didn't . . . Anyway, I'm sure my husband could fix it if it . . . The plunger? Oh yes, I saw it right behind . . . No, no, I'm not calling about the lease either, we *love* living here . . . Oh, I'm so sorry . . . Shouldn't call you before 10:00 a.m., then. I'll remember that . . . Mrs. Cor . . . Mrs. Corbett, the reason I'm call- ing . . . The sink? *No!* It's fine too. I'm calling about the yard. There's something you should . . . Yes, Jack has already cut the grass, a couple times . . . Oh yes, he does the edging too. But, Mrs. Corbett, I'm calling to tell you about the chrysanthemums . . . Oh, they were? Best ever last year . . . Burgundy. Bronze and gold too. Yes, I bet they were lovely. Mrs. Corbett, did you have any white ones? . . . You don't like white? Doesn't show up against the white siding . . . You go for drama. I see. Well, Mrs. Corbett, my husband and I spent half of Saturday replacing . . . Yes, I said replacing . . . Why? Well, because I pulled them up . . . Yes, roots and all; I thought they were weeds . . . Perennials? No, I don't know the difference . . . Aha! Come back every year. I'm so sorry, Mrs. Corbett. I really . . . should have just cut them back? Yes, I see. What colors? Well now, I'm afraid they're all white, Mrs. Corbett. That's the only color the nursery had . . . No. No burnished bronze . . . Yes, they were sold out . . . No, Mrs. Corbett, really, I'm not calling about the lease . . ."

Saffee watches the liquid bubble. Is this what is supposed to happen? She reads the directions again. "Brush on, wait ten minutes, scrape off." Sounds easy. She anchors her ponytail more securely to the top of her head and waits. Shouldn't the remover come with a clip for her nose? Time to scrape. It's immediately apparent that the project will take much more effort than she expected. She repeats the process and sighs. She hates the table. She will remove the paint only because Jack wants her to. Only because underneath it all, *he* sees beauty.

Robert Scott, also an aspiring actuary who works in Jack's office, invites Jack to play on his church softball team. "No practices, just games on Saturday afternoons," he promises.

Jack digs through still-unpacked boxes to retrieve his ball and glove, and that evening, taking more study breaks than usual, he sits on the love seat, slapping the ball into the pocket. *Thwap, thwap, thwap.* Saffee finds the repetitive noise an irritating intrusion into their almost blissful state of marriage. But on Saturday, she has to admit it is fun to watch her husband run around the bases like a happy kid.

After the second game, Robert walks with Jack and Saffee to the parking lot. He says that someone has made some new rules at his church. Now, everyone who plays on the team has to attend church, at least Sunday school.

"Ah," says Jack. "What church do you go to?"

"Baptist."

"Okay," Jack says.

When they are alone in the car, Saffee exclaims, "Baptist? I didn't know there are Baptist churches in Minnesota. Aren't they like holy rollers?" She says she doesn't think she'll be going with him . . .

*"I'm not going!" Joann's green-handled hairbrush flies through the air* . . .

On Sunday, when Jack comes home, he tells Saffee that the adult Sunday school class was interesting. He stayed for the service too because it seemed like that was what was expected of him. He assures her he saw no unusual behavior.

The following week, when he returns, he says he thinks she would like the church and that the preacher gives a good message from the Bible.

She disagrees but senses it would not be wise to contradict Jack without knowing what she's talking about. She'll go. Once. Why couldn't it be a Lutheran ball team?

Brother Fred *(Whose brother? And don't Baptists believe in last names for their clergy?)* wears a suit rather than a robe; a tie, not a clerical collar. The sermon *is* thought-provoking—something about not burying a kind of money, called talents, in the ground. However, some of the congregants are huggers, and visitors are asked to *stand and announce their names.* Why hadn't Jack warned her?

Sunday afternoon Saffee answers the doorbell and is taken aback to find Brother Fred on the front step. He wears a short-sleeved shirt just like plain folks. Saffee invites him, their first guest, to come into the living room and calls Jack to join them. She doesn't think to offer any refreshment.

Although the preacher is friendly and nonthreatening, Saffee plunges into nervous chatter. She tells him that she was "saved"—the Baptists seem to like that term—in fourth grade, read *Egermeier's* as a child, and in college began a habit of Bible reading. She neglects to mention that the habit had not taken a full hold and has been sorely neglected for some time.

Sounding hopeful, Brother Fred tells her that the church needs help with the fifth-grade Sunday school class. Would Saffee like to "volunteer"? The morning at church *had* been fairly pleasant—nice people, good sermon, a choir that sang with gusto. But what kind of a church invites perfect strangers to teach their children? Her opinion plummets.

"Me? Well, I'm not sure . . ." She backpedals. "I don't really know the Bible very well at all," she says. "I wouldn't be able to teach it. You wouldn't ask if you knew how unqualified I am."

"Wonderful," Brother Fred says. "This is your opportunity to learn. We have teaching guides for every lesson, and as you prepare by studying the Scripture, just think how much you'll learn."

Saffee is speechless. She has never taught anything to anyone in her life. She is shy. She knows little about the ways of children, having had practically nothing to do with them when she was one herself. Why is this "brother," whom she has just met, smiling at her with an expression that says he knows she will do it?

He tells her that she would not be the lead teacher, rather an assistant to Robert Scott's wife, Mary. Nice woman. Saffee wouldn't have to do much teaching the first few weeks until she is comfortable.

She remembers her mother's lament that the only time anyone from church called her was when they wanted her to do something. In her case, to bake a cake.

On the other hand, hasn't God said . . .

Saffee hears herself agree to help, at least to try. How much more intimidating will this new life become?

# CHAPTER FORTY-TWO

# GIRL TALK

The open garage door, necessary for ventilation, must look inviting, but Saffee wishes Gail, her bubbly, chatty neighbor, hadn't popped into the garage unexpectedly. As usual, Saffee prefers to be alone . . .

*"Don't be bringing people into our house. It's not a good idea . . ."*

. . . but she tries to be gracious.

Her college dorm room had seen a parade of girls—drawn into her roommate's circle of affection, certainly not by Saffee's aloof manner. She wishes she were warm and welcoming like Gloria, whose influence seems to have only gone so deep, her mother's much deeper. Can't Gail see that Saffee is preoccupied with an arduous project? She's worked four mornings to remove layers of paint from a very small square of surface and her attitude rivals the chemicals for unpleasant.

Saffee suggests that Gail could sit in a lawn chair a couple of feet outside the small garage to distance her pregnant self from noxious fumes. Then she turns down the volume of a favorite string quartet playing on the radio.

Gail launches into a cheery monologue about a recent family

wedding. The smitten mother gushes about Jenny Rose scattering rose petals down the aisle, describes in detail what the attendants wore, how she always gets emotional at weddings, and on and on. The neighbor pauses for breath, smoothes her maternity shirt over her prominent belly, and encircles her unborn child with her short arms.

Saffee wishes she knew how to say that she too feels a little emotional at the moment and would like to be alone. But Gail would want to know what is so emotional about stripping paint and she'd never understand. Saffee isn't sure she understands either.

She tugs another roll to the sleeves of Jack's old white shirt, too worn at the collar for the office, and wonders what she should say if Gail inquires how the table came to have such inordinate layers of paint. With a quiet sigh, she counsels herself to be polite and scrapes with determination at a patch of glutinous red as Gail recounts more wedding details. They thread Saffee back to her own wedding . . .

*"The flowers you got me . . . Look! . . . Brown, ugly carnations! Dead! . . . I saw the gorgeous orchids you got for Jack's mother! Shows what you think of me! . . ."*

"Saffee?"

Saffee looks up at Gail and realizes she's asked a question. "I'm sorry, Gail. What's that?"

"Your wedding cake, when you got married, what was it like? Who made it?"

Embarrassed, and trying not to sound it, Saffee explains to Gail that the church secretary put her in contact with the special events committee who took care of all the details. She must have sounded like an idiot. She doesn't suppose that other brides pass on decisions to strangers. At the time, however, she had been grateful.

"Oh! Well, that's one way to get married, I guess." Gail sounds surprised, but not critical. "Bet you had classical music," she says, nodding toward the radio that plays a dramatic piece suddenly unsuitable for garage background music. Saffee turns it a notch lower.

She tells Gail that there had been a trumpet and organ processional.

"Trumpet? Cool!" says Gail. "I'll have to remember that for Jenny Rose's wedding."

Saffee, with a change of heart, flashes a smile at her neighbor. Gail's good-humored banter is entertaining, taking attention off her stiff hands. She scrapes with renewed energy.

It becomes Saffee's routine to coax paint off the Norway table for about two hours each morning before she catches the bus for work at noon. Returning to the duplex about 8:00 p.m., she usually finds Jack studying dull-looking graphs and formulas as he prepares for exams late into the night. She decides that it is good they both have challenging projects.

Gail's husband, Bill, occasionally persuades Jack to leave his books long enough to take in an evening baseball game. They are becoming good friends. Saffee has proved to be what every talkative female needs—a good listener—and somehow Gail seems to know when Saffee is in the garage. With Jenny Rose in a preschool two mornings a week, and pregnancy sapping her energy, she seems to relish spontaneous forays next door. Saffee's mother's word for Gail would be *loquacious*, and Joann's voice whispers the label every time Gail appears.

One day, as Saffee vigorously rubs a rough surface with sandpaper, Gail interrupts her own monologue to ask why Saffee doesn't rent an electric sander.

"Guess that would make the job easier," Saffee says, considering. "But for some reason, I just need, well, I mean, I have to put my own sweat into this project."

Another day Gail asks sweepingly about Saffee's childhood. Saffee remembers childhood in moments, disquieting, specific moments she does not want to share. Since the inquiry was not about moments, she replies in kind.

"Fine," she says with a warm smile in hopes to disarm Gail. "It was fine." She wonders how much trust is needed in a girlfriend relationship before she can speak freely about moments. It might be soon.

"You know, Gail, how I always have the radio tuned to a classical station when you come by, and then after a while I turn it off?"

"Yeah, I guess you do," Gail says. "How come?"

"Because having you here is never a Mozart moment—you always put me in a rock 'n' roll mood."

Gail sputters apologetically and Saffee clarifies, "Don't worry, Gail, rock 'n' roll is always more fun. It's definitely a compliment."

The demonstration draws to a close. Party guests complete their orders for Tupperware essentials that perky saleswoman Lucy has convinced them no kitchen is functional without. More than bowls and such, Lucy's effervescence and bouffant hairdo, purple miniskirt befitting a slimmer woman, and white go-go boots have held the roomful of young women in her spell for the last hour.

Gail had invited Saffee to the event, which is hosted by Gail's cousin. Seated beside her neighbor-become-friend, Saffee checks "Large Mixing Bowl Set," turns in her order form, and waits for the others to finish. She watches Gail's attractive cousin carefully arranging multi-colored napkins into a fan design on the refreshment table. The young woman wears a satisfied expression as she surveys a stunning floral centerpiece and tiered serving plates piled with dainty confections.

"All right, ladies, are we ready?" Lucy inquires, collecting the last of the order forms. "Before refreshments, it's that time we've all been waiting for—the drawing for the door prize!" The guests, still atwitter under Lucy's spell, admire an arrangement of gifts from which a lucky one will choose her prize. Saffee eyes a set of red gelatin molds. They would be perfect to shape Christmas tree salads, a Kvaale tradition she thinks she can comfortably carry forth.

But there is a "catch" to the drawing. The winner not only goes home with a gift but also promises to host a Tupperware party within the next three months. For Saffee, this is out of the question. Host a party? She has almost no one to invite, she doesn't have any experience baking, and she can't accommodate a group in her small living room. Those guests who for some reason are unable to host a party are asked not to draw. Saffee counts the women present and notes she has a one in thirteen chance of being the winner. The odds are good. Why not at least play along for the fun of it? And who knows, maybe if she wins, Lucy might let her keep . . . without . . .

The slips of paper are randomly selected. Saffee's is marked "Winner!" There are "ohs," "ahs," and expressions of disappointment.

"Ladies"—Lucy squints at the winner's name tag—"Sapphire here is the next Tupperware hostess!" There is a polite clap. "And here are your lovely Jell-O molds, dear, just sign the date of your party on this clipboard."

"Oh. Well . . ." Saffee stretches upward in her chair toward Lucy's ear to address her as confidentially as possible. "I . . . but I really don't want to have a party. You see, I . . . I just wanted to play the game. I took a chance and . . ." How she yearns to run out the door.

Lucy stiffens and the room goes silent. Her expression changes from aren't-we-having-fun to a drama of disbelief. "One of the most significant responsibilities in life, Sapphire," Lucy intones, "is to be a woman of truth. A woman's word is her bond." She punctuates each word as if she holds a judge's gavel. "Her yes must be yes, and her no, no. A civil Christian society depends upon it."

Saffee is mortified. No one yells, "Preach it!" but from the wide eyes and ever-so-slightly tilted noses, there is no mistaking what the women are thinking.

Her face burns. She is shocked, but stupidly so, to be taken as a liar. Truth telling is part of her life. (She had sorely repented for lying to her mother, telling her she was "fine.") But who would believe that now? Hasn't it just been proven otherwise? To be a part of the fun, and foolishly hoping to get something for nothing, she had played her chance without considering the consequences. Harmless intentions or not, she'd been wrong and is exposed.

Coming to her rescue, dear Gail whispers, "No problem, Saffee. I can have it at my house, we'll do it together. I'm sure my bridge club will come."

Saffee doesn't dare look at Lucy, who quickly snatches the set of Jell-O molds from Saffee's hands and gives it to Gail. Before leaving, Saffee makes heartfelt apologies to Lucy.

A few weeks later the two neighbors host ten women in Gail's living room, which is identical in size to Saffee's, and serves well as a venue for Lucy's animated sales pitch.

With the help of Betty Crocker, Saffee contributes two layer cakes. One, coconut lemon; the other, chocolate marble. Two guests ask for her recipes.

# CHAPTER FORTY-THREE

# THE WOODEN BOX

affee has evaded Gail's questions about the table, but as their
friendship grows, she begins to share snatches of its history. She
relates that her great-grandfather made it in Norway and that it
traveled from there to North Dakota, then Minnesota. She tells how
a prairie fire prompted eight terrified siblings, her mother among
them, to seek refuge under it.

Eventually she confides that her once clever, talented mother fell
into a disturbed mental state and how the old table seemed to prompt
within her confusing delusions of good and evil. Under its strange
influence, real or imagined, Saffee says, she obsessively applied the
layers of paint.

"So, why are you stripping it?" Gail asks.

Saffee sighs. "Well, it's hard to explain, and sometimes I'm not
sure myself. But Jack says restoring the table will help me not be
mired down by memories of being raised in a troubled home—more
than I already am. I trust his judgment," Saffee says, giving her scraping tool an extra hard push. "I just hope that something good comes
out of all this labor."

After the conversation, Saffee feels lighter, just as she had when she first shared her life with Jack.

Throughout the summer, the two neighbors share a certain joy as each new area of raw wood becomes completely exposed. In hot July, during a mini-celebration with glasses of Gail's lemonade, Saffee blurts, "Gail, thanks so much for being my cheerleader. I've really needed one." And she means it.

How odd it is to share this closet, this *small* closet. Business suits and sport coats and half a dozen dress shirts cram against her wrinkled blouses. A number of ties drape over her green silk dress. Black and brown wing tips jumble with pink slippers, red and navy pumps, and basketball high-tops. Removing the three boxes carted from Saffee's former life might make room for a little order. She slides them out.

Sitting on the floor, she shuffles through mementos that mean little to her now.

She finds her sixth-grade report on the Battle of Gettysburg, with Mr. Mason's affirming inscription, "You made me feel like I was there!" The words still make her feel warm. She replaces the paper and pushes the box under the bed.

She finds that the second box is mislabeled. Perhaps once it did hold April's keepsakes, but now it contains her mother's spiral notebooks. Over a dozen of them, filled with poems, short stories, and who knows what else. It was logical that her dad left what he thought was April's box with Saffee's. Reading the notebooks would be a journey into both her mother's joys and angst. Someday. She shuts the box and shoves it, too, under the bed.

The third box is the one made of wood they had found in the basement. Inside are newspaper clippings, turned brown, dating from the 1920s and '30s. Beneath them, dating from the late 1800s and into the next century, is a pile of yellowed papers, most of them legal documents.

She finds several birth certificates, vaguely recognizing the names of her mother's siblings. One is for Joann Mabel Kirkeborg, born March 4, 1913. There is a manifest from a cargo ship that lists her grandfather, Knute Kirkeborg, age eighteen, as a worker on board.

And here is her grandparents' marriage license.

She opens an envelope that contains her grandmother's certificate of death.

"Clara Isabella Kirkeborg . . . Cause of death . . . exhaustion from hysteria and acute mania. Place of death . . . State Hospital for the Insane, State of North Dakota, May 4, 1920."

Saffee's heart thumps. Hysteria? Acute mania? Hospital for the Insane? The words glare like neon lights. Her mother *and* her grandmother? Insane? What was that term she learned in psychology? Evolutionary lineage. For an instant, for only an instant, her chest tightens.

*But God.*

God has promised her—her life will be different. She must believe that this box contains a view into other people's lives, not hers. At the same time, she is saddened to learn about her grandmother. Exhaustion would be expected after bearing, how many children? Nine? Maybe there were also miscarriages. Joanne had told her that her mother's last baby, a girl, was given away. What happens to a mother who carries a baby within her body and then it is taken from her? What might she be driven to? In her grandmother's case, it seems to have been mania.

Another question burns within Saffee. Had her mother ever looked into this box? Had she read the "Certificate of Death of Clara Isabella Kirkeborg"? She probably had. If so, maybe she concluded that mental illness was very likely her destiny also.

Saffee goes to the kitchen, pours a glass of iced tea, and sits for a while on the back step. Perhaps Saffee's grandmother Clara was at wit's end trying to love and care for all of her brood. She thinks about her mother's decline into darkness and kinship with the table. By default, perhaps Joann was unloved, or at least felt so. What could give greater pain? Pain so deep it could never be covered over, least of all by paint.

Painting was Joann's intentional action, as Jack calls it, against powers that beset her. But painting the table hadn't spared her from mental illness. Has Jack been wrong?

Words of comfort from the past return. *I will lead you and guide you with my eye upon you.*

Saffee concludes that action in and of itself is not the answer. It must be the right action. Her mother's painting was done in torment. It created ugliness—for the painter, and for the painted. Saffee's work, in contrast, is to search for goodness and to restore beauty.

Her perspective renewed, she goes back to the bedroom, wondering what else is in the old wooden box. In a yellowed paper folder, she finds six fragile pages printed in Norwegian that look to have been torn from a magazine. A faded photograph of a weathered, somber-looking man and woman appears on the first page. The names beneath are Anders and Maria Kirkeborg. She recognizes them as the names burned into the underside of the Norway table, her grandfather Knute's parents. Another generational jump backward, to what?

Saffee looks into the rugged face of the man who, in a sense, she already knows. A sensitive artist, the skilled craftsman who many years ago labored to make a table. She hopes that the wife beside him was a good woman, a woman of strength and wholeness. The pages appear to be biographical. If only she could read them.

Seated at the circulation desk, Saffee looks up to see a graduate student she recognizes in line. She rightly assumes that Leif Bergstrom is waiting to check out research materials on plant pathology, as he often does. She's been hoping for days, ever since she opened the old wooden box of papers, that he would show up again. It's Saturday morning, a time she usually doesn't work, but today she agreed to substitute for a coworker and now is glad she did. The folder, with the article featuring her great-grandparents, is in a paper bag at her feet.

She has never spoken to this student, other than to answer his brief questions, but by his name, and more so his accent, she is fairly certain he is Norwegian.

"Mr. Bergstrom?" she says as he reaches the desk. "I was wondering, I mean, are you, I mean, do you ever . . ." She takes a deep breath and begins again. "I have something I need translated. You are Norwegian, aren't you?"

Leif Bergstrom looks a little surprised and says, "Yah. I am from Norvay."

Saffee removes the folder from the bag and hands it to him across the desk. "Is it possible that you, or do you know someone, who could translate this for me? It's six pages. I think it's a biography of my great-grandparents, and I'd love to know more about them."

The student looks at the article and politely tells her that he is way too busy to help. He's preparing his dissertation for his PhD, he says, but perhaps his wife, Ingrid, would be interested. How much would she pay?

They agree on twenty-five dollars and he looks pleased. Leif Bergstrom leaves the library with the old folder tucked into his Scandinavian-looking knapsack. She had not had the presence of mind to get his phone number.

## CHAPTER FORTY-FOUR

# NEWLY WED

affee returns home from the library in the early afternoon. She finds Jack studying baseball stats, his lanky body draped over the end of the love seat. She drops her purse, leans over, and pecks him on the forehead.

"Hi," she says, tousling his thick brown curls.

"Hi, sweetie." His eyes only momentarily leave the sports page.

She's eager to tell him about perhaps finding a translator for the biography, but he looks preoccupied. "I'm starved," she says. "Have you had lunch?" Three steps take her into their tiny kitchen, and from the clutter she knows the answer. Her hands go to her hips.

"You wouldn't make a very good Indian," she says under her breath.

"Mmm?"

"Jack, do you know you leave a trail *anyone* could follow?" Her head does an upward twitch.

"Yeah, it was an amazing graze," he quips, without looking up.

Mess had never been tolerated in Saffee's upbringing and was certainly no joking matter. Its appearance catches her off guard. "I bet I can tell you *everything* you've done while I was gone."

Not inquiring if he wants to hear, she begins a litany. "For start-ers, you ate some of the leftover meatloaf." She claps down the cap on the ketchup bottle, shrouds the remaining inches of meat with plastic wrap, and spirits them both into the refrigerator, shutting the door with enough vigor to rattle the jars inside.

"Aha! It was a meatloaf *sandwich*," she says, shoving slices of bread back into their bag. Gathering momentum, Saffee addresses the saltshaker as she thrusts it into the cupboard. "Just in case the pepper misses you," she says with animation.

*Clunk.* She throws a Pepsi can into the wastebasket. Hard. Soft drinks were only allowed for the most special of occasions in her home. She probably had only three or four in her entire childhood. And those certainly did not contain caffeine. Saffee darts a glance at oblivious Jack, who must be focused on something of great impor-tance. *Is he even listening?*

"You sat here at the table," she continues, a little louder, jerking one of the stainless steel chairs into place and snatching up a hand towel that dangles from its red plastic seat.

She picks up a postcard from the table. It's from April, the first one in months.

Hey, you two Love Birds! I called Daddy and he told me you got married. Congratulations! So sorry I couldn't be there. Hope you understand I'm pretty busy looking for my own Romeo—I sure dig these Italians!

Love and Kiss, Kiss!
April

Saffee's eyes do a big-sister roll. She drops the card and continues her mission.

"Ah! A crossword puzzle while you ate," she chortles, picking up the completed work, a ballpoint pen, and a smeary plate.

"I *am* impressed you do crosswords with a *pen*," she huffs. "I'll give you credit for *that*." She carries the plate to the sink where a bar of soap has slid off the counter, leaving a sudsy path before plopping into a puddle of water.

"Jack washed his hands. Give him another point. Only *three* cupboard doors open?" *Slam. Slam. Slam.*

With this, Jack turns his head and gives her a long, quizzical look.

She waits, daring him to respond.

Finally, he says, matter-of-factly, "I live here," and returns to his reading.

Saffee is muzzled. She pours herself a glass of milk, picks up a box of graham crackers, and goes out the back door. She sits on the top step to munch and mull. This isn't the first time she's been huffy about Jack's disregard for keeping their small house tidy. Weren't husbands, as well as wives, responsible to keep things neat?

It wouldn't be difficult to pick up after him—but would that be *fair*? She doesn't like to think he regards her as his maid.

Her mother was employed as a maid when she and her father met, and again maid and caregiver during the war years in San Francisco. As in other things, she isn't eager to follow suit. But throughout Saffee's childhood there was little need for Joann to pick up after Nels. For all his lack of polish, he was as fastidious as she. Certainly no crumbs ever fell off *his* plate.

A magazine lying on a chair flickers in her memory. Young Saffee had carelessly left it there. "How can anyone sit in this chair if you don't pick up after yourself?" her father had demanded, shaking his finger at her. The reprimand had stung and helped to foster a lasting conviction of how things "ought to be."

But wait. Why would she want to perpetuate a mind-set now that had, in part, made childhood so unpleasant? The troubling thought plays over and over in her mind. She flinches as her own petty, disapproving words ring in her ears.

She thinks of Jack's mother. From the first time Jack had taken

Saffee home to meet his parents, she couldn't help but notice how Harriet adored her less-than-orderly husband and attended to his needs without complaint. It seemed to give her joy to serve him. Of course, Saffee had heard no complaint from James either.

Roles and rules in Jack's home were quite different from those in Saffee's. So . . . Jack must presume . . . while Saffee presumes . . . oh dear. Her shoulders slump; she takes another cracker.

Okay, not so fast. The new bride juts out her chin. Jack lives here, but she does too. Why is *she* the one expected to change?

*"Your mother ain't happy unless she's mad about somethin'."*

*. . . Your life will be different . . .*

Again, recollections bring a clarifying moment. Saffee considers that there are times in life when she will have to *make* things different, *make* things better. It will not just happen with a touch of some celestial wand. Change might involve struggle, might take time. Hadn't she watched her mother take the trivial things of life way too seriously, leaving no energy to deal properly with matters that were truly important? What terrible thing had Jack done? Merely made a bit of a mess. While she—she had smattered an unredeemable half hour with rubbish much more difficult to clean up.

From her perch on the step, she has been staring into the backyard, not seeing it. Now the lawn mower, covered with grass clippings, comes into focus. While she was gone, Jack had cut the grass. That was nice. But he could have cleaned the grass off . . . *Stop! It's trivial.*

Saffee hurries around the house to the garage and finds a broom. Returning to the backyard, she is arrested by its charm. Jack had not only mowed that morning but edged the perimeter. And she sees a mound of pruned, dead branches, tied and stacked against the house. The redbud trees proclaim a flurry of spring color—color that, in her bad mood, she hadn't noticed. She admires the thriving, newly planted young chrysanthemums they had put in the ground *together*, even though she alone had done the prior ruin.

She leans on the broom beneath a brilliant blue sky, drinking in the heady scene. Their first yard. Even if it is rented, it is, for this time, their yard. Her whole life is filled with beautiful gifts—Jack being the best. How could she have been so easily seduced to criticize him?

She looks down at the broom.

*"Did I tell you that she hit my legs with a broom handle?"*

Saffee quickly brushes grass off the mower and pushes it around the house and into its place in the crowded garage. She'll go in immediately to apologize.

Exiting the garage, she collides with Jack coming around the corner.

"Hey, hon, how about going to the baseball game tonight?" he says. "Bill's got some extra tickets." In one hand he holds the broom she had dropped in the backyard and in the other is her forgotten milk glass. The box of graham crackers is under one arm. She looks into his face and grins sheepishly.

"I'd absolutely love to," she says, taking the broom. "Who's playing?"

Maybe she will go to the concession stand. Maybe she will drink a Pepsi.

## CHAPTER FORTY-FIVE

# TENDRIL TANGLE

Early on an August Saturday, Saffee slips out of bed, being careful not to disturb Jack. He had grappled with actuarial formulas until 2:00 a.m., and she had worked until nearly eleven under lamplight in the garage, enjoying the cool evening silence. When she saw a celebration of fireflies blinking in the velvet dark, she rushed inside and pulled Jack away from his books out into the diamond-studded night.

They stood close, surrounded by the enchantment, until Jack said he must go back in.

"Aww," she objected, "you know what they say, 'All work and no play makes Jack . . .'"

"So, 'they' think I'm a dull boy?" He laughed.

"Never," she said emphatically, planting a kiss on his lips.

Now, in robe and slippers, she pads into the dark garage and raises the door. The morning sun, as if eagerly waiting, floods inside.

She turns and admires the tabletop, finally free of its multicolored past. She glides a hand along the silky surface. Last night she sanded its fine grain until it yielded a delicate sheen. Its daylight debut is even better than she'd hoped. But there is much more to do.

Today she'll begin restoring the apron, that intimidating four-inch-deep carved piece that rims the perimeter.

At eight o'clock, Saffee drives the VW to the hardware store and outfits herself with two gallons of stronger, smellier remover, a wickedly stiff wire brush, and a blunt probe to remove loosened paint from deep crevices. And more gloves. And more sandpaper.

Back in the garage, Saffee clips her swinging ponytail to the top of her head and pours a quantity of the new remover into a work bucket. Wrinkling her nose, she drags a brush full of the amber liquid onto a small area of carved vines. The serpentine twists and turns have always suggested to her some struggle between good and evil. They probably represented something similar to her mother. Joann frequently had pointed out dualities, such as truth versus lies, beauty versus ugliness.

She imagines her great-grandfather Kirkeborg coaxing the wood to release the enigmatic motif with his chisel. She wonders if he, like her mother, had imagined a certain presence. Her talented ancestor would undoubtedly be terribly disappointed to know that his lovely work had been reduced to a trap for paint.

The remover bubbles. She tries the new brush, applying pressure to the stiff bristles to test them. She's learned that many layers of paint can be scratched and grooved without jeopardizing the wood beneath. Progress is almost imperceptible and Saffee has abundant time to muse while she scrapes. Being unfamiliar with Norwegian lore, to her the design suggests something Shakespearean.

*Whose reptilian head lurks in yonder braided vine?*
*Whose sin'ster eye leers my very soul?*

She chuckles, just like her mother used to, entertained by her own strung-together words. Jack advised Saffee to be grateful for gifts from her mother. She's not sure if composition is one of them. Did Joann write something about this vine? If so, it might be in one of those spiral notebooks. Saffee debates again whether or not she wants to read them.

She wonders if the vine has a botanical name. She'll have to ask Leif Bergstrom, the Norwegian plant pathologist (pathologist, how fitting)—if she ever sees him again. He seems to have disappeared.

How many times as a young girl did Saffee see her mother apply wet paint over dry with the intensity of a combatant? Her mother's every stroke seemed to increase her agitation. But conversely, as Saffee wages a new war, this one to loosen and remove those painted layers, she senses liberation. In fact, a triple liberation. She dares believe that the wood, and she herself, and her mother also . . . "Oh, God," she whispers. "Please, Lord, set her free!"

She's trying to establish a habit of calling her dad every Sunday afternoon. She's learned that Joann seems to be coping acceptably well and showing interest in minor decorating of their new mobile home. He does not suggest that she and Jack visit. Neither does Saffee.

Coming from their street-side mailbox, Jack appears on the driveway. He steps into the garage, waving a postcard.

"A princess!" He sounds amused. "They made her a princess!"

"Who? What are you talking about?" She puts down the bristle brush and takes the card from him, trying not to stain it with her gloves.

It's from April. Saffee recalls that the last they had heard she was in Italy. Wrote she couldn't get an audience with the pope, so she settled for a Swiss guard or something like that.

Saffee reads aloud, "'I'm on Samos—a tiny, picturesque Greek island. Gorgeous. The villagers have made me their princess because of my blond hair.'"

"Well, that sounds like April," she says. "She was always pretending something."

"I look forward to meeting her someday," Jack says. "She sounds pretty adventurous."

On the driveway, Jack raises the small hood at the back of the

VW in order to change the oil. Saffee slops more remover onto a layer of cracking blue paint and continues to think about April. She regrets her own years of rudeness designed to keep kissy-huggy April at arm's length. But if her postcards are to be believed, April sounds okay and Saffee is happy for her.

A song she heard on the radio a few days ago has since been maddeningly stuck in Saffee's head. Pouring more remover into the bucket, she absentmindedly sings,

> *Sometime an April day will suddenly bring showers*
> *Rain to grow the flowers for her first bouquet*
> *But April love can slip right through your fingers*
> *So if she's the one don't let her run away . . .*

# CHAPTER FORTY-SIX

# JOANN'S NOTEBOOKS

Saffee pulls a box from beneath the bed and removes a pile of spiral-bound notebooks. Her fingers are sore from working so long on that stubborn carved vine. Today she will give them a rest. She turns pages of familiar handwriting that ranges from neatly penned to scrawls of jumbled emotion. Hatch marks slash through paragraphs deemed unacceptable.

Saffee skims the rambling "essay poem" Joann had written after attending the Miller's Ford sewing club—*"rhythms of boisterous chatter . . . raucous undercurrent . . . guttural pieties . . . boorish sticks and stones . . . rude cacophony . . ."*

She shudders at the display of criticism. What insidious powers had countermanded Joann's gifted mind so that a few women gathered to gossip had prompted this troubled torrent? She quickly exchanges the notebook for another and reads curious lines entitled "Night, From Under a Table."

> *Benches bar the world; benches mark the dark.*
> *A snore. A rustle. The last ember falls.*
> *Who whispers there?*

*Will Someone come?*
*Or will she always be alone?*
*Pull the blanket tight, child.*

Saffee can only guess what the words refer to. Any reference to a table must indicate the Norway table. Why would her mother have spent the night under it?

The cover of another notebook reads, "Herein lies evidence to hang, beatify, or bore."

She grins. There was no denying that Joann could sometimes be witty. Inside, she reads a scathing account of her altercation with the minister and subsequent withdrawal from the church. A poem follows:

*My days are troubled and few*
*Am I but a flower that fades?*
*Is there not hope for a tree cut down to sprout again?*
*Its root may grow old in the earth*
*Its stump may burn*
*Yet, at the scent of Water it will bud!*
*Oh, God! Hide me!*
*Conceal me 'til your wrath is past that I may not be burned*
*Find my transgressions sealed, O God*
*My iniquity covered over*
*My flesh pains; my soul mourns*
*Your holy fire purifies*

The last line is scrawled to be almost unreadable—

*Or is the inferno meant for me?*

Saffee rereads the muddled words. Does "a tree cut down" refer to the wood of the Norway table as well as to Joann herself? By scraping away the desecrating paint from the dead table, Saffee hopes, like the poem says, to make it "sprout" and "bud" again. The process is giving her, too, a sanding and scrub, stretching her to bloom. Yes, Jack was right.

*Oh, Lord, forgive my lack of love and sympathy for my ill mother. For years I practically denied her existence. Remove my own ugly, self-centered layers—and thanks for not using a wire brush! Bring forth new life in me. And the table. And Mother.*

Although she is emotionally exhausted, Saffee moves on and finds what she has been hoping for, a poem called "The Vine." It is dated shortly before the fateful Thanksgiving Day now so indelibly stamped into family memory. A catch in her chest makes her momentarily hesitate to read what might trigger the emotion of that night, but she is too curious not to.

> *The vine, that vigorous vine*
> *has gone astray*
> *Has become foreign to Him*
> *The outcast vine grows with the tares*
>
> *Shoots, planted by abundant waters*
> *Spread branches turned toward Him*
> *And commune with the stars*
> *Roots, turned toward others*
> *Will not thrive*
> *Joy, sorrow*
> *inextricably*
> *intertwined*
>
> *He will pull up the roots*
> *Cut off the fruit*
> *Leave it to wither.*
> *The vine, that vigorous vine*

*has gone astray*
*Has become foreign to Him*
*The outcast vine grows with the tares*

It seems possible that the table's carved vine had suggested these words. Considering what happened in the Petersons' yard, Joann must have meant them to be literal. That night it seemed as if she were fulfilling some personal directive to uproot the plants, the "tares."

Saffee reads the enigmatic poem to its conclusion, aware she will never fully understand words sprung from Joann's delusions:

*The pruning shears*
*will come*
*must come*
*The cast-out branch is thrown into the fire!*
*I cling to the vine!*
*The pruning shears*
*will come*
*must come*
*"I give unto them eternal life; they shall never perish,*
*Neither shall they be plucked from my hand."*

Saffee whispers, "Oh, Lord, I pray that in spite of her delusions, Mother knows that You are the Vine, and that You are truth."

## Chapter Forty-Seven

# Stuffed Ribs

What began as a relaxing evening catching up with the newspapers suddenly changes when Jack looks up and suggests they should invite his boss and wife to dinner. Saffee, lounging on the love seat, drops her paper and sits up straight. "You're kidding, right?"

After Saffee's angst when she cohosted the Tupperware party with Gail, he knew he could expect some hesitancy. "It would be a good way to get to know them," he says. "Good for all of us. And you'll like Leonard Johnson. He's a really nice guy. I'm fortunate to work for him." Jack tells her that his boss was recently transferred to Minneapolis, so he and his wife probably know few people in the area and would appreciate the invitation.

"Where are they from?"

"Louisville, Kentucky, I think. Somewhere down south."

"Southerners? Oh, Jack. I'm not ready to compete with southern hospitality yet."

"But, Saffee . . ."

"No, Jack. I'm sorry."

Jack settles back into the turquoise vinyl chair and picks up his softball and glove. He thwaps the ball into the pocket a few times, a habit Saffee is still trying to get used to. She knows the matter is not settled.

Her memory shuffles through snapshots of her mother's pathetic attempts to entertain. She feels a queasiness not unlike that she used to experience before playing in a piano recital.

From the lumpy love seat, she scans their hand-me-down furniture.

"Honey, look at this place," she says. "You know I love it—it's great for you and me, but . . . your boss? They probably live in a very affluent neighborhood."

Jack says nothing.

Then she looks into the nook they call a dining room and knows the clincher. "Look, Jack, all we have in our so-called dining room is a Modigliani poster that's not even framed." The stylized, long-necked portrait seems to smirk at her, daring to be compared to the "real art" that must hang in the Johnson home. "We absolutely can't have company for dinner without an appropriate table. The stripping won't be finished for weeks . . . maybe months. We'll just have to wait on entertaining."

Jack's expression says he doesn't accept her arguments. He gestures toward the kitchen and their small Formica dinette set with its tubular stainless steel legs and four matching chairs with red plastic seats.

"Honey, *that* table works just fine. Don't *we* use it every day? We'll just carry it into the dining room and throw a tablecloth over it."

He moves to sit beside her. Crestfallen, she drops her head onto his shoulder. He doesn't get it. Neither one speaks for a few moments. In his gentle way, Jack asks, "Did you ever have any *good* times around the Norway table?"

"I . . . I can't remember any."

"Let's change that."

She looks dubious.

Family tables are more than just places to eat, he says. Much of his young life was around a table. Jack laces his fingers behind his head and gazes upward, as if childhood scenes replay on the ceiling. The dining room table was where he glued balsa airplanes together, he tells her, and where he played a million games of cribbage with his brother. His mother did her daily crossword puzzle there, and his dad paid bills and studied the stock market.

"When we had company," he says, "I remember more than the food. I remember my uncle recounting the same war stories over and over. And my cousins telling such unfunny jokes we howled." Jack's eyes linger for a moment, the corners of his mouth turned up. "Oh yeah, and Mother always cautioning me not to eat so fast—when sometimes I was slipping my food down to the dog. What a great place it was to be—for all of us, not just the dogs."

She is jealous beyond words of his memories. She can't believe he has even more to tell.

"When Danny and I got older," Jack says, "after meals we all lingered at the table drinking coffee, talking about life—God, politics, philosophy. I've realized that those conversations became foundational to my entire belief system. It was the place where Dad encouraged us to formulate what he called a worldview. Oh, if tables could talk," he says, summing up his reverie.

Jack's account helps her to better understand why he has a social consciousness, as well as an intellectual life. It had been built over the years with the help of his family and their guests, and now he was sharing it with her. Saffee is relieved tables can't talk.

"Oh, Jack," she blurts, turning to face him, "I really want to have what you describe. It's silly to be afraid of good experiences." She swallows the lump in her throat. "I must get over this."

Jack puts his arms around her. "Honey, you'll do just great . . . I can hardly wait for the boss to meet my lovely bride."

❖

Saffee finds the recipe in Sunday's *Minneapolis Star and Tribune*. Stuffed pork ribs. It shouldn't be difficult. With the addition of chopped apple, the stuffing is similar to the dressing her mother always made at Thanksgiving. She will make it Saturday—for the Johnsons.

That morning she swishes a dust cloth over the furniture. The carpet looks the same whether vacuumed or not . . . she chooses not. Vacuuming that doesn't show might be considered a trivial thing.

Later, as she begins to prepare the meal, she hears the *thunk, thunk* of Jack's basketball on the backboard that he and neighbor Bill put up at the edge of the driveway. Their masculine exuberance as they contend makes her happy. She so much wants the coming evening to go well, and to make Jack proud of her.

She chops an onion. A childhood scene flickers through her mind . . .

*"Nels!" In the kitchen, Joann stares aghast at the irregular chunks of meat he has cut. "This is a rump roast!" she hisses so guests don't hear. "People slice rump roasts, not hack them! Don't you know the difference between a rump and a chuck?"*

Saffee lectures herself. *I'll cry over an onion, but nothing else! Not even when eight legs bump under that little table . . . Having company for dinner only requires common sense.*

*Oh, God, help me emulate only what Mother did right, and do other things better. Let this day honor her . . . and You.*

Leonard and Betsy Johnson are warm, unpretentious, and chatty. They sip iced tea and tell about their experiences adapting to northern ways. Betsy recounts recently ordering a meal at a restaurant.

"The waitress came to our table and said, 'So, whatcha want?'"

Leonard laughs heartily and adds, "In the South, they ask me, 'What'll you have, *honey?*'" Now they both are laughing.

"I wouldn't like someone speaking that way to *my* husband," Saffee says with a smile. "Northerners aren't used to speaking with familiarity to strangers."

Leonard nods with understanding. "You'd probably want to 'wop her upside th' haid,' as they say in Loo-ih-vuhl!"

"That's for sure. I don't mind people being friendly, just don't call my husband 'honey'!"

The conversation drifts to other matters. The queasiness in Saffee's stomach has all but gone away. She sighs with relief and excuses herself to serve the meal, still within earshot of the conversation. *God, help me do this.* She tosses the salad and carefully lifts the hot pan of savory ribs from the oven. Perfect. She divides generous portions onto four plates. The Formica table is too small for a platter.

She can hear the living room talk return to eating out. Jack recommends Minneapolis restaurants the newcomers might enjoy. "There's a great barbeque place just a little to the west," he says. "Best ribs in town."

"Now that's the only way to have ribs," Leonard gushes. "Barbequed! Not the way *we* had them last night!" It is clear he is teasing Betsy.

"Oh, Leonard." Betsy laughs. "I know they were terrible! I found a new recipe in Sunday's paper," she explains to Jack. "Maybe I didn't cook them long enough."

"That wasn't the only problem, my dear. There was some kind of *mush* in between the ribs! And no barbeque sauce at all!"

*"Mush!"* Betsy chortles. "Leonard, it was called stuffin'!"

In the kitchen, Saffee freezes. She grips the edge of the counter for several moments until she can think.

Saffee senses that Betsy is used to her husband's humorous chiding, but she must be careful not to embarrass Jack's boss. She takes a deep breath. Here goes.

She pokes her head around the corner. Jack gives her a weak smile. Summoning her best southern accent (having college friends from the South can come in handy), Saffee announces, "Y'all're gonna love this new recipe for ribs! Ah found it . . ." She gulps. "Ah found it Sunday . . . in the *Stahr and* Tri*bune*!"

Leonard groans. "Oh no!" With a red face, he tries umpteen ways to backpedal. Both he and Betsy insist that although something had seriously gone awry with their dish, they are sure Saffee's pork ribs and stuffing will be marvelous—it certainly smells wonderful!

That night Jack holds her tightly in his arms and whispers, "I'm so proud of you. You made the best of a delicate situation . . . and the ribs, the whole meal, it was delicious."

"Thanks, hon, but I'm afraid I didn't manage to spare the Johnsons from embarrassment."

"That would've been impossible, and I bet it won't be long 'til they laugh about it."

Encouraged more than he will ever know, Saffee smiles in the dark.

## CHAPTER FORTY-EIGHT

# RAINBOW HEART

By late August, fall threatens an early appearance. The garage floor feels chilly. One day the cap from the paint remover can slips from her stiff fingers and rolls under the table. Retrieving it, she catches a glimpse of the words burned into the underside. She gets a pencil and tablet and carefully copies them. More Norwegian that needs translation, but Leif Bergstrom has not reappeared.

That evening she and Jack carry eight discarded cement blocks from the back property line into the garage. Jack, with Bill's help, lifts the table onto the stacked blocks. Saffee watches them, disappointed that her project is going so slowly. At least now she can work from a chair rather than the floor.

While Bill and Jack are discussing the upcoming football season, Saffee hears the phone ring and hurries inside to answer. She learns that Mary Scott is sick. Can Saffee teach the Bible lesson to the fifth graders on Sunday? She feels obligated to say yes, even though she too will be ill, from nerves, long before the class begins. So far, she has only helped by playing the piano and assisting with crafts.

Each morning during the remainder of the week's tedious work on the table, she has plenty of time to think about teaching the Old

Testament story of Joseph. The thrust of the lesson, according to the teacher's guide, is forgiveness, and Joseph had a lot to forgive. She runs through the injustices he suffered: sold into slavery by his brothers, falsely accused of assault by his employer's wife, thrown into prison for years, forgotten by man—but not by God.

She considers the summary points she'll make: Joseph persevered in hardship and was greatly honored; he forgave his brothers; he understood that his trials were part of God's plan for the preservation of nations.

Saffee wants the children to know that God can give them, like Joseph, a good future. That with Him good things can come from bad. Or, as the lesson book says, beauty from ashes.

As she slops more chemical remover on a paint-encrusted area, she thinks of the blessings that have come into her own life. This table, for example. It could have become ashes when flames whipped across the prairie. If it had burned, her mother would not have survived, and she and April would never have been born. The table endured considerable misuse, yet, like Joseph's honor, its former beauty is being restored.

By the time Sunday morning comes, Saffee has thought a lot about Joseph the overcomer.

Warmer weather returns. Gail sits in her usual place in the late summer sun. Saffee realizes she's never told her neighbor about the words inscribed on the table's underside. She crawls beneath and tries to read them out loud. The foreign sounds make them laugh, and they wonder about their meaning. Saffee says when she was young she imagined the words chronicled Viking conquest and buried treasure.

"No way," says Gail. "It's prophetic. It says"—she puts her hands around her mouth like a megaphone—"'There will be eight Andrews children eating at this table.'"

"No way yourself, Gail, but I guess it's no surprise you think like a mother," Saffee says, glancing at Gail's ever-growing belly that at the moment has a naked baby doll perched precariously on its slope. Jenny Rose, the doll's barefoot owner, scampers after yellow butter-flies in the grassy front yard.

In privacy, Saffee has catalogued the reasons she feels negative about having a child. Her baby sister, April, had taken Saffee's place in her mother's heart. In various ways, babies had complicated Joann's life. Her mother suffered an early death because of the tragic circumstances of her last baby. Then there was Saffee's distasteful memory of Joann begging Nels for a baby, long after there was hope of offering another child a normal home. No, having a baby holds little appeal, but there had been no reason to share why with Gail, or even Jack.

Suddenly Jenny Rose bounds into the garage, throws her arms around Saffee's neck, and proclaims, "I love you, Miss Saffee!" Saffee, kneeling on the cement floor, wire brush in hand, is so startled she sinks backward onto the cement and the little girl settles into her lap.

"Oh! Jenny Rose!" Saffee has never held a child before, never felt a child's hug. The little girl is warm and soft and smells of fresh air. "Oh my!" is all Saffee can say. As quickly as the little sprite had come, she is off to twirl and play in the summer sun.

Gail wears an amused expression, then nods toward the table. "Saffee," she says, "when I look at this big wonderful table, I can't help but think about what its future will be like."

Saffee is puzzled. "What do you mean?"

"Events around it, you know, fun things, like birthday parties, children coloring Easter eggs, your kids sorting out their Halloween loot and . . ."

She's reminded of what Jack shared of his childhood. "Gail . . . I just don't know."

"Aren't you and Jack going to . . . ?"

"Jack and I are fine without any children," Saffee says, trying not to sound curt.

Gail's imagination is not deterred. She says in her mind's eye she sees a high chair pulled up alongside and a little one kicking the table with her foot.

Saffee makes it clear that after all her hard work she wouldn't appreciate anyone kicking her beautiful table. Gail rattles on, naming kinds of shoes there will be, or at least could be, sharing space underneath during meals—sneakers, sandals, little slippers with bunny ears . . .

Saffee joins in. "Don't forget *adult* high heels and black wing tips."

"Right. And don't forget the bare feet," Gail goes on, "big ones, little ones, long legs and short, all under this table."

Jenny Rose's doll tumbles from its perch. Saffee picks it up and asks Gail if she had played with dolls as a child.

"Of course. Why?"

"Just wondering," Saffee says. For some reason she's wondered if playing with dolls taught a girl how to be a mother. She grins at her neighbor. "Anyway, if we ever decide to have a baby"—even the word is hard to say—"which I doubt, you'll be one of the first to know."

"Miss Saffee! Miss Saffee!" Another day Jenny Rose comes running across the driveway and into the garage where Saffee is peeling off another pair of shredded rubber gloves. It has been a productive day.

"Look, Miss Saffee, I made you a heart!" Jenny Rose waves a crayon drawing in the air.

Saffee kneels down and puts one arm around the exuberant little girl. "I like all the colors. It's *so* pretty, Jenny Rose. Tell me about it."

"Well, this is the 'splanation . . . My heart is a *rainbow* heart!"

"Jenny Rose, what a beautiful thing. A rainbow heart."

"You can put it up in your garage and look at it while you work."

"I will. I promise."

Jenny Rose skips out of the garage. "I gotta go now. I love you, Miss Saffee! Gonna make a heart for my daddy! G'bye!"

Saffee calls after her, "Thank you, Jenny Rose." Silently, with a lump in her throat, she adds, "I love you too, Jenny Rose."

Saffee suddenly feels unsteady. She sits down in "Gail's chair." How can one's long-held, stubborn mind-set change in an instant, making all of her reasons for it completely invalid? Her heart, her "rainbow heart," feels ready to burst—all because of love. Motherhood no longer seems out of the realm of possibility. Not at all.

Saffee is at the stove browning chicken when she hears the VW pull into the driveway. Before Jack can put down his briefcase, she meets him with a warm embrace.

"Mmm, don't you look happy," he says, pulling off his tie.

"Well, I should."

"Why?"

"It's because," she says, smiling, "I have a rainbow heart."

"A what?"

She kisses him. "Come in. I'll 'splain it to you."

## CHAPTER FORTY-NINE

# THE WEDDING GIFT

Saffee hastens toward the library exit after a day's work.

"Mrs. Andrews?"

She stops abruptly. "Oh! Hello!" She is pleased that Leif Bergstrom remembers her name.

"I'm sorry I did not return this to you earlier," he says, pulling her folder from his knapsack. "I have been so busy . . . My wife, she wrote it all out. She said it vas interesting."

Saffee opens the folder and sees the original article along with a stack of handwritten pages. She rummages in her purse to find the folded bills she's carried for some time, waiting to see him again.

"Ingrid, my wife, she said it vas a good vay to practice her English. She didn't use the typevriter because she had to revise a lot. It vas easier to use a pencil . . . vit eraser."

"This is wonderful. Please thank her for me." Saffee presses the money into his hand.

"Thank *you*," he says. "I'm glad I see you today; ve go back home soon."

Going home? Saffee remembers the inscription she copied from the table and pulls the piece of tablet paper from her purse. "You're leaving? Oh, but there's something else . . . um . . . something short . . ." She hands him the paper.

"It is from the Bible," he says. "Do you vant me to translate? It vill just take a minute." Together they find an empty library table and sit across from each other as he writes. Upside down she reads two words: *wife* and *vine*.

Saffee curls up on the love seat with a cup of tea and the handwritten, translated article about her great-grandparents, Anders and Maria Kirkeborg. It is a compilation of interviews with their children and various acquaintances from their Valders Valley community. She skims the words, hoping to find a reference to Anders's woodworking skill and maybe even a mention of her table.

She reads at length about their being a hardworking couple whose days were filled with the arduous tasks of farming and raising children. In addition, Anders and Maria "were known as 'the hands and feet of Jesus,' as they attended to the needy. The salvation of every soul in the valley was the passion of their lives." Saffee is so warmed by numerous such glowing accounts, she forgets her tea.

"Anders was a master craftsman . . ." Ah, here's what she is looking for. She reads about her great-grandfather's ability to make his own farm implements, sleds, carriages, and . . . fine furniture. He used "neither nails nor glue, but fitted one piece into another so snugly they stuck fast. He frequently ornamented his work with traditional decorative designs. No one else in the valley carved with his skill."

Saffee marvels. One piece of this man's artistry stands in their garage. She reads quotes from a daughter: "Mother and Father led prayers after each evening meal. All the family feared God's name. We and the hired help and their families gathered at the table . . ." *Around the Norway table!* ". . . and that was the best time of the day.

Everyone was welcomed and loved. We sat crowded on long benches, parents holding children. We sang psalms, followed by Father's Bible reading and prayer. Thus we carried on our heritage . . ." Saffee thinks about how in contrast this is to what happened later.

Other pages record that the oldest of the family's seven children was Knute, who emigrated to America. Anders wrote in his testament that the family table, "the wedding table he had made for Maria," would pass to Knute. "Jergen, the second son, took the table to his brother when he too went to America in 1910."

Wedding table! The inscription that Leif translated today now makes a little more sense. Saffee pulls out the tablet paper. How does it begin? "Your wife shall be like a fruitful vine . . ." She blushes.

Smiling, she cannot sit still, but jumps up and spontaneously twirls. Originally, the atmosphere around the Norway table was one of happiness and hospitality. No longer will it suggest darkness to her, but a symbol of flourishing life.

"Jack!" Waving the pages, she hurries to his study. "The table, our table, it was made as a gift of love, a wedding gift!" She holds the pages against her chest, grinning. "This article, along with all my work, of course, has lifted all the heaviness I've experienced over it."

He gives her a loving hug and his pleased look says, "Didn't I tell you?"

The next day, as she heads to the garage, Saffee catches her smiling reflection in the hall mirror. Funny thing, smiles. They seem to be standard adornment on some faces—lately they often appear on hers too. She lifts the garage door and pulls on yet another new pair of rubber gloves. She thinks about the portrait of her great-grandparents on the front page of the biography.

The text revealed that there was a special joy in Anders and Maria Kirkeborg's Norwegian home. Their sober faces probably reflected the hard times they lived in, when smiles indicated foolishness. But nowadays, smiles are commonplace. She is filled with gratitude that her new way of seeing things, thinking about things, is not only an *internal* exercise, but shows on her face. Also, she is grateful for Jack. Sometimes so much so that her smile muscles ache.

She looks out at the birches across the street. All summer she has fancied them to be kin to her table. Their limbs, changing into yellow garb, sway in the light wind, sweeping wispy clouds from the morning sky.

Today she will coax away another layer of paint.

## CHAPTER FIFTY

# THE STROKE

Machines gurgle, beep, and whirr. Tubes regulate fluids.

Saffee watches Nels gently massage her mother's motionless arm. Nels called her four days ago from the hospital, the day Joann had a stroke. She could tell by his voice that he wanted her to come. Needed her with him. She felt guilty that she hadn't seen either of them since the wedding. She hurried to the hospital, through a cold October rain, filled with anxiety, hating that she was nervous to see her mother—in any condition.

The doctor called the stroke massive. It remained to be seen, he said, if she will ever speak again, or move.

Today, as she lies there, Joann looks much older than fifty. Her hair, once strikingly dark, is ribboned with gray. Her face is sallow, her eyes closed. Does she hear them? A place in Saffee's heart, long fiercely guarded, is broken into unexpectedly. "I'm so sorry, Mother. I'm so sorry." The words come forth with sobs. Nels puts his arms around her. She tells him she'll be back the next day.

The next day, with cold, sore fingers, Saffee wraps fine sandpaper around the end of a screwdriver and absentmindedly rubs along the contours of her great-grandfather's carved masterpiece. Outside it has begun to rain.

"*I'm sorry, Mother.*" The words Saffee spoke in the hospital reverberate in her head. Joann's eyelids had fluttered for an instant. Her small dark eyes pierced Saffee's with an accusing look that seemed to say she took Saffee's apology to be an admission of guilt—guilt of conspiring against her, of being the perpetrator of her miserable years. Saffee is still stunned. Does Joann believe that her own daughter was the villain?

In spite of two layers of clothing under her sweatshirt, Saffee shivers. Her intent had been to express that she was sorry her mother has suffered, sorry that her life has been haunted and crazed. The apology also meant, "I'm sorry I didn't come home to see you during the college years. Surely I could have done something to ease your pain. Surely I could have helped you, my own mother. I'm sorry I did not. I'm sorry!" But she hadn't said that. Jumbled emotion, and her mother's unexpected glare, stifled the words.

Perhaps Saffee's neglect did contribute to Joann's pain. If so, she *was* the villain. If so . . . Now she whispers, "Oh, Mother, forgive me."

Saffee looks back into her childhood. She had been sullen and pouty. "Owly" had been her mother's word. But are these signs of villainy?

Her eye catches Jenny Rose's "rainbow heart" taped to the garage wall. Had Saffee ever scribbled such a gift for Joann? Once, when she spilled similar self-condemnation to Jack, he said, "Saffee, it was never your job to fix your mother, only to love her."

Well, she hadn't done a good job of that either. Hiding away at college wasn't loving. Rarely writing a letter, never calling on the phone wasn't loving. Perhaps she should have persisted in nagging her father to seek help for his sick wife. Why had she stopped? Saffee's thoughts jump to the day Joann demanded Saffee to assess if there was something wrong with her. *No, Mother, you're just fine!* The words choke her, as if she is swallowing sand. What could she have said?

Saffee is learning to interact better with others, but any opportunity to establish a satisfying relationship with her mother was lost long ago. In the chilly garage, she listens to a steady drizzle patter into the gutters. She drops the screwdriver to the floor and cries.

Late Indian summer suddenly becomes wintry. From the kitchen window, Saffee watches the first snowfall begin to blanket the grass. The warmer asphalt driveway is still bare, but it too will be white by the time she and Jack come home from work tonight. Then they will enlist Bill's help to disassemble a table that now displays a split personality—three legs still suffer variously colored layers of paint, while the rest of the table breathes free. They will prop its pieces against a garage wall for a few months and, for the first time, drive the VW inside. She has done her best to finish the project before winter. Come spring, she will.

## CHAPTER FIFTY-ONE

# CHRISTMAS

In early December, Jack tells Saffee there is an office Christmas party planned for the sixteenth.

She momentarily squints her eyes, wrinkles her nose, and then asks calmly, "What in the world should I wear?"

He looks at her blankly.

The next Saturday Saffee takes the bus downtown. At Peck and Peck, she finds an emerald green silk suit. It fits like a glove.

Back home, she models the new outfit for Jack and receives his unreserved approval. She reads a tag attached to the label. It says, "Love me for my imperfections." She guesses it refers to the slubby silk fabric. She wonders why it doesn't say, "Love me in spite of my imperfections."

Saffee muses over the notion. Sometimes she still wonders what her husband sees in her. "Jack," she says, reaching for a hanger, "do you love me for my imperfections, or in spite of them?"

Jack admires her reflection in the closet door mirror. "You're testing my powers of self-analysis," he says. "I'll say I love you just as you are. Not perfect, of course. Perfection would be boring."

She considers the thought. Her former life had been boring, but such a far cry from perfect. She hangs the suit in the closet. "Well, Mr. Andrews, I think *you're* perfect and not at all boring," she teases, remembering how this morning he'd left shaving cream slopped on the bathroom counter and toothpaste spattered on the mirror. Other than that, what could she fault?

At the party, holiday merriment has a life of its own and makes few demands on her. The executives' wives are older than she and seem to have known each other for years. Saffee's modest efforts to join in are only somewhat successful. She exchanges pleasantries with Leonard and Betsy Johnson, who again praise that never-to-be-forgotten meal of stuffed ribs. Smiling, but self-conscious, she stays fairly close to Jack most of the evening, listening as he banters with coworkers.

A couple of days later an invitation arrives for a New Year's Eve party given by some of Jack's high school classmates. Forgetting former resolutions to rise above old fears, Saffee considers that she has paid her party dues for one season. This time she'll stand her ground. But Jack insists they go, saying that his friends are her friends too. Hadn't they come to their wedding? Her memory of that day is a blur; she'd have to check the guest book. She tells Jack that she had endured the office party because she rightly assumed that group would have little interest in her and expect little in return. A party with people near her own age was another matter. There she would face unspoken competition, and she would lose.

Happy-faced Jenny Rose bursts in the door about noon. Gail has asked Saffee to keep her an hour or so after morning kindergarten until she returns from her baby's medical checkup. "Thanks, friend," Gail had said, "there's no one else I'd rather trust her to than you."

The little girl's cheeks are flushed, and dark curls spill across the shoulders of her bright pink jacket. "Look, Miss Saffee, I made a present for Mommy and Daddy for Christmas!" With mittened hands she holds up a green gift bag tied shut with a red ribbon.

"Nice, and what a pretty bow, Jenny Rose. Did you tie it yourself?" Saffee unzips the girl's jacket.

"Sure I did. And it's a really good present . . . but don't ask me what it is," she whispers loudly, her eyes dancing. "It's a secret!" Jenny Rose carefully places the gift bag on the coffee table and slides out of the jacket, mittens dangling from the sleeves. Saffee pulls off her matching pink boots.

"I bet you're going to put the present under your Christmas tree."

"Of course, if I can find room. There's lots and lots of presents under there!"

They go to the kitchen, Jenny Rose cradling the green bag in her arms. Saffee ladles hot soup into two bowls, puts crackers on a plate, and pours glasses of milk.

"Miss Saffee, now remember, don't ask me what this is, okay?" she says, stretching to place her gift in the center of the Formica table.

"Okay."

"Cuz I can't tell you!"

They both gently blow on spoonfuls of soup to cool it and Jenny Rose says, "Well, I can tell you"—her voice becomes mysterious—"it's something white!"

"The gift is white? That's nice."

As she munches a cracker, Jenny Rose contentedly kicks a rhythm on a table leg. "I guess I'll tell you one more thing," she says, her eyes on the bag. "I made it out of *wax*."

"Mm, wax?"

"And I can tell you something else . . . There's a string in the middle of it!"

Saffee laughs and says, "Now I really wonder what it could be."

Jenny Rose looks thoughtful. "Miss Saffee . . . well . . . maybe I can tell you one more thing." She whispers, "You're s'posed to put *fire* on top of it!"

"Ohhh," says Saffee, "fire!"

"Now don't ask me any more questions. You'll just hafta see it after Mommy and Daddy open it up." With this final pronouncement, Jenny Rose drains her milk glass, picks up the gift, and, with a self-satisfied look, holds it against her chest.

Gail had said there was no one else she would rather entrust this treasure of a child to, at least for these few minutes. Saffee found that surprising, but she can remember few compliments that have given her more pleasure.

"Okay. Let's see if I've got the lineup straight," Saffee says as the last hours of their first Christmas together wane. "The first row: rook, knight, bishop, queen, king, bishop, knight, rook. And pawns across the second row."

"Right. And remember, the white queen goes on white, and black on black."

"Got it." She knew if she bought this elegant chess set for Jack he would love it—and she would need to stretch again. Games. She's trying so hard to like them, to see the point.

When it's almost ten o'clock, Saffee figures she's spent enough time for one night learning chess strategy, but she doesn't want the day to be over. Outside it's snowing. Jack suggests a walk and she happily agrees.

They decide to walk along the mini-forest of birch trees across the street. But first, holding hands, they stop to admire their Christmas tree, twinkling through the front window. Saffee recalls the year her mother made the solemn decision to refrain from turning on holiday lights out of respect for those who had perished in tree fires. It had not seemed like one of the "good things" Saffee wanted to retain.

They cut across the yard until they are in front of Bill and Gail's corresponding window. Below it, surrounded by unblemished snow, are the kneeling, life-sized forms of Mary and Joseph keeping watch over Baby Jesus. Saffee stops to brush white flakes from the holy family's heads and shoulders, and then she and Jack walk diagonally toward the street. She turns to view the tableau again. From this angle, a vigorous flame atop a white candle inside refracts bold rays of light toward the nativity. Jenny Rose's secret gift now proclaims its surprise. More than a candle—her gift is the radiant star of Bethlehem.

At six twenty on New Year's Eve, Saffee, wearing a blue quilted robe, removes eight jumbo, prickly rollers and finds her hair more unruly than usual. Winter's furnace-dry air makes it flyaway, snapping at the brush with static electricity. She puts the brush down in chagrin and glares into the bathroom mirror. She still has about twenty minutes before they need to leave. Maybe they can be late.

She begins to apply makeup, unable to avoid seeing her mother's resemblance in her reflection, hearing her parents' voices . . .

*"Joann! We're late! What's holding you up?" "I'm not going! You and the girls go."*

*"Joann! It's Palm Sunday! Now put yer coat on . . ." Nels dodges the green-handled hairbrush as it flies . . .*

Joann is in a nursing home now, only thirty minutes away. The hospital helped Nels make the arrangements two months ago when it became clear that she would not return home after the severe stroke. She has regained partial use of one arm, but the rest of her body shows no sign of recovery. Saffee takes the bus to go sit by her side as often as possible; there is no certainty that Joann recognizes her. The visits bring back the past as Saffee sits there, trying to sort things out. They take an emotional toll on her. Sometimes these emotions, in various forms, spill over at home.

Even though Saffee is twenty-two, some of her teenage complexion lingers. She impatiently dabs eruptions with cover-up. "Glop!" she addresses the mirrored face.

"What did you say?" Jack calls from the living room. He's watching the evening news on their small black-and-white television, a Christmas gift from his parents.

"Nothing," she replies.

She plans to wear a black sheath that often brings compliments. Then again, tonight black might look like death-warmed-over.

Saffee begins to cry. What has happened to the modicum of composure and confidence that she had achieved over the past months? The office Christmas party, by no means a disaster, had seemed to set her back. She had been tongue-tied, afraid she reflected poorly on Jack. She crosses her arms and hugs the robe as if to prevent her body from falling apart. Sniffling up tears, she goes to Jack. Surely he will understand why she can't, they can't, go. She wouldn't even mind staying home alone, but she knows he wouldn't leave her on New Year's Eve.

Surprised, Jack makes room for her on the love seat. Before he can ask her what's wrong, the phone rings on the small table beside Saffee. Instinctively, she wills her voice to be normal and answers, wishing she hadn't.

"Oh. Hi, Daddy."

Nels says he will be spending the evening with Joann at the nursing home. His drive from Red Bridge takes a little less than an hour. Will Saffee and Jack join him, at least some of the evening? "Unless you have plans," he says.

Saffee's mood tempts her to retort that of course they have plans—it's their first New Year's Eve since they've been married, they're young, they like to go places. She reddens. Why would she pretend she has become some *bon vivant*?

"We're going to a party, Daddy," she says, "but it doesn't start 'til late." She casts Jack an inquiring look. He nods. "We can meet you for a while first at the nursing home."

"It's New Year's Eve, Muzzy. Nineteen sixty-four already!"

Saffee has not heard her dad use that nickname for years. The three visitors sit flanking Joann's bed in the warm, cramped room, Jack at the foot. Their winter coats drape over the backs of the chairs.

Nels pats Joann's good arm. "You know what? The world still celebrates this night, the night we met. And that was twenty-five years ago."

Her head turns. Dim, watery eyes appear to fix on him. It has been determined that Joann is blind in one eye from glaucoma; she had refused vision tests for years. The stroke affected the other eye; her distorted mouth sags to one side.

"Do you remember that night, Muzzy?" He looks with hope into her vacant face, even though he knows there will be no answers to his questions. In spite of his years of matrimonial trials, it is typical of Nels to bring up only good memories.

Several times Saffee has heard the story of her parents' first meeting, at a dance, of course. With pride, Joann told her how popular she had been at dances, and how Nels had quickly claimed her as his own.

"You sure look nice, Joann," Nels says. "You always did look good in red." She wears a shapeless bed jacket. "Someone's cut your hair." The salt-and-pepper hair is short, very short. "When it grows a little I'll give 'em some extry cash to give you a permanent," he says. He's always liked curls.

*"Sapphire! When I'm old and infirm, promise you'll cut the hairs on my chinny-chin-chin. Promise me now . . ."*

Since their arrival, Joann's face has been without expression, but her eyes slide from side to side. Saffee picks up her chair and carries it around the bed, placing it near Nels where perhaps her mother can see them both at once.

What goes on in her mother's head now? If the stroke quelled her delusions, as the doctor seems to think, perhaps it was a blessed thing. Too long was she caught in cycles of fairly acceptable behavior when medicated and full-blown schizophrenia when she refused drugs. No longer will there be scandal because she runs down the street scantily clad or knocks on neighbors' doors to warn of apocryphal dangers. Nels no longer will suffer the humiliation of obtaining court orders to recommit her to the state mental hospital. No more calls for police assistance. At great cost, it appears her torment is swept away.

"Mother . . ." Saffee's words have come with great difficulty during prior visits. Tonight she must try harder to bridge an emotional hurdle. Ignoring how warm she is in her black sheath, she begins. "Mother, I just want you to know that I'm fine, being married and all, I mean. I'm really good. I have a good life . . . and . . . a lot of credit for that goes to you."

There is no indication that Joann comprehends, but Saffee continues, "Mother, remember the vegetable soup you always made for us? Now that the weather's cold, I make it too. Just like you did. Jack really likes it."

Saffee glances at him. She knows he must be a little uneasy, but he smiles and says, "That's right, Joann, it's very good."

"I just want you to know that I appreciate that you always made us good meals." Nels nods at her, approving her effort to communicate.

Joann's eyes steady on her daughter's face. Saffee searches for more, anything more. "I remember once you told me to never serve liver and brown beans and chocolate cake at the same meal—too much brown."

"Ugh!" she hears Jack breathe. "Please don't!"

Saffee laughs. "Funny, the things that stick with a person, right, Mother?"

She searches how to extend her awkward, one-way chatter.

"Oh! Guess what Jack bought me for Christmas—a sewing machine. Singer, of course. You always said they're the best. I'm going to try to make curtains for our kitchen. Like you did. I couldn't begin to count all the curtains and draperies you made over the years."

She feels a duty to carry on the stilted conversation. Nels, never much of a talker, probably runs out of things to say during his frequent solo visits. Jack is quiet. Saffee crosses and uncrosses her legs, being careful not to brush against the bed rail. A run in her sheer black hose would not be good at the party.

"Remember when you used to draw a lot, Mom? Even tricky things like faces and cute little squirrels and rabbits. And all those floor plans for the Cottonwood Point house. You were so good at it. I'm planning to learn calligraphy. If I do it well, it will probably be because you passed on some of your artistic talent."

Saffee's heartfelt urge to inventory her mother's contributions to her life surprises her. She wants to continue. Wants to tell her gifted, fractured mother that she loves classical music because of all the records Joann used to play. But the eyes have closed. They hear a soft snore. Music can wait until another visit.

Jack looks at his watch and Saffee reaches to retrieve her coat. Then suddenly she knows there is one more thing she must say, even if it is not heard.

"Mother," she declares, "I'm taking the paint off the Norway table." She would not be surprised if Joann's eyes popped open at this announcement. But there is no movement.

"I hope that's good news, Mother. I . . . I hope you're glad about it. I never understood why you painted it all the time, but I just know that paint must come off." Saffee rambles a bit, saying that she suspects painting the table served to heighten her mother's trauma. She tells her that the removal is not a defiant or rebellious act, but a necessity. "The work is, well, therapeutic for me." She glances at Jack. "It's been healing, and I didn't even know I needed healing. And also, Mom, I began to imagine, and hope, really hope . . ." She chokes, making it hard to go on. "I hope that as I release layer after layer of paint, you, too, might be released from the grip of . . . well . . .

"I'm sure some people might think this sounds strange, Mom, but out there in the garage all summer, I felt that the presence of God was with me, showing me things." She takes a deep breath. Mentioning God in this familiar way is so un-Minnesotan. "I've asked Him to heal you of the emotions and agonies of the past. I really, really hope He has, and will." Saffee leans to give her mother a kiss on the forehead. "I love you, Mom. I'll be back soon."

Nels reaches out and squeezes Saffee's hand, then plants his own kiss on Joann's cheek.

Hurrying across the parking lot, Saffee holds tightly to Jack's arm. She's unsteady, not only from emotion, but also her black suede, toe-pinching high heels.

"Careful, it's getting icy," he says.

When they get to the car, he reaches into his coat pockets. Then into the right pocket of his blue blazer, and the left.

"The directions to the party," he says, "they were right on the dresser. I must not have picked them up."

He starts the motor and switches on the heater. "It would be a lot of driving to go back to the house, then back this way, and then to the party."

He looks at her and says, "You know what? There'll be other parties and I'm starving. Let's get some Chinese takeout and go home." He laughs. "We can watch the Times Square celebration on TV— like a couple of old folks."

"Okay," she says, trying not to sound relieved. Seeing her helpless mother confirmed that life needs to be lived fully and enjoyed, parties and all, while a person is able. But, as Jack says, there will be other parties.

Jack eases the car over icy patches on the road. He reaches for her hand and offers her a smile filled with love and approval.

## CHAPTER FIFTY-TWO

# WAITING

1964–1976

Dim, misty years drift by in monotonous discomfort. Joann can manage to slowly turn her head and raise one arm in response to those around her but is unable to speak. Throughout endless, wakeful nights she revisits regrets. Slumber disjointedly jumbles the pleasures and pains that were . . . and calls of things yet to come . . .

. . . *The soft touch of her mother's hand . . . "Joann . . ."*
. . . *The harshness of her father . . . "High school? Not yet, Joann, not 'til eighteen . . . You'll clean da guest cottages four years, just like da odders done."* . . .

"Where are her partials? I've looked everywhere. I'm sure I put them in this morning. Look at the chart—she's hardly taking any food."

"Her partials? Do you think she dropped them in the—no, how could she?"

"That's it! I wheeled her into the bathroom, had to leave for a minute before I got her on the commode . . . maybe she leaned forward, just let them fall out."

"Only strained food for you now, Joann. Can't fit new dentures for someone who doesn't talk, you know . . . Have you seen the abscesses on her gums?" . . .

. . . "Mom? Are you awake? I've come to read to you . . ."
*The Lord is my light and my salvation; whom shall I fear?*
*The Lord is the strength of my life; of whom shall I be afraid? . . .*

. . . "Oh, Nels! The pain was fierce; I didn't think I'd live through it! *Who'd think a baby would put me through such pain. I feel so weak . . . I'm going to be a modern mother—no nursing for me. Bottle-feeding's the rage . . . I'll get some rest that way." . . .*

. . . "Joann. Wake up. Nels is here, your daughters too. Look, see how much your grandson has grown." . . .

. . . *"Rolf! Get away from me! Stop it! I'll yell for Pa!"* . . .

. . . "Mom? Can you hear me when I read?"

*When the wicked . . . came upon me . . . they stumbled and fell.*
*Though an host should encamp against me, my heart shall not*
*fear . . .*

. . . *"The psychotropics, we've tried them all, Joann, none seem to have*
*helped . . . all that's left is shock . . . If you don't consent, it will be a*
*long trip through the courts . . . It's the only way you have a chance,*
*Joann." . . .*

. . . *"Saffee's a Kirkeborg through and through, Nels, but this one, look*
*at those blue Kvaale eyes! This one takes after her daddy." . . .*

. . . *One thing I have desired of the Lord, that will I seek after;*
*That I may dwell in the house of the Lord . . . to behold the beauty*
*of the Lord . . .*

. . . *"Joann . . ." The soft touch of her mother's hand . . .*

. . . *Memorize the words, memorize the words . . . Hysteria . . . Acute*
*mania . . . Hospital for . . .*

. . . "Open up, Joann, here comes the applesauce. Mmm. Now, Joann, don't push it away, see there, you've spilled on your bib! Here, let's try again." . . .

. . . *"Yes, Joann. You're beautiful. You always will be."* . . .

. . . "Mom, listen to these words." . . .
*When my father and my mother forsake me,*
*Then the Lord will take me up* . . .

. . . *Hospital . . . Hospital for . . . Hospital for the Insane . . .*

. . . "I see your pictures on the board, Joann. You were some looker! Nice family. Can you see them up here? Look, I'll point." . . .

. . . "It's Sunday, Joann. Nels will be coming. He always does, you know. Let's see . . . what should we wear? You look nice in this flowered blouse, and here're some matching beads." . . .

. . . "Mom, the Scriptures I always read to you are from the book of Psalms. They're wonderful words, Mom. I hope they comfort you." . . .

*For in the time of trouble he shall hide me in his pavilion:*
*In the secret of his tabernacle shall he hide me . . .*

. . . "Hungry? Sure you are. Let's roll to the dining room. Here, Joann, right up to the table now." . . .

. . . *Wait on the Lord: be of good courage, and he shall strengthen your heart;*
  *Wait, I say, on the Lord! . . .*

## CHAPTER FIFTY-THREE

# KITE LESSONS

1964

andpaper in hand, Saffee kneels on the garage floor. Nels's car pulls into the driveway and she gives him a wave.

"Hi, Daddy," she says as he approaches, "Look, I'm working on the third leg." Since the first real thaw of spring, she has devoted more time than ever to the table project, terribly eager to be finished.

Nels admires her progress and finds a tarp on a back wall shelf. He folds it into a cushion. "Here," he says. "Save your knees."

Last summer Nels didn't seem to fully understand her zeal for restoring the table. Saffee wasn't surprised. He's never been one to see connections between emotion and action. For years his assessment of Joann went no deeper than to observe, "She thinks too much." But ever since New Year's Eve, when he heard Saffee share with Joann about stripping the table, he's concluded that his daughter is the best judge of how she must deal with the past.

He settles into the webbed chair.

"How was Mother today, Daddy?" He often comes from the nursing home after visiting her.

"She looked good. Dressed in a nice blue blouse and pants." These days, if Joann is awake and able to train her one dim eye on him during visits, Nels is happy. If she is asleep, or struggles to lift her left arm as if to wave him away, he is disappointed.

"I've been reading the Bible to her when I visit," Saffee says. "I hope she hears me." Nels looks appreciative.

There's a streak of moving color in the yard. Saffee waves to Jenny Rose.

"Miss Saffee! Come see my kite!" the child calls.

"Dad, there's the adorable little girl from next door I've told you about."

Nels steps onto the driveway. Jenny Rose beams contagious delight.

"See my kite!" She holds it out for inspection. "My daddy got it for me."

"It's very pretty, Jenny Rose," Saffee says, joining Nels in the sunshine.

"Daddy's gonna show me how to fly it *way, way* up in the air!"

Bill appears from the adjacent garage with twine and colorful strips of plastic. "Hey, Jenny Love," he says, "I found the string and just what we need for the tail." He notices Saffee and Nels. "Hi, Saffee. What do you think of our kite?"

"Perfect for this breezy day." Saffee introduces Bill to her dad.

"Nice little girl you have there," Nels says, smiling.

Bill agrees. Saffee and Nels watch the pair kneeling on the grass. Patient, large hands show smaller ones how to tie the plastic tail strips. Bill attaches the line to the frame and unwinds a length from the spool.

"Are we ready, Daddy? Let's make it fly!"

Bill gives the kite a strong toss into the wind.

"Look!" Jenny Rose exclaims as she runs beneath the rising,

twisting kite. "It's so high!" She scampers back to Bill, her long dark curls tossing in the breeze. "Daddy, can I fly it?"

Together they hold the spinning spool. The kite soars and dives like a magnificent bird. Saffee tries to remember if she has ever flown a kite. She doesn't look at Nels.

"Hold tight, Jenny!" she calls.

The kite loops crazily in the wind, gently tugging Bill and Jenny Rose into the next yard. Saffee returns to the garage and picks up her sandpaper. Nels follows and sits without speaking in the webbed chair. The scene of devoted father and carefree daughter replays in Saffee's mind. She wonders what her dad is thinking.

Nels clears his throat like he does when he's embarrassed. "Saffee," he says. There is a long pause. "They were . . . those two . . . I mean." More silence. He clears his throat again. "Saffee. I know I wasn't the best father."

She stops sanding. He's apologizing. The few words are all "Daddy's little girl" needs to hear. The humble admission fills her heart with love.

"Oh, Daddy." She rocks back from her knees to sit on the floor and looks up at him. His eyes get teary so easily nowadays. "You didn't have a father to teach you how to be one, just like Mother had no mother. But you did fine. Look at me, Daddy. Didn't I turn out okay? You must have done a good job."

"Yes, I know, you're fine, but . . ." Nels shakes his head. "But I shoulda done better . . . Mother, she . . . but it's not Mother's fault. I . . ." He leans forward with head down, hands on knees. "And April . . . goin' off like that. She needed a mother . . . and a father."

"She's okay, Daddy. I'm excited that she's found Kyros. He sounds pretty special. And I'm sure you're happy they're planning to move to the States when they can."

Over the winter there had been a flurry of letters from April, extolling her newfound Greek friend, Kyros, who soon became more than a friend. In February, April wrote that they had been married on the island of Santorini. The sisters had missed each other's weddings but promised by mail to make amends in the future.

"Mother's condition made your life really hard, Daddy, and . . . and sometimes it was hard for April and me too. Mother was too broken to love us well. But for us, everything is okay now. Really, Daddy."

*I am loved. My life is different. I am not my mother. I am different.*

Nels pulls out his handkerchief and blows his nose. "I dunno what else to say. But you're a good girl, Saffee. I, well . . . I dunno what to say." The handkerchief goes back to its pocket. Nels drums the arms of the chair for a moment, then stands abruptly. "Wonder if there's some coffee left?"

She smiles. "Sure, Dad. In the kitchen."

He ducks into the house and Saffee goes out to catch another glimpse of the kite. It flies like young Jenny Rose, wonderfully tethered, wonderfully free.

Saffee has commented more than once that she and Jack would be "just fine" with no children. But now, after watching Gail and Bill nurture their daughter and new baby, she can see that life is supposed to be more than just fine. Investing, *investing*, in a child is an opportunity to give the world a Jenny Rose. Again, Saffee has watched, and listened, and learned.

An early morning rain stops abruptly and moves on, leaving behind an overcast sky and a vigorous cool wind. Saffee switches on the garage ceiling light. The Norway table, its rich honey-toned wood finally bare but for a fresh coat of varnish, stands as if on center stage. The heirloom piece closes a circle begun years ago when a young man planed hand-hewn planks of birch and carved an enigmatic vine. The circle has compassed spiritual blessings, hardships of everyday life, terror, shelter, and demonic delusion. It survived the tyranny of a paintbrush and the excoriation of chemicals and sandpaper.

Clouds begin to part in the eastern sky. A strong shaft of yellow sunshine bursts onto the table, as if blessing it.

Saffee spins the radio dial until orchestral magic befitting celebration fills the air. She's grateful for the day at Joann's bedside when she thanked her for imparting love of classical music. For years, mother and daughter shared this spiritual grace, this communion, unspoken. She boosts the volume, exhilaration surging with the harmonies. She gathers empty paint remover cans and newspapers that litter the floor and throws them into the trash.

Saffee looks out across the road where the stand of young birches bend and sway as if in rhythm with the music. Shimmering green leaves fling showers of raindrops into the air.

"Oh," she breathes. "God, You have choreographed the trees to worship You."

She lifts her arms to join them.

"Thank You, Lord, for Your gifts," she whispers. "I have seen Your Spirit at work. You have ushered goodness and healing into my deepest being, giving my life a new lyric. You have chosen my inheritance. I needn't fear." She lowers a hand to touch the restored wood—wood that once had stood in sun and rain and swayed in the wind.

As rings mark the age of a tree, circles of life also close and begin again.

Tonight, the Norway table will take its welcome place in their home.

## CHAPTER FIFTY-FOUR

# REDEEMED

1975

"I made this egg into a bunny. Look, Mom, he's got ears and a cotton tail." Seven-year-old Grace holds up her creation for Saffee to admire. The Norway table, covered with a vinyl cloth, is littered with containers of dye, stickers, crayons, and other essentials for Easter egg decorating. The children's enthusiastic creativity gives Saffee great pleasure.

Nels is napping, but she knows he would not want to miss out on the traditional fun.

Saffee asks Daniel, age nine, to keep an eye on Benjamin, three and a half, whose enthusiasm matches his brother's and sister's but, of course, not his skill. Saffee goes to her dad's room to see if he has awakened. His face looks peaceful; how can she interrupt him?

Thinking how pleased she is that he is part of the household, she stands for a moment watching his chest rise and fall. When Saffee and Jack bought the four-bedroom home eight years ago, they thought there was a possibility Nels would move in with them. Soon after Grace was born, he did.

For a moment, her eyes scan the room. On the bureau is the yellow ceramic dancing girl Nels gave Joann in her happier days. Saffee wonders what he thinks when he looks at it now. Her thoughts are interrupted by screeching protests in the kitchen and she quickly returns to investigate.

A cup of purple dye somehow was spilled across the table. Daniel, rather than minimize the mess, is smearing his fingers through it and exuberantly flicking purple dye onto his sister and brother. In a flash Saffee yells, "Daniel, stop! Stop! Stop!" Grabbing his arms, she glares at him. "Daniel, that's hateful! What are you doing? Are you crazy?" Her outburst surprises the children, and later prompts her own discouragement.

That night when the children are asleep, Saffee and Jack hide the eggs. When they finish, Saffee sinks into a chair and relates the afternoon's unfortunate scene.

"Daniel reminded me of Mother, madly smearing her hands and arms through paint on that same table. I could almost see her spattering colors through the air with those Jackson Pollock results. The memory stabbed right through me, Jack, and before I could think, I lost my temper.

"He wasn't being hateful, just childish," Saffee continues. "He thought I was mad about the mess. But I guess some old table angst reared its ugly head and I fell for it."

"Don't be so hard on yourself, Saffee. I don't suppose unpleasant memories ever completely go away."

"Maybe not, but I don't want the children to be affected by my sensitivity to the past."

Jack bends down and tilts her face up to his. "You've learned that lesson very well and I'm proud of you. But you're human—a wonderful wife and mother who can make a mistake." She gives him a grateful smile and relates how she and all of them cleaned up the mess together. Both Daniel and Saffee had sincerely apologized.

Jack wraps his arms around her. "You might even get Mother of the Year award!"

"Ah, go on," she chuckles, rolling her eyes.

Sunday morning Saffee sits at the Norway table, reviewing the Easter dinner menu. The table, without yesterday's paraphernalia, is the stunning centerpiece of the spacious room. She makes a note to ask Jack and Kyros to add all three table leaves before dinner.

She'll put the glazed, spiral-cut ham into the oven before the guests arrive at one o'clock; scalloped potatoes are under way; April is bringing her broccoli cheese casserole and homemade rolls. Did Kyros say he's making baklava? She smiles. April's lovable Greek husband of nine years never passes up the opportunity. Grammy Andrews promised two lemon meringue pies and a fruit salad; the green salad can be tossed at the last minute.

What else? Oh yes, the coffee, and the molded Easter bunny chocolates she couldn't resist at a candy store.

She pauses to admire the white trumpeting blossoms in the center of the table. Jack has brought her a lily every Easter since the table made its debut in the dining alcove of their rented duplex twelve years ago. Yesterday the family took an Easter lily, the symbol of resurrection, to Joann, as they always do. Joann's condition has improved little since she was admitted to the nursing home. Several times a week, month after month and year after year, Nels sits by her side. He whispers sweet love words and massages her hands and feet.

"Your dad's a prince," an aide more than once has commented to Saffee. "A lot of the residents here go for months without even one visitor. We've never seen a man as loyal as Nels."

School pictures of Saffee and Jack's three children smile down from a bulletin board, and the walls display their artistic endeavors. When they visit, the children sing or recite poems and Bible verses. They can only hope Joann enjoys their efforts.

Saffee removes the lily and folds away an embroidered runner she made, thanks to Joann, who years ago insisted she learn to embroider dish towels. The tabletop reveals accumulated blemishes. Among them, a phone number carelessly impressed through a piece of paper, irregular printing that spells "Daniel," a divot from a slip of an X-ACTO knife, and at least two white rings from sweating water glasses.

When she notices the flaws, which she rarely does, she thinks of the maxim "Love me for my imperfections." The layered paint of years ago, and these more recent scars, are mere neutral reminders of where life has been. She needn't go back to them emotionally. Long ago she decided this.

She spreads a white paper tablecloth, coaxes its stiff edges to drape downward, and places a gumdrop tree, made from a brambly branch, at the center. One more thing. She puts boxes of crayons handy on the buffet.

It is eight o'clock; the hot cross buns go into a pan to warm; she hears Nels puttering in his bedroom. The children will be waking soon. Anticipating the impending merriment, she rearranges the cellophane grass nestled in straw baskets. Any moment her tribe will fill the house with glee as they scamper to hunt for eggs. There will be just enough time for breakfast before the eleven o'clock church service.

Saffee hears Benjamin's infectious laughter as he comes scooting down the hall from his bedroom. "I found a egg! I found a egg! Grandpa Nels! Get up, get up!" He appears, one hand clutching his slipping pajama bottoms, the other holding aloft a blue and yellow egg. "My first one! It was under my pillow!"

Jack returns from walking Skye, their Scottish terrier, leaving him in the backyard. "Look, Daddy!"

"Good find, Benji," his father says. "Mom's got a basket here for you to collect more," he says, bending to tousle Benjamin's hair.

Grace appears. "Mom! Me too, where's my basket?" She's closely followed by the oldest pajama-clad child.

"I'm gonna find the most, cuz I'm the tallest and can reach the highest," Daniel boasts.

"Daddy! Daddy! I found the one with my name on it. See how nice I wrote it?"

"Good going, Amazing Grace," Jack says.

Nels, unshaven, joins the happy throng. Benjamin crawls under the rocker, although it's clearly not a hiding place that Saffee and Jack selected.

"Benji, you're gettin' warmer," Nels hints. "In fact, you might get burned around that there rocker." The little boy wriggles backward and quickly snatches a yellow egg from under the rocker cushion.

"Thanks, Grandpa!" He races elsewhere.

The hunt is in full swing. Saffee watches the hurry and scurry, joins in the banter, lives the moment.

When no more eggs can be found, Saffee pours orange juice, puts the hot cross buns on a platter, and summons her family to the table. "Mommy, I'm so hungry!" Daniel rubs his stomach. "Can I have *three* hot cross buns and *three* eggs this year?"

"Me too," says Benjamin. "Grandpa Nels, can I sit on your lap?"

"Right here, Benji, up you go. Say. You're gettin' heavy."

Saffee makes a mental note that they'll need four additional chairs for the dinner guests. They won't match, but so be it. Years ago, when she and Jack bought six ladder-back chairs, she couldn't imagine they would ever need *that* many.

They join hands and Jack prays.

He thanks Jesus, the Christ, for His sacrifice of death on the cross and His resurrection from the grave. He thanks Him for promising and providing eternal life. He thanks Him for the family gathered around the table and those who will arrive later. They all chorus, "Amen!"

The children *tap-tap-tap* eggs against their plates, breaking and scattering shells. The youngest licks frosting from the top of his hot cross bun.

Grace asks if they can decorate the paper tablecloth like they had at Christmas.

"That's why I brought the crayons," their mother says, reaching for the boxes.

"One of the best things I like about Easter is getting gumdrops for breakfast," says Daniel, his teeth sticking together as he speaks. Saffee smiles as she refills Jack's and Nels's coffee mugs. Someday she'll tell her children about the gumdrop bush of her own childhood.

The crayon boxes are passed and everyone, young and old, selects a handful. Between bites of food they scribble and draw, with no regard for lack of artistic talent. It isn't long before mostly recognizable brown bunnies, yellow chicks, and lengthy daisy chains abound across the paper. Together, Daniel and Grandpa Nels draw a large cross. It is yellow, outlined in brown.

"We drew the cross window at church," Daniel says. "It's yellow cuz the sun is shining through it."

"Gracie, what's those *green* things you're makin'? Green eggs?" Benji asks, his mouth full and a splash of juice on his chin.

"I know what they are!" Daniel says. "Green eggs and ham, like in the book."

Grace shakes her head and continues to make circles with a fat green crayon, first stretching her arm in front of Saffee on one side, and then in front of Daniel and Grandpa Nels on the other, so as to rim the table edge. Coming to the extent of her reach, she jumps up to color the paper in front of Jack.

"Okay, finished!" Gracie says when she has encircled the entire table, obviously enjoying that she has puzzled the others. "Give up?"

"I think you drawed a necklace, Gracie," Grandpa Nels says.

"No-o-pe."

"It's a train!" exudes Benji.

"No-o-pe."

"We give up. Tell us, Grace," Jack says.

"Olives!" Grace sings out in triumph.

"Olives? Don'tcha know olives are black?" says her big brother.

"Not *mine*! Cuz mine are still *growing*!"

Smugly, Grace waves her crayon in the direction of the framed calligraphy that Saffee penned for the wall—the ancient blessing that Leif Bergstrom had translated, the words Saffee's great-grandfather had burned into the wood under the table almost one hundred years ago.

"I made lots of green olives around our table, just like Mommy's picture says!"

Saffee is more pleased than Grace could know. She looks at Jack; he winks back. Saffee has read the words to her children, telling them it means they are a special promise from God.

"Why don't you read it to us, Gracie?" Saffee says.

Grace pushes her chair to the wall and stands on it for a better view, and also, Saffee suspects, for effect, reminiscent of her theatrical Aunt April.

Grace reads:

*Your wife . . .*

"That's Mommy, Benji," she informs him.

*. . . shall be like a fruitful vine*
*in the very heart of your house.*
*Your children . . .*

Grace expansively gestures toward her brothers. "And that's *us*!"

*. . . like olive plants around your table.*
*Psalm 128*

## 1976

She sleeps in earth's darkness . . .

*"Joann, My beloved, Joann, My Joy!"*

. . . and awakens to brilliant Light.

*Jesus takes her hand. "Come, My Joy. Come to My banqueting table."*

The unread morning paper rests on Nels's lap as he sits in his recliner. From the kitchen, Saffee watches her father, wanting to share new happiness with him, waiting for the right moment. Although he is looking in the direction of Benjamin who is revving matchbox cars over and under sofa pillows, she suspects he is lost in sadness and sees nothing. Skye sleeps on the floor beside him. Nels's right arm extends downward, his hand slowly strokes the dog's black fur. Saffee suspects that her father has been thinking about what might have been and wondering why.

The midnight call from the nursing home came two weeks ago. Nels's vigil by his wife's side was over. Regarding her father's long devotion, "Love me for my imperfections" is an adage that Saffee has replaced with another:

*People are not perfect—until you fall in love with them.*

The funeral was small. Attending were Nels, Saffee's family, April and her husband, and two caregivers from the nursing home. Also, out of respect for Saffee and Jack, Gail and Bill and a few people from church were there. When it was over, Saffee and April fell into each other's arms.

"I think we'll always have a part of Mother tugging at us," April said.

"That's right," Saffee agreed, "the best part."

Since April returned from Europe, still her perky self, but more worldly-wise, she and Saffee have become best of friends.

"Want to join me for a cup of tea, Dad?"

He snaps out of his reflection and takes on his usual lighthearted voice. "Nah . . . you know I don't drink that stuff. Tea's for women-folk. I had my coffee."

"I knew you were going to say that." Saffee draws up a chair beside him. "It's been a sad time, hasn't it? I can see it in your face today." He nods in agreement.

"Tell me something, Saffee." He interrupts himself to search through his pants pockets for a handkerchief. "Here it is." He doesn't use it, just holds it at the ready and continues, "Tell me"—another pause—"tell me why you think your mother had to go through so much hell."

"Oh, Daddy. I don't know. But, Daddy"—she covers his hand with hers—"I want to tell you about a wonderful dream I had about her last night."

"Oh yeah?" He looks into her eyes, eager to hear anything that is wonderful.

"It was about Mother in *heaven*, Daddy. And, Daddy, get this." Saffee squeezes his hand. "She was *dancing*!"

"Dancin'?"

"Yes, Daddy, it was a marvelous sight, since she hadn't even *walked* for years, had hardly even *moved*, couldn't smile or say a word. But, Daddy, I saw her dancing. Twirling round and round and laughing, Daddy, *laughing*!"

Nels tries to say something, clears his throat, and tries again. "She . . . she . . . when we was young . . . she loved to dance, just like that yellow, whatcha call it, figurine I got her. I still got it, you know." He looks into the distance. "That's how I like to remember her."

"I know."

Nels refocuses. "She was laughin', you say?"

"Yes, Daddy. But that was the end part. The beginning of the dream was when Jesus, surrounded by brilliant light, walked toward her, stretched out His arms, and embraced her. Then, get this, Daddy, He gave her a sparkling white stone and told her to read what was written on it. She was smiling so big when she read the stone. And then I heard *her voice*—that none of us heard for years. She said, 'It says "Joy"!' And Jesus said, 'Yes, Joy is your new name. You are *My Joy*!'"

Nels sits a little straighter, his eyes wide. "What happened then?"

"That's when she started dancing, and oh, Daddy, she was so happy. And there was music like you've never heard. Beautiful, beautiful music I can't describe. I wanted to stay right there in the middle of it myself—but that's when I woke up. Then I just had to wake up Jack to find out if *he'd* heard the music of heaven."

"Did he?"

"No, but I wish he had. I will *never* forget it."

Nels's closed eyes are brimming. Saffee wraps her arms around him and their wet cheeks touch. They rock a little, back and forth.

Nels smiles. "Dancin'," he says hoarsely. "She's dancin' to music . . . Dancin' . . . in heaven."

# Reading Group Guide

1. How does Joann's mental illness affect Nels, April, and Saffee?

2. Discuss the role of fire in Joann's life.

3. What are the consequences of emotional neglect?

4. In what ways is it possible to avoid taking on the negative aspects of the people who raised you?

5. How does Saffee honor Joann? How does she dishonor her?

6. Birch trees appear throughout the novel. What might they represent?

7. Joann, Nels, and Saffee are each restricted by personal fears. What fears play a part in your life? How might this story help you deal with them?

8. Discuss the Norway table and its symbolic role in the story.

9. What leads to Saffee's growth and wholeness? Do any of Saffee's

experiences or moments of enlightenment apply to your family legacy?

10. Discuss how the main characters find redemption.

# Acknowledgments

eartfelt thanks, Sandi and Scott Tompkins. Your professional expertise and encouragement made a way for me and many others to take the first steps toward becoming published authors. Your perceptive, gentle counsel was vital to this work.

Thank you, all my writing friends in the remarkable Kona Writers' Group. Your support and helpful criticism were beyond value.

Patti Hummel, my creative, tireless agent: you recognize possibilities and then make them happen. I am deeply grateful.

Thank you, Daisy Hutton and Ami McConnell of HarperCollins Christian Publishing for believing in me and my story. Also, thanks to Ruthie Dean, Becky Monds, Zachary Gresham, and Kristen Vasgaard. Each of you played a part in nurturing the various aspects of the book.

Nicci Jordan Hubert, you understood my heart and the nuances required to convey it. Your sensitive edits were appropriate and welcome.

To my Norwegian cousins, Leif and Anders, *Tusen takk!* Your gracious hospitality inspired me to learn and write about my ancestry. I am blessed to be part of the same family.

Thank you, Nancy Ann Field. When you cried in all the right places, you became one of my first encouragers. You were joined early on by Irene Periera and Barbara Fessendon. Thank you, dozens of friends and acquaintances, who went out of their way to spur me on. Particularly, Pat Weed, Vicky Scott, Joanne Archerd, and Carey Haivala. Also Judy and Gary, Rose and Jerry, Bob and Joan, Skip and Jerrien, Debra and Dennis, as well as the Prairie Life Center friends. Your interest and enthusiasm were unexpected and wonderful.

Thank you, Carol Lamse and Janet Kronemeyer and Ruth Arthurs, for believing in the message enough to share it with others.

How amazing it has been that several diverse groups of people have met to explore the story. Thank you, organizers and hosts: Linda Swygard, Char Grothues, Susan Befort, Debbie Ball, Sharon Bighley, Kathy Bondurant, Lee and Gwen Cure, and the other gatherings of readers I have never met.

Thank you, Mary Ann Shotzko and Mary Mathowicz and your staffs at St. John, for your sacrificial benevolence to my loved ones. By extension, you are part of the story.

Thank you, Holly, for your always patient, uncomplaining techy help. You knew how much I needed it. Thank you, Meeja, for your very enthusiastic promotion. And Andrew, for your expression of chagrin about a different table. Your comments planted ideas. Thank you, Sarah, for your willing support and interest. Also, thank you, Cammie. Because you lived it, you were often the only one I could consult for advice.

Thank you, Ted, my loving husband. You patiently endured, listened to me chatter endlessly about the writing without complaint, read every word, and gave me your valued perspective. You never complained when dinner was in doubt.

Most of all, I acknowledge God the Father, Son, and Holy Spirit, in whom I live, and breathe, and have my being.

# ABOUT THE AUTHOR

© Lifetouch Church Directories and Portraits Inc.

Suzanne Field, a graduate of the University of Minnesota, has taught English as a Second Language in China, Ukraine, and Hawaii. She has also been a magazine editor and home-school teacher. Suzanne writes to encourage others to rise above memories and embrace the goodness found in each day. She and her husband have five children and divide their time between Dallas and Hawaii where she is a tutor and mentor.